LANGUAGE AND LITERACY SERIES

Dorothy S. Strickland and Celia Genishi
SERIES EDITORS

The Complete Theory-to-Practice Handbook of Adult Literacy:
Curriculum Designs and Teaching Approaches
*Rena Soifer, Martha E. Irwin, Barbara W. Crumrine, Emo Honzaki,
Blair K. Simmons, and Deborah L. Young*

Literacy for a Diverse Society:
Perspectives, Practices, and Policies
Elfrieda Hiebert, Editor

The Child's Developing Sense of Theme:
Responses to Literature
Susan Lehr

The Triumph of Literature / The Fate of Literacy:
English in the Secondary School Curriculum
John Willinsky

The Child as Critic: Teaching Literature
in Elementary and Middle Schools, THIRD EDITION
Glenna Davis Sloan

Process Reading and Writing:
A Literature-Based Approach
*Joan T. Feeley, Dorothy S. Strickland,
and Shelley B. Wepner, Editors*

Process
Reading and Writing:
A Literature-Based
Approach

Edited by
Joan T. Feeley
Dorothy S. Strickland
Shelley B. Wepner

Teachers College, Columbia University
New York and London

Published by Teachers College Press, 1234 Amsterdam Avenue
New York, NY 10027

Library of Congress Cataloging-in-Publication Data

Process reading and writing : a literature-based approach / edited by
    Joan T. Feeley, Dorothy S. Strickland, Shelley B. Wepner.
        p.   cm. — (Language and literacy series)
    Includes bibliographical references and indexes.
    ISBN 0-8077-3118-8. — ISBN 0-8077-3117-X (pbk.)
    1. Reading (Elementary) — United States.   2. Literature — Study and
teaching (Elementary) — United States.   3. English language —
Composition and exercises — Study and teaching (Elementary) — United
States.   I. Feeley, Joan T., 1932–   .   II. Strickland, Dorothy S.
III. Wepner, Shelley B., 1951–   .   IV. Title: Literature-based
approach.
    LB1573.P76   1991
    372.4 — dc20   91-30766

Printed on acid-free paper

Manufactured in the United States of America

98 97 96 95 94 93 92 91   8 7 6 5 4 3 2 1

To our children
    Maura, John and Judy, and Brian and Scott
    Mark and Kimberly, Randy and Cindia, and Michael
    Meredith and Leslie

And to teachers of children who, like us,
    are still learning about reading and writing

Contents

Foreword

- This book should only be read if you want to get to know the vibrancy, fun, nature, and possibilities for improving literacy teaching.
- The book is definitely two thumbs up.
- Truly an unprecedented addition, important to those interested in educational change and what must be viewed as one of the most significant pedagogical movements of the century.
- The stories the teachers, principals, and superintendents tell are alive, fresh, and real.
- The book presents a wonderful collage-like discussion of teachers involved in the development of literacy programs that are child-centered. The book invites you into the minds of teachers and places you side by side with them as they pursue their quest for developing literacy experiences that connect reading and writing to real people through real books including those developed by classroom authors.
- The editors should be thanked for organizing this volume to include and support the voices of teachers, administrators, and others working at a variety of levels and in numerous settings.

You may be already asking, "What is he doing with this foreword?"

Some are apt to expect the foreword to be an advance organizer for the book in which reference might be made to the themes of the book and the various chapters within each section. Others are likely to expect the foreword to compliment the contributors and place the book historically. Still others might expect the foreword to be an opportunity for one who shares a kindred affiliation with the authors and editors to say how the work relates to their own thoughts. Still others will expect the foreword to serve a function not unlike a pep rally. Yet others will not read the foreword simply because they did not take notice of their tendency to expect very little.

Let me explain. I wanted to capture some of my gut reactions before getting too tied up in any of my lengthier ramblings. Now let me say a little more about some issues which emerge throughout the volume.

First, I was reminded of my own experiences with implementing changes in classrooms in which I had to learn what must be akin to the three cardinal principles of golf: Watch the ball, Watch the ball, Watch the ball. As I was pursuing changes in literacy teaching, the teachers and I became stalled, awkward, and schizophrenic as we focused on how we as teachers acted or on what we were doing. I can't recall what turned us in the direction of the student, but this shift proved key. I struggle with the verb, but feel sure that the three cardinal principles of teaching are Watch the child, Watch the child, Watch the child. The ease with which the contributors talk about themselves, including their difficulties, successes, and especially their quests — a term I am borrowing from one of the contributors (Fred Burton) — seems to come from their focus on the child. In other words, one of the essentials that seems to be at the heart of teacher change in every setting is the emergence of the student as the focus of classroom life.

Second, I was struck by the quality and character of the contributors as a group — people on the cutting edge of their field who are innovative, dedicated, and down-to-earth. You will enjoy the company of these teachers, especially the quality of thinking they bring to the study of their students. These teachers are themselves readers, writers, and members of communities of learners. They are working side by side with ideas, other teachers, and students. In the spirit of research and development, they approach literacy instruction neither with a blind acceptance of the status quo nor with the view that instructional improvement involves simply replacing the old regimen with a new one. They discuss the tensions they experience as they learn to trust themselves, learn to take risk moment by moment, and search for ongoing feedback on what they and their students are doing.

It is notable that their view of literature extends beyond the traditional curriculum-based views of old to views that value the social nature of literacy, the functions that literacy serves, the students' meaningful engagement in collaborative reading-writing activities, the students' exploration of issues and themes and rich discussions emerging from what they read and write. This book should serve as a wonderful source book for teachers interested in exploring the transition from traditional classrooms to more literature-based reading-writing classrooms with whole-language orientations. Unlike other books that describe such transitions or suggest such pedagogy, the current volume offers multiple case studies from teachers in different regions with students of varied backgrounds.

Third, there is an excitement about the stories as you journey with these teachers and administrators into the unknown. The volume represents reflective practitioners who are risk takers and who are on the move. As the changing views of literacy suggest, their classroom literacy programs are everchanging. Furthermore, as these teachers themselves change, their views of the children they work side by side with also change. I found my interest sparked by a number of the various plots that unfolded and my intellectual curiosity aroused by the topics addressed. A number of the teachers' explorations piqued some of my own special interests: the concern for teaching and assessment on the run, the notion of the student as researcher, and their strategies for helping students select books, engaging students in projects that involve more than just cutting and pasting ideas from multiple resources, involving parents in the education of their children, and creating literacy experiences that connect literacy to the students' lives outside of schools.

Obviously, there is a great deal more that can be said about the volume. Hopefully, I have piqued your curiosity enough. Enjoy.

Robert Tierney
Ohio State University
Columbus, Ohio

Preface

There has been a quiet revolution going on in American elementary schools during this past decade. Writing, the long-forgotten stepchild of the language arts, has come into its own as teachers initiate writing as process in their classrooms. Following models suggested by research-practitioners such as Donald Graves, Lucy Calkins, and Nancy Atwell, teachers have begun to develop young writers through a workshop approach. Instead of teaching writing through textbooks or workbook drills, teachers have taken control of their composition programs. Children write daily on topics of their own choice, read their pieces to classmates for reaction, and revise accordingly. Those pieces selected for publication are edited with the teacher to reflect standard form. Children begin to see themselves as authors, critically examining their own writing and that of others; they say they like to write and look forward to the writing workshop.

Writing process teachers quickly become disenchanted with the basal reading programs found in 80% of our classrooms. They want children to become just as excited about reading as they are about writing. The next step for most is to try to apply the writing process model to the teaching of reading. Basal readers alone are no longer adequate; teachers who have been reading children's literature to and with their children in writing workshops now want to use real books in their reading programs.

In 1987, California led the way for change when the legislature adopted the now-famous California Initiative. In an article in the Fall 1988 issue of *The New Advocate*, Superintendent Bill Honig describes the program outlined in the English-Language Arts Framework (the document written to make the initiative operable) as a literature-based reading curriculum that is integrated with the teaching of writing, speaking, and listening. California districts are now mandated to cut back on the use of workbooks and dittos and to increase the use of trade books from a recommended list of children's literature.

While many teachers in California and throughout the country welcomed the Initiative, they were uncertain about the implementation of a literature-based, integrated program. Questions arose about materials, teaching-learning strategies, and organization.

The purpose of this text is to help educators move from teaching reading in a lockstep, skills-oriented, basal-driven fashion to a more holistic, process-driven, literature-based approach. In global terms, most basal reader programs focus on the teaching of discrete word-attack skills, emphasize "product" responses (correct answers to questions on story content or workbook exercises), and suggest that children read their selections in sequence. On the other hand, a process approach focuses on how readers negotiate text and how teachers can aid the process. Teachers may use trade books or a combination of basals and trade books and give children some choice in what they select to read. Skills are taught as needed through real reading situations in small or large groups, and children are encouraged to respond to what they read in logs, eventually sharing their thoughts with peers and the teacher in group discussions. Workbooks and dittos are replaced with journals, logs, and specific writing assignments.

There is no magical "one way" to move from traditional basals to a literature-based, process reading program. Teachers develop their own programs that work in their teaching situations. We have identified exemplary process reading classrooms and schools that span the grade levels and have asked teachers and administrators in these schools to share their programs with others.

The book is divided into five parts: primary (K–2), middle elementary (3–5), upper elementary (6–8), special populations, and perspectives beyond the classroom. In each of the first four parts, besides the teachers' chapters, there is a piece written by or about an administrator. In the overview for Part I, "The Primary Grades: Great Beginnings," Dorothy Stickland deals with current issues in early childhood education, such as emergent literacy and appropriate literacy programs for the kindergarten years. The chapters that follow are by first- and second-grade teachers who plan their literacy programs around themes, genres, and authors. The section closes with insights from a principal from Dublin, Ohio, who encourages a literature-based approach.

Joan Feeley sets the stage for Part II, "The Middle Elementary Grades," by describing what children in middle childhood are like, both in general and as readers and writers. Chapters Five, Six, and Seven are written by teachers of 7- to 10-year olds who have used a workshop approach to teach reading, writing, and social studies. Chapter Eight is a report about an elementary school in Brooklyn, New York, in which teachers and administrators have worked together to initiate change.

Part III deals with teaching reading and writing in the middle-school years. In the overview, Shelley Wepner outlines the characteristics of children in the "wonder years" of early adolescence and suggests ways in which the schools can better meet the needs of these developing readers and writers. In Chapters Nine, Ten, and Eleven, teachers of sixth-, seventh-, and eighth-graders describe their reading workshops with many examples of their students' responses to literature. This section closes with a report of an unusual storytelling program, conceived by a language arts coordinator and an English teacher, in which middle-school students continue to develop as readers and writers as they create original picture books that they share with preschoolers and kindergarteners in their own district.

Irene Gaskins, principal of the Benchmark School in Media, Pennsylvania, which caters to children with learning problems, introduces Part IV, which deals with special populations within the schools. She tells how Benchmark teachers were introduced to the writing process and went on to embrace a "process" philosophy. While Chapter Thirteen describes how a Reading Recovery teacher works with at-risk first-graders, Chapter Fourteen presents a model program in which special education students learn to read and write through realistic experiences with the computer and authentic materials such as trade books and newspapers. In Chapter Fifteen, a veteran process teacher from Fairfax County, Virginia, shares her reading program for gifted third-graders. The two remaining chapters in this part focus on populations common to most school districts, children who need remedial help and are usually served through Chapter I–funded instruction and children for whom English is a second language.

Entitled "Perspectives Beyond the Classroom," Part V is designed to move the reader from the microstructure of the classroom to the macrostructures of the school and district. After an introduction by the editors, a language arts coordinator from Kalispell, Montana, shares her district's story of change. This chapter is followed by an interview with a superintendent of schools in a suburban district who promoted just such a transition.

The book closes with an epilogue in which the editors tie together the common threads running through all the chapters and offer guidelines for promoting change.

We would like to acknowledge and thank the many people who helped to enhance the quality of this text: Sara Biondello, Peter Sieger, and Kathy Rutz, editors; Cathy Labate, photographer; Jean Sawey, typist; Jane Bambrick, college librarian; John LaVigne, Erika Steinbauer, Peter Heaney, and Philip Caccavalle, administrators and supervisors who shared ideas; all the classroom teachers who taught us so much along the way; and all the students who generously contributed their writings, along with their parents who graciously cooperated with all our requests.

Process
Reading and Writing:
A Literature-Based
Approach

Part I

THE PRIMARY YEARS: GREAT BEGINNINGS

DOROTHY S. STRICKLAND
Rutgers, the State University of New Jersey

David sits on his potty reading a book. At three years his chubby legs, bent to accommodate the low seat, form a comfortable lap for holding a book. He alternatively examines the pictures by touching different parts of them and then carries on a "conversation" with the characters shown. Then he "reads" the page. His version is a fairly accurate rendition of the actual words printed. The sense of the story is completely intact. Before he turns the page, he sometimes plays a little guessing game with a character illustrated by saying, "I'll bet you don't know what's gonna happen next, . . . but I do!" Then he turns the page and continues with the story. (Jewell & Zintz, 1986, p. 3)

Monica, Paul, and Anthony have just completed an elaborate structure in the block area of their kindergarten classroom. They have worked all morning to get it just the way they want it to be. They discussed the height of various buildings and decided that some had to be adjusted to make them match each other. This prompted considerable size comparison of blocks and conjecturing about which blocks should be added or eliminated. Since this was to be a city, tiny people, cars, and other items were added from the classroom collection of small manipulatives. At times other members of the class came by to watch and make suggestions. There was a great deal of activity and talk. When clean-up time arrived, the children sought permission to leave their city intact for another day. Leery of trespassers, they decided to post a sign to ensure its safety. After considerable discussion about the proper writing materials and wording to use for their sign, "KP T" was posted in large red letters — a warning to all to keep out.

Incidents such as those described above are rather ordinary events in homes and classrooms where children are fortunate enough to grow and learn in print-rich environments. Three-year-old David has no doubt been surrounded by books since birth. He has been read and sung to. He has had access to crayons and markers along with his trucks, stuffed animals, and sand pail. His interest in stories and language is just as natural to him as his interest in making mud pies and racing toy cars. Each day brings new opportunities to explore and experiment through his own growing awareness of language, both oral and written. According to Jewell and Zintz (1986), David's mother often wished that he would take care of learning "first things first." "After all, whoever heard of a body reading in wet training pants?" (p. 3). David, however, seems to be perfectly satisfied with the way things are. He is learning to read within the natural course of his day-by-day activities — *all* of them.

Monica, Paul, and Anthony are in a kindergarten classroom where print finds its natural place in every aspect of the learning. Labels on cereal boxes and other food containers are read in the housekeeping area as a natural part of the play activity, and notes are frequently written in children's scribbling or invented spelling and posted on the refrigerator there. A news center, in the form of a chart attached to an easel, lists interesting messages dictated by children to the teacher each day. "Mary's mother cut her hair" was a hot news item recently. Recipes and other directions for making or doing something of interest to the children are frequently posted and referred to by students and teacher.

Children in Western cultures, such as ours, live in print-filled environments. To be sure, some have the benefit of more active involvement with print than others. Virtually all children in our society, however, come to school with some notion of the functions and conventions of print. Most of what they learn is done through playful, social interactions with others — sometimes children like themselves, but most often responsive and caring adults who are genuinely interested in sharing ideas and information with the child.

During the past two decades, researchers interested in young children's language and literacy development have made extensive observations of children learning to read and write in naturalistic settings (Harste, Burke, & Woodward, 1984; Hiebert, 1981; Teale & Sulzby, 1986). Young children have been observed in settings — both at home and in classrooms — where invitations to experiment independently with written language were a part of their everyday experience. This research has added immensely to our understanding of young children's emerging literacy. It is not surprising that much of what was learned about how young children learn written language parallels what is known about how they learn oral language, which many feel is the most remarkable accomplishment of humans.

Similarities between the learning of written and oral language exist in many ways. For example, like oral language, learning to read and write begins early in life. Young children recognize the graphics associated with their favorite fast-food restaurants, storybooks, and recordings as early as age 1 and 2 with apparent ease. As with oral language, young children play a major role in constructing their own knowledge of written language. They are not passive consumers. At every point, they are active participants in the process, asking questions and demanding to know. Most often their desire to learn about language and literacy is embedded in a search for some other end. Questions such as, "Where does it say it?" or "How do you write it?" are often prompted by the need to use the information for their own genuine purposes. As they grow in their ability to use language, their interest in it becomes greater and greater. Whether oral or written, language is used by children as a tool to comprehend and create meanings. It helps them make sense of and regulate the world around them.

Educators who advocate the implementation of practice consistent with the way children naturally learn are said to hold an "emergent literacy" point of view. The term *emergent literacy* comes from the work of Marie Clay (Clay, 1982), whose observations of young children provide much of the foundation for the ways we study and think about early literacy today. This view differs from widely held assumptions about language learning that have typically dominated prekindergarten, kindergarten, and primary-grade curricula. For example, the concept of emergent literacy is fundamentally different from reading readiness, which suggests that children are not ready to read and write until they are approximately 6 years old. Prior to age 6, the role of parents and teachers is regarded largely as one of preparing children for the awesome task of learning to read and write in the primary grades. Getting them ready implies the systematic and sequential teaching of a predetermined set of skills and knowledge thought necessary for success with literacy.

When we extend that reasoning to the primary grades, learning and teaching for first, second, and third graders continue to be viewed as the transmittal of information from the bearer of knowledge (the teacher) to the consumer of knowledge (the child) with the primary purpose of getting them ready for each succeeding level. Little attention is given to making the process functional and meaningful for the child at his or her current stage of development; little attention is given to helping children learn how to learn for themselves.

It is not by accident that the move toward an emergent literacy point of view has developed hand-in-hand with the trend toward teaching writing and reading as process. Both of these ideas are congruent with the current emphasis on providing a developmentally appropriate curriculum for early childhood learners — prekindergarten through Grade 3. The same theoretical underpinnings underlie all of these trends. Together, they are causing tremendous changes in the way we approach the teaching of reading and writing during the early years.

Throughout the country, teachers of kindergarten and primary-grade children are re-examining their curricula to determine how learning to read and write might be better supported there. They are using the principles of emergent literacy and process approaches to reading and writing to plan developmentally appropriate experiences for their students.

OBSERVATIONS FROM A KINDERGARTEN

Chris Bluestein is a kindergarten teacher at Public School 199 in New York City. For the past several years, Chris has been experimenting with various approaches to strengthening the literacy instruction in her classroom. She was already an avid enthusiast for the use of children's literature when she began attending workshops involving the writing process. Although somewhat hesitant about the application of these ideas to kindergarten, she and her students plunged right in to give writing a try. Having already made extensive use of literature and language charts to immerse the children in a print-rich environment, Chris found that many of them knew more about written language than she had anticipated. Some produced writing that revealed various degrees of awareness of how words, letters, and the sounds that letters represent work together in our language. Others relied solely on pictures and scribbling as written communication. Very often, combinations of all of these were used. Chris observed that in the beginning, no matter how much knowledge about print children demonstrated, they sought constant assurance that they could "really" write. Building an atmosphere in which children felt they could take risks became an important part of her teaching strategy.

One of the most significant additions to Chris's literacy program has been the extensive use of big books. These enlarged texts permit children to actually see the text as she shares stories and poems with them. The highly predictable language of these books encourages children to join in from the very first reading, giving them a sense of what it means to be a reader. Making use of these texts as models of reading and writing has served Chris as a key method for helping children begin to understand what it means to be literate. Today, journal writing and the use of big books are two of the most important components of Chris's literacy curriculum.

The writing component has been especially valuable in helping Chris track children's developing understandings about print. She uses checklists and anecdotal notes to document what children demonstrate they know about language through their writing and their responses to literature. Chris has discovered that skills related to identifying letter names, sound-letter relationships, and the concept of "wordness" are better taught and assessed through the children's writing than through the phonics workbooks used in many kindergarten classrooms in her district.

When one of her students accompanied a vivid picture of Batman with 'I wt tse btmn' to tell about going to see a Batman movie, Chris was delighted with the confidence with which he used his knowledge of sound-symbol relationships, wordness, and sentence structure to produce a coherent message about his own personal experience. Most important, just as Chris has become more self-assured in these techniques, so have her students gained in their confidence and competence as readers and writers.

The "great beginnings" that Chris Bluestein and other kindergarten teachers like her are attempting to give young learners provide the foundation for helping children become active, independent learners. That foundation is strengthened and extended throughout the primary grades in classrooms such as those described in Part I. Cindy Perkins Weaver and Betsy O'Brochta build on children's emerging literacy to offer an integrated language arts program in which reading and writing are taught throughout the day and across the entire curriculum of their first grade classes. Mary Mulcahy has typically stressed writing in her combined first- and second-grade classroom. The children's enthusiasm for reading books has been enhanced, however, by the bridges they construct from their own writings to that of professional writers and vice versa. Dawn Harris Martine has always used an abundance of literature in her teaching. Children are read aloud to daily and poems are put on charts and read chorally by children during storytime. Her extensive use of children's literature as the basis for minilessons during writing workshops was a natural forerunner to the integration of reading and writing in her second-grade classroom. Principal Fred Burton, who regularly shares literature with his students and encourages his teachers to experiment with new ideas, wants his school to become a "community of learners."

All of these educators have several things in common: They are intensely committed to improving the learning and teaching in their classrooms; they are willing to risk trying something new even though it may require "retrying" in several different ways until it is right for their situation; they are readers and writers themselves; they have a natural curiosity and desire to learn; and they are all reflective about their own learning and that of their students.

REFERENCES

Clay, M. (1982). *Observing young readers*. Portsmouth, NH: Heinemann.

Harste, J. C., Burke, C. L., & Woodward, V. A. (1984). *Language stories and literacy lessons*. Portsmouth, NH: Heinemann.

Hiebert, E. H. (1981). Developmental patterns and interrelationships of preschool children's print awareness. *Reading Research Quarterly, 16*, 236–260.

Jewell, M. G., & Zintz, M. V. (1986). *Learning to read naturally*. Dubuque, IA: Kendall/Hunt.

Teale, W. H., & Sulzby, E. (1986). *Emergent literacy: Writing and reading*. Norwood, NJ: Ablex.

CHAPTER 1

Linking Reading and Writing Through Thematic Teaching in a First Grade

ELIZABETH POMEROY O'BROCHTA
CINDY PERKINS WEAVER
Barrington Informal Elementary School, Upper Arlington, OH

Barrington Informal Elementary in Upper Arlington, Ohio, is a very busy and exciting place to be. Everywhere you turn, you are greeted by children's work. In the classroom, displays of work hang from the ceiling, are mounted on doors and window shades, and line walls. In the hallway, a patchwork of children's pieces is woven throughout the corridor — a kindergartener's collage of *The Very Hungry Caterpillar*, a first-grade class's comparison of age and the size of feet, and a second grader's mural of an aquarium seen at a local fish store can all be found. Children's work is valued here in the place where we teach.

In 1972, the board of education accepted the Informal Program, serving kindergarten through eighth grade, as a parent-choice alternative for the Upper Arlington City Schools. The teachers within the program are guided by, but not limited to, the broad goals and mission statements that serve the entire district. They are committed to reaching these goals through teaching and learning processes that have developed from the field of Informal Education.

The foundations for Informal Education stem from the ideas of Froebel, Montessori, Dewey, Isaacs, and Piaget. More recently, the research of linguists and educators such as Graves (1983), Goodman and Burke (1985), and Clay (1985) have shaped the Informal classrooms into the active classrooms they are today, emphasizing constructive language learning that occurs through functional, purposeful use. Informal Education refers to a style of teaching that:

Values child choice and decision making in the education process

Utilizes more small group and one-on-one instruction than it does whole-class instruction

Works to integrate the different areas of the curriculum through theme teaching

Provisions classrooms with a range of materials so that learning can grow out of first-hand experience

Values a holistic approach to reading, writing, and oral language learning

Values exploratory play as a prerequisite to systemized learning

Encourages flexible use of classroom time and space

Values the aesthetic experience of life as a central and vital dimension of a child's overall school experience (Carter et al., 1986).

We are very fortunate to teach where we do because we are in an established and supportive program where our beliefs are nurtured rather than questioned. Our energies go toward reviewing and implementing our curriculum, which has been structured by the teachers around themes popular with our children.

The topics for a thematic approach in our classrooms stem from the children's interests and the content areas of literature, science, social studies, health, math, and the arts. We try to integrate each content area within the theme; in a well-balanced academic year, we center a study around each content area at least once. In each of our first-grade classrooms, the degree of integration within a theme differs according to when it is studied during the school year. For example, a theme in the beginning of the year usually lasts for a shorter period of time and is less integrated, with big chunks of time devoted solely to acclimating the children to school, to the room and its materials, and to one another. Early in the year children read self-selected books in small groups with and without the teacher.

In writing workshop children generate their own texts on any topic and draw a picture to go with their writing. First, entries in journals may consist of a picture with the text represented only by the beginning sounds in the words (Fig. 1.1). We label the items in the room and play games with words and the children's printed names to begin exposing children to meaningful print.

By midyear, a thematic study is more in depth, and the content areas blend in with one another as the day unfolds. Blocks of time are devoted to our theme both in the morning (quiet work time) and afternoon (theme work time). Activities often extend over days and build on one another. At this point, the children generate more of their own text and begin to

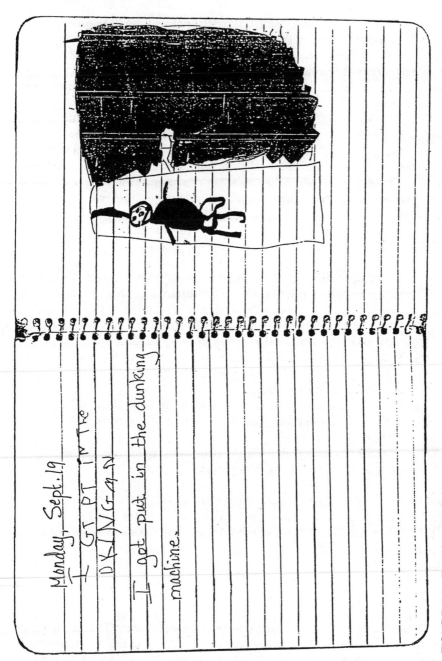

FIGURE 1.1. Early journal writing

distinguish between their own and conventional spelling. Second drafts are done on selected pieces, with the children first circling those words they feel need to be changed to conventional spelling. Only these words are then changed. The written language in their pieces also changes, reflecting a move to "story" or "book" language because of the exposure they have had to literature.

We have found that certain themes lend themselves readily to the beginning of the year, to the middle of the year, or to specific content areas. Themes such as family, bears, farms, and self get us off to a comfortable start, while folk and fairy tales, magic, and animals are appreciated more at the end of the year when the children are more able to read them. Mid-year we often study themes such as food, dinosaurs, water, and the sea.

Regardless of the theme, there are certain questions we ask ourselves while planning such as:

1. What opportunities does this theme provide for oral language? What opportunities are there for discussing, sharing, reporting, storytelling, choral reading, dramatizing, and asking questions?
2. What opportunities does this theme provide for personal or imaginative writing and for describing or explaining?
3. What opportunities does this theme provide for experiencing and enjoying literature? What opportunities are there for using reading as a source of information?
4. What modes of response can we encourage from the children (e.g., artistic representation, poetry, dramatizing, constructing models, informative writing)?
5. What is an appropriate culminating activity for this theme (e.g., a class book, a parent night, a play)?

To emphasize the progression of theme development over the course of a school year, we would like to share two themes. Betsy O'Brochta describes a theme done at the start of the school year, and Cindy Weaver describes one done midyear.

"ME, MYSELF, AND I": INTRODUCTORY THEME

The beginning of first grade can be a stressful time. On that first day at our school, a first-grade teacher is met by anxious children and parents. I have found that a study of self (entitled "Me, Myself, and I") seems to ease some of those anxieties and build confidence in the children. (They already have a wealth of information to bring to the study!) From past experience, I know that this theme and its activities allow me to introduce various materials within the room and establish guidelines for using them.

Planning

Prior to the children arriving that first day, I sat down and thought about what I really wanted to accomplish with this theme. I wanted the children to become comfortable, to learn the routines of the day, and to begin to see and write functional print.

Next I gathered theme-related books from our school library, the public library, and my classroom. Knowing that Ohio State's quarterly publication, *The WEB—Wonderfully Exciting Books*, had previously reviewed books on this theme and had also done a detailed web of activities, I grabbed this teacher reference, collecting as many books as possible. Pooling ideas from each book and sorting those which lent themselves to whole-group activities, small-group activities, and independent reading, I then webbed the book extensions and other activities by content areas study. Figure 1.2 shows my planning web for this three-week study. Since my goal for the theme was to get the children acquainted with school and our class routines, field trips and guest speakers did not seem necessary.

Developing the Theme

I opened the theme by reading Miriam Cohen's *Will I Have a Friend?* (1967) and then having the children draw self-portraits. After drawing, the children wrote about themselves with invented spellings. This gave the children a starting base for introducing themselves and it gave me a valuable first piece of work to put into their writing portfolios. Word-attack strategies were noted from their written pieces, and sophistication in drawing (Were all the facial features included? How much detail was used?) was seen from their art work.

The completed drawings and writings covered a broad range in ability! While the pictures ran from stick figures to side profiles, the writing ranged from prephonemic random letters (no connection to the words intended) to complete sentences. This activity provided a complete profile of the class.

That same first day, the children did their first graph, the first of many to come in this theme. Before they arrived, I had folded a large piece of chart paper into four columns, labeled and illustrated with four choices: I walked, I rode my bike, I took the school bus, I came by car. On a sentence strip I wrote "How did you come to school today?" On four-inch sections of

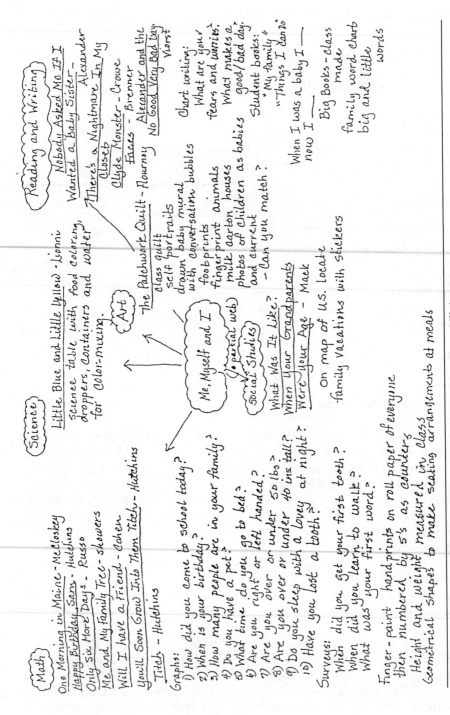

FIGURE 1.2. Planning web for content area using "Me, Myself, and I" theme

sentence strips I wrote each child's name. That afternoon we sat in a circle with the graph lying in front of us and discussed how we came to school, pointing to the columns as ways were mentioned. I took my name and placed it on "I came by car." Then the children took turns graphing. When everyone had had a chance, we counted up each column, wrote the number at the top, and talked about which number was the biggest, smallest, etc. We usually graphed every other day during this theme on topics such as "How many people are in your family?" "What kind of pet do you have?" and "What color are your eyes?"

From that day on, I shared at least two theme-related books a day with the whole group. In small groups, we made big books such as "I Can" and "After School." These books consisted of a sentence starter and the children's dictated version. For example, the dictated version of "I can" might be "I can run." As the children gave their ideas, they were written down on a large piece of paper and handed back to them. They then copied underneath the writing and drew pictures to go with the text. After this, we would write the text on a strip of paper and the children "read" the words as the strip was cut apart. Next we jumbled the words and I had the children assemble them in order. These "puzzles" were put in zip-loc bags and hung on hooks in the room for the children to come back to during worktime. The finished pictures and text were assembled into big books to be put in our class library. Small-group activities also included written or dictated books on families, things they could do, their pets, etc.

A successful book extension was centered around *The Patchwork Quilt* by Valerie Flournoy (1985). One of the messages in the story is that a quilt can tell a story about the people who made it. With fabric crayons we each designed a block about us doing something we enjoyed. A parent volunteer then sewed the blocks together, sandwiched the stuffing and backing, and headed up a small group to tie it. The quilt was proudly hung in our room, telling the story of us.

Assessment and Evaluation

Prior to the first day of school, first-grade teachers in our district are given the opportunity to meet with the children to assess reading strengths. We use three procedures from Marie Clay's Reading Recovery (1972): a dictation sentence measuring word attack, a ten-minute written vocabulary test in which children write all the words they know and can read back, and running records on selected level books (see Chapter 13 in this book on Reading Recovery). This opportunity is invaluable for the children and the teacher. It provides that rare occasion when teachers can give their undivided attention to each child. It is also a wonderful time for developing teacher-student rapport.

During this theme and throughout the year, I kept individual running records, notes on observations made of each child, and selected written pieces that showed specific strengths in spelling strategies or story development. All of these records would later be used to fill out the first progress report (Figure 1.3).

Culminating Activity

The culminating activity was the schoolwide Parent Information Night, designed to give the teachers the opportunity to talk about their individual classrooms and personal teaching philosophies. It was a thrill to see the pride and enthusiasm of these parents as they wandered around the room enjoying their children's work. Parents were asked to write a letter or draw a picture to put in their child's mailbox. This strengthened the role of writing and let the children know that their work had truly been appreciated. The next morning when those notes and drawings were enjoyed by the children, the pride seen on the parents' faces was mirrored in the faces of their children!

"THE SEA": MIDYEAR THEME

By December the children were experienced with theme work. They knew how to go about exploring their individual interests while meeting teacher expectations. While the students' input had been valued and accepted, the previous studies primarily were teacher-initiated. However, based on their experience with decision-making and their growth as readers and writers, I knew they were ready to take on the responsibility of choosing and planning our new theme.

During the initial brainstorming session in late December, we discussed possible themes for the new year. The children were full of enthusiasm and creative ideas. The most difficult decision we faced was the selection of a single theme from many wonderful suggestions. Following a lively voting session, the winning theme proved to be "The Sea." While the children decided to spend some of their winter vacation searching for books and other materials, my responsibility was to begin the pre-planning process.

Pre-Planning

The pre-planning process began with a phone call to several local libraries. While the librarians collected children's literature about the sea,

TEACHER COMMENTS

I. PERSONAL AND SOCIAL GROWTH

	Nov	Jan	April	June
1. Expresses positive self-image				
2. Complies with established classroom rules				
3. Works and plays cooperatively				
4. Follows through on activities and projects				
5. Works and plays independently				
6. Organizes time, work, and personal belongings				

II. INTEGRATED CURRICULUM
A. THEMES

B. SOCIAL STUDIES

	Nov	Jan	April	June
1. Is developing knowledge of social studies concepts				
2. Participates in cooperative decision-making and critical thinking				
3. Uses beginning research skills				

C. SCIENCE

	Nov	Jan	April	June
1. Is developing knowledge of science concepts				
2. Uses science process skills				

D. HEALTH

	Nov	Jan	April	June
1. Is developing responsible attitude and knowledge of personal health and safety				

Effort
1 = Tries most of the time
2 = Tries with encouragement
3 = Puts forth little effort

ASSESSMENT KEY

NOTE: The effort grade for each section represents all subskills unless otherwise noted.

III. LANGUAGE ARTS
A. READING

	Nov	Jan	April	June
1. Enjoys and responds to literature				
2. Selects appropriate reading materials				
3. Uses a variety of reading strategies				
4. Comprehends				
5. Makes good use of reading time				

B. WRITING

	Nov	Jan	April	June
1. Enjoys and initiates writing				
2. Develops ideas				
3. Is developing knowledge of the mechanics of writing				
4. Forms and space letters and words legibly				
5. Uses appropriate spelling approximations				

C. LISTENING AND SPEAKING

	Nov	Jan	April	June
1. Demonstrates courteous behaviors				
2. Participates in class discussions				

IV. MATHEMATICS

	Nov	Jan	April	June
1. Estimation				
2. Surveying and Graphing				
3. Geometry				
4. Addition _____				
5. Subtraction _____				
6. Time				
7. Money				
8. Measurement				
9. Problem Solving				

Individual Performance
+ = Outstanding performance
✓ = Satisfactory performance
- = Needs improvement
= Blank space indicates not applicable at this time

FIGURE 1.3. The Progress Report

15

including fiction and nonfiction, I pulled books from our classrooms. After reading each book, I recorded the title, author, possible extension activities, and interesting links to other reading materials. Based on my reading, I decided to develop a web listing titles of books for all the facets of our unit. Figure 1.4 shows my planning web for topics (animals, treasures, oceans, the seashore, and boats), trips, speakers, songs, and media.

My next step was to identify resource people within the community to serve as speakers and possible field trip opportunities (i.e., aquarium, pet store, zoo, scuba diving school). After gathering all this information, I set out to discover an appropriate starting point for our study of the sea.

Developing the Theme

The children returned to school with excellent ideas and exciting plans for our new study. Postcards, pictures, books, and bags full of shells quickly filled the round tables. Our theme was off to a roaring start. We spent the first week reading, building our web, charting ocean words, and labeling objects for the theme table. Many discoveries were being made and many questions were asked. The children couldn't wait to find out more about life in the sea.

A trip to the local aquarium was scheduled for the second week of our study. We had the opportunity to hold hermit crabs, sponges, newts, and even a starfish. The children asked numerous questions and made many interesting observations. Upon returning to school we decided to compose a group story about our exciting trip to Byerly's Fish Aquarium. We began by making a list of the important information to include in our story. Our list quickly grew to an unmanageable size, which meant we had to make some important decisions. After a lengthy discussion we decided to limit the list to ten key ideas. We spent the next two days writing, questioning, and rewriting the text. The children were very proud of their final drafts, and I was pleased with the work that had gone into developing the story. In a meaningful way, we had worked on plot development, sentence structure, spelling, and punctuation.

These two weeks had been a time of great discovery. The children loved sharing and charting various ocean facts, such as "Did you know that mother sharks sometimes eat their babies?" Big books, murals, graphs, aquatic dioramas, and large stuffed sea creatures were displayed throughout the room. A few weeks later we were off to the zoo. The children planned a bake sale to earn the money for our trip. Posters were created and announcements were made to advertise the sale. We practiced making change, so our math focus was on money. This theme developed nicely and took us in many directions.

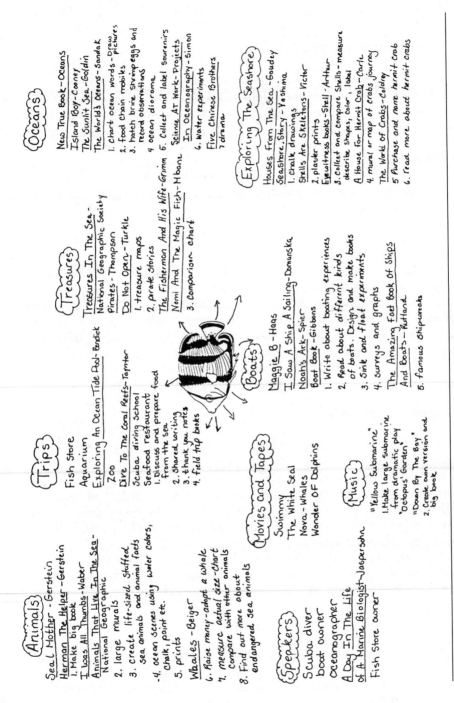

Animals
Seal Mother – Gerstein
Herman The Helper – Gerstein
I Was All Thumbs – Waber
Animals That Live In The Sea – National Geographic
1. Make big book
2. large murals
3. create life-sized stuffed sea animals and animal facts
4. ocean scenes using water colors, chalk, paint etc.
5. prints
Whales – Beiger
6. Raise money – adopt a whale
7. measure actual size – chart compare with other animals
8. Find out more about endangered sea animals

Speakers
Scuba diver
boat owner
Oceanographer
A Day In The Life Of A Marine Biologist – Jaspersohn
Fish Store owner

Movies and Tapes
Swimmy
The White Seal
Nova – Whales
Wonder Of Dolphins

Music
"Yellow Submarine"
1. Make large submarine from dramatic play "Octopus' Garden"
"Ocean By The Bay"
2. Create own version and big book

Trips
Fish Store
Aquarium
Zoo
Exploring An Ocean Tide Pool – Berdick
Dive To The Coral Reefs – Tayntor
Scuba diving school
Seafood restaurant
1. Discuss and prepare food from the sea
2. Shared writing
3. thank you notes
4. field trip books

Boats
Maggie B – Haas
I Saw A Ship A Sailing – Domanska
Noah's Ark – Spier
Boat Book – Gibbons
1. Write about boating experiences
2. Read about different kinds of boats. Design and make books
3. Sink and float experiments
4. surveys and graphs
The Amazing Fact Book Of Ships And Boats – Rutland
5. famous Shipwrecks

Treasures
Treasures In The Sea – National Geographic Society
Pirates – Thompson
Do Not Open – Turkle
1. treasure maps
2. pirate stories
The Fisherman And His Wife – Grimm
Nomi And The Magic Fish – M bani
3. Comparison chart

Oceans
New True Book – Oceans
Island Boy – Cooney
The Sunlit Sea – Goldin
The World's Oceans – Sandak
1. Chart ocean words – Draw pictures
2. food chain mobiles
3. hatch brine shrimp eggs and record observations
4. ocean diorama
6. Collect and label souvenirs
Science At Work – Projects In Oceanography – Simon
6. Water experiments
Five Chinese Brothers
7 drama

Exploring The Seashore
Houses From The Sea – Goudey
Seashore Story – Yashima
1. Chalk drawings
Shells Are Skeletons – Victor
2. plaster prints
Eyewitness books – Shell – Arthur
3. Collect and compare Shells – measure describe shapes, color, label
A House for Hermit Crab – Carle
4. mural or map of crabs journey
The World of Crabs – Goldey
5 Purchase and name hermit crab
6. read more about hermit crabs

FIGURE 1.4. Planning web for content area using "The Sea" theme

Assessment and Evaluation

Evaluation took on many forms during this theme. I observed the children as they worked and interacted with one another. In addition to examining the products created on a daily and weekly basis, I conferenced with individuals and small groups. To keep an ongoing record of the student's growth and development, my observations were recorded in my teacher log.

The children were also encouraged to evaluate their own learning and the learning of others. While they were busy with their projects, experiments, and literature extensions, they recorded predictions, observations, and conclusions in their journals. We gathered at least once a day to share, discuss, and orally evaluate each other's work, which aided in the development of the work in progress.

Classroom newsletters and personal evaluations were completed at the end of each week. The children wrote and illustrated the newsletter each Friday. The pages were filled with fascinating ocean facts, interesting stories, and exciting weekly events. The personal evaluations, including my comments, gave the children the opportunity to reflect upon their own growth and achievements as well as set goals for the following week. Figure 1.5 shows a form children filled out weekly to communicate with parents about work completed and goals set for the following week.

Culminating Activity

The children decided to conclude our ocean theme with a rather unique evening open house. A small room connected to our classroom, known as the project room, was transformed into a yellow submarine, and the classroom became an underwater world. A great deal of time and effort went into the preparations. While the captain, safety director, and weather person were busy practicing their lines, the rest of the class created signs, pamphlets, and invitations.

On the night of the open house, the children came early to set up. As the parents arrived the "travel agents" passed out schedules and tickets for the submarine ride. When everyone was seated, the captain welcomed our guests, the weather person gave a brief forecast for the trip, and the safety director demonstrated the proper technique used to put on a life jacket.

With the captain at the wheel, the crew entertained the parents with a variety of sea songs, including "Yellow Submarine" and "The Ship Titanic." When the yellow submarine reached its destination, our guests were escorted off the boat and into our underwater world. A tape of ocean sounds played softly as the children proudly shared their work. This theme

FIGURE 1.5. Self-evaluation form

Name_____

Date_____

I finished my musts every day this week.   _____yes   _____no

I used my time wisely.   _____yes   _____no   _____some of the time

I respected other people and their work this week.   _____yes   _____no

I helped ____

I've been reading __

I've learned: ____

I'd like to work on: _____

Comments from teachers:

---

was a success because the children played active roles in their educational process. By creating a balance between teacher-directed and child-centered activities, I was able to present basic concepts and ideas while encouraging the children to pursue individual interests and participate in the decision-making process.

By SHARING TWO SUCCESSFUL THEMES from different points in our year, we have attempted to show how we integrate the process of reading and writing in our classrooms and how the handling of themes change over time. While we used similar approaches with both themes, there were clear differences in the levels of sophistication employed.

As children grow in their ability to make appropriate choices in their reading, writing, and other work, theme development becomes more child-directed, and the teacher's role becomes more that of a facilitator (as in Cindy's mid-year theme "The Sea") and less an initiator (as in Betsy's beginning of the year theme "Me, Myself and I"). We believe that through thematic studies children become active learners and skilled decision-makers, skills we feel are invaluable for life-long learning.

RESOURCES IN OUR CLASSROOM LIBRARY

Our classroom collections contain a wide variety of reading materials, including children's literature (fiction, nonfiction, and poetry), magazines (*Ranger Rick, Zoo Books, Highlights for Children*), newspapers, and pamphlets. Books are housed on labeled bookshelves and in plastic tubs. The children are encouraged to check out classroom reading materials by signing the "book chart." Laminated envelopes are used to protect the books, and the children are responsible for returning them the following day.

Big books may be purchased or created by students and/or teachers. We bought many of our big books from the following sources:

The Wright Group, 10949 Technology Place, San Diego, CA 92127

Rigby, Inc., P.O. Box 797, Capital Lake, IL 60014

Richard C. Owen Publishers, Inc., 135 Katonah Avenue, Katonah, NY 10536

Scholastic Inc., 730 Broadway, New York, NY 10003

We also use several sets of books, including Story Box Readers and Sunshine Readers (The Wright Group). These books are categorized according to level of difficulty and placed in colored baskets for easy access. The children enjoy reading and sharing these predictable books. We use these books for individual reading conferences and regularly send them home in the children's nightly reading folders.

REFERENCES

Carter, M., Clark, E., DeLapp, S. R., Gee, M., Hatcher, F., Hodges, J., Koehl, J., O'Brochta, B., Webb, B., Williams, L., Yarletts, J. (1986). *Upper Arlington informal curriculum handbook*. Unpublished manuscript, Upper Arlington, Ohio, Public Schools.

Clay, M. (1985). *The early detection of reading difficulties*. Portsmouth, NH: Heinemann.

Cohen, M. (1967). *Will I have a friend?* New York: Macmillan.

Flournoy, V. (1985). *The patchwork quilt*. New York: Dial.

Goodman, Y. M., & Burke, C. (1985). *Reading strategies: Focus on comprehension*. Katonah, NY: Richard C. Owen Publishers.

Graves, D. (1983). *Writing: Teachers and children at work*. Portsmouth, NH: Heinemann.

CHAPTER 2

Literacy Lessons from a Combined First and Second Grade: A Journey

MARY MULCAHY
Richard E. Byrd School, Glen Rock, NJ

John H. Westerhoff (1987) used the metaphor of a pilgrimage to describe teaching. The curriculum, says Westerhoff, is the route over which the person travels, the student and the teacher are both travelers, and the process is a shared journey over some planned route. This metaphorical description reflects my experiences in a cross-graded school in Glen Rock, New Jersey. My first- and second-grade students and I have been on a journey, searching for ways to make learning meaningful, dynamic, and collaborative. Our journey really began in 1984 when I enrolled in the summer writing institute at Teachers College. As the two-week institute drew to a close, I was already making plans for my classroom in the coming school year.

I instituted a writing workshop in my classroom, and over the next two years I watched it become stronger and stronger. During writing workshop we learned much about writing and about each other. We learned about style, technique, and listening for the author's voice. As my students grew and developed as authors in their own right, they became more and more attuned to the work of other (professional) authors. They began to feel a kinship with Judith Viorst, Bernard Waber, and Chris Van Allsburg because they knew from their own experience what it meant to be an author. As time progressed, we found ourselves automatically drawing parallels between what we were reading and what authors were writing. My students intuitively made the "reading-writing connection."

I began looking for ways to make this connection more real and more consistent for my students. My success and strong belief in my process approach to writing encouraged me to look at my traditional basal reading program to see if that, too, could be changed. And so, I began making changes to create an environment that fosters all aspects of language development: reading, writing, speaking, and listening.

CHANGES: LOOK BEFORE YOU LEAP

Each time I read about a new teaching technique built upon the philosophy of whole language, I immediately jumped in and decided this was for me! I had to do this in my classroom! Unfortunately, I discovered that it doesn't always go exactly as the book says. One of the most important lessons I've learned during the past several years is to take it slowly and not get discouraged. My students were not guinea pigs with whom to experiment. I could not justify using them to try out all of the latest educational innovations. They needed consistency and so did I. I therefore began making gradual rather than drastic changes in my reading program.

The first change I made was to try to incorporate more literature into my present reading program and to reduce the amount of money and time spent on skill sheets and workbook pages. The money I saved by not ordering any new workbooks was used to purchase multiple copies of paperback books at varying reading levels. In this initial purchase I chose titles and authors with which my children were familiar. My justification for not purchasing workbooks came from *Becoming a Nation of Readers* (1985), which stated that students were spending far too much time on decontextualized activities and not enough time on "real" reading. During the summer, I read through all of the paperback books I had purchased and created comprehension questions and vocabulary lists to correspond with each book. I also set about the task of creating what the literature called a "print-rich environment": I displayed books everywhere, and I decorated the room with poems and charts containing print that was purposeful and stimulating.

That September I began my reading program by grouping my students homogeneously, as I had in the past. Four groups were formed, ranging in ability from beginning first- to middle third-grade levels. The groups were based solely on reading ability, *not* grade level. Therefore, first graders and second graders were often in the same group. Because my students were accustomed to the combination of first and second graders, they accepted this arrangement readily. But, instead of using the basal text as the primary reading source, each group was assigned a paperback book deemed to be appropriate for their reading level.

The beginning readers used small paperback versions of big books we had in class. These books were part of the Wright Group Story Box program. They contained very predictable and often rhyming text. This group later progressed to books characterized as early I-can-read books. Syd Hoff and P. D. Eastman were popular authors at this level. The middle readers used regular I-can-read books. The Frog and Toad series by Arnold Lobel, the Little Bear series by Else Homelund Minarik, and the Nate the Great series by Marjorie Sharmat proved to be ideal for this group. The more advanced readers enjoyed the Dorrie series by Patricia Coombs as well as books by Judy Blume, Chris Van Allsburg, and Bernard Waber. Chapter books were also used by this group. Each group met with me so that I could introduce the story and discuss new vocabulary before students read silently and answered my comprehension questions.

At first, the students were very excited about their new books and their "new" reading groups. They were reading familiar titles by familiar authors. But I realized after the first few months that my paperback reading program was not all that different from the already-existing basal program, minus a few extra skills sheets. I was, in essence, doing what much of the professional literature called "basalizing literature." The results were not what I had hoped for: My basalization of literature was not bringing the excitement of literature to my students as I had intended. So, I continued reading and learning in the hope of finding a new suggestion, a new way.

I found myself again looking back at my writing program in an effort to see what had made it so successful. The factor present in my writing program and missing from my reading program was the freedom to choose. In writing, the students were free to choose their own topics. They wrote about what was interesting and important to them. In reading, I was making all of the choices. Choice was one of the key motivating factors mentioned by Jane Hansen in her book, *When Writers Read* (1987), for initiating student interest in reading. But the students needed to be taught how to choose. I looked carefully at my present reading schedule and decided to restructure by using my writing program as a model.

THE READING WORKSHOP

My class has reading from 10:00 to 11:20 every day. This block of time is now designated as our reading workshop. I decided to begin my reading workshop just as I did my writing workshop, with a minilesson. This reading minilesson always began with my reading aloud to the class. By reading to them I would be modeling reading behaviors and introducing them to some of the best children's literature. I would read picture books, big books, poems, and songs—anything that would stimulate their interest in reading.

My reading, though, always had a dual purpose: first and foremost, to introduce the children to the world of books and to entice them to take part in the adventure of reading; and second, to model a particular reading strategy that would help them when they read independently. These strategy lessons focused on a particular aspect of the reading process. For example, by using a poem copied and illustrated on chart paper, I could zero in on several reading skills. We would first look at the illustration for picture clues so we could talk about what the poem might be about, thus establishing a mindset for reading. Then, after an initial reading, we could focus more specifically on a particular phonetic element that was repeated in the poem. Repeated readings by students reinforced sight words, built confidence and fluency in oral reading, and provided a nonthreatening forum in which students could practice their newly acquired reading skill. The poem was then displayed in the classroom to be read and re-read individually or by small groups of children during the reading workshop time.

The reading process was also reinforced when I shared a picture book with the class. Again, before reading, we always spent time discussing what we thought the story might be about based upon the title, cover illustration, or perhaps what we already knew about the author. This discussion helped focus students on setting purposes and making predictions as they listened to or read stories.

Author studies also became an important aspect of this oral reading time. Oftentimes we would spend an entire week or more reading the work of one particular author. The students became very familiar with the style of the author and the topics about which he/she usually chose to write. This made the reading-writing connection very real to my students. They began to look at authors as people, like themselves, who wrote about that which they knew and found most interesting. Judith Viorst, for example, was an author they related to quite readily. They viewed her as a mother, much like their own mothers, who wrote about her children. They thoroughly enjoyed her books because she wrote about everyday problems and situations faced by children their own age. The students also began to become drawn to particular authors and they themselves began bringing in their own collections of books by that author for me to share with the class. Parents began coming in to tell me that they couldn't believe the change in their children, who would daily return home bubbling over with stories about books they had read in school or I had read to them.

In addition to author studies, we often focused on a particular genre of literature. We spent a week or so on each genre: wordless books, ABC and counting books, fairy tales, or stories about characters facing real and sensitive issues. The students became familiar with the many options available to them in the world of books. Some quickly found their reading niche and were drawn always to a particular type of book, while others continued to experiment with many different genres and authors. Everyone now found the world of books more exciting, more real, and more accessible. This was what I had been searching for as a teacher! The process of reading had become real and important, not just to the strong readers, but to all of my students.

Besides reading to the students, time needed to be consistently built into the schedule for the students to read independently and in small groups and to talk about what they were learning. Time also was needed for me to meet with students to guide their learning and help foster greater independence in reading. This appeared to be a monumental, if not an impossible task, but I again took my time, tried different things, and eventually found what worked best for my class. The structure I decided upon was not uniquely mine but rather came from suggestions made by educators in the field of whole-language learning and literature-based reading programs.

Our daily minilesson usually lasted about 20–30 minutes, depending upon the length of the selection being read and the skill or reading strategy being reinforced. Immediately following the minilesson, 15–20 minutes was set aside for silent reading time. During silent reading the students were free to read books of their own choosing. As mentioned before, students needed to be taught how to make appropriate book choices. Many of my minilessons addressed this very important topic. As a class we discussed the importance of finding a book that was "just right" as far as readability and individual interest.

Together we came up with a framework of how to tell if a book was "just right"—not too easy or too hard. The students learned that after looking at the first few pages they could usually tell whether or not the readability level was appropriate for them. They also had learned to try to use all of their reading strategies—picture and context clues as well as phonics and decoding skills—before judging a book as too hard. The ability to comprehend and enjoy the book they had chosen was the overriding factor for making a choice. The beginning readers were encouraged to read the pictures as well as the words. And, of course, there were always wordless books and easy I-can-read books available in the classroom library. At times the children were also allowed to read with a "book buddy." Quite often a more able reader would be the partner of an emerging reader and would read to him or her. This was excellent oral reading practice for the more capable reader and provided a wonderful model for the emerging reader.

After only a few weeks, the students became quite adept at making their choices. Sometimes they deliberately chose a book that they knew was very easy for them just for the sheer pleasure and satisfaction of knowing it was easy. On the other hand, sometimes they chose a book that they knew was too difficult for them, but they would try it with the hope that someday that book would be "just right" for them. This book became a challenge, a goal for which they could strive. The most exciting moments for me were when an exuberant student would announce to the class that a book that was too hard for him/her in January was now "just right" in March. Allowing the students to choose for themselves enabled them to measure their own growth, take responsibility for their own learning, and feel great pride in their own accomplishments. As their teacher, I too was able to keep track of their growth. It was no longer measured by the completion of a level or book in a basal program, but by what I was observing and recording about their reading growth and performance.

In order to help the students and myself keep a record of their progress, each student kept a daily reading journal. The journal served many purposes, but the first was to provide an accurate record of what the students had read, when they read it, and what they thought about it. Time was provided each day during silent reading time for students to write down the name of their book, the author, a readability rating (easy, just right, or too hard), and a brief statement about the book. The students were also encouraged to jot down any new words they learned as they read or words they couldn't figure out. The reading journals were a great source of pride to the students as they were readily able to see how much they had accomplished in a short period of time. I looked at these journals each day in order to see what types of books each student chose or if there was any particular situation that needed to be addressed. The journals also provided me with something concrete to show students' parents when they asked how I was able to measure their progress without the structure of a standardized basal reading program. I also kept a spiral notebook, divided into sections marked off for each student, in which I made comments about students' book choices, as well as notes about decoding or comprehension difficulties. These problem areas were then addressed during whole-group lessons, small-group meetings, or individual conferences.

At times the journals were also used as an offshoot of a daily minilesson. For example, if during a minilesson we were discussing story setting, I might ask the children to write a description of the setting of their story in their journal. Or, when we were discussing character analysis, they might be asked to write a letter to the main character of their story. When used this way, the journals provided me with an opportunity to zero in on various comprehension strategies and note existing strengths and weaknesses.

Perhaps the highlight of our reading workshop was the reading response group time. Response groups were made up of four or five students who met immediately after silent reading and journal writing time. The members of the groups were chosen by me and remained constant for approximately two weeks. The groups were determined in several different ways: by ability level, by interest in a particular type of book, and by my deliberately mixing children with varying interests and ability levels. The students chose their own books for their response group meetings.

Each group had a leader. The leader changed each day. It was the group leader's responsibility to direct the discussion, providing an opportunity for members to tell about their book, share an excerpt, or relay a discovery they made about themselves as readers. Sometimes I asked the groups to focus their discussion on the day's minilesson by responding to a teacher-prompted question. My role during this time was to become a member of one or more of these groups, sometimes as an equal partner sharing what I myself had read, other times as teacher addressing a particular skill I felt the group needed. Direct teaching like this happened most often when the groups were determined by ability.

After each response group meeting, the group leaders were asked to share with the class something interesting that their group discussed or learned that day. The other members of the class were then free to ask

questions or comment on the group's activities. Students learned so much from each other as they shared their reading from the day. Often they were able to recommend a book to a friend or share a strategy that they had used to figure out a hard word. They took this response time very seriously as they sought to share and help each other. A true sense of community, of helping each other achieve the same goal, had developed in my reading class when compared to the very rigid basal reading groups I had used in years past. Yes, the students were well aware of who were the strongest and weakest readers in the class, but they also were aware of some of the strengths the weaker readers possessed, such as their ability to persevere and to utilize many strategies in order to read and comprehend successfully. The class became a team whose goal was to read and share the excitement of reading together.

Response groups have also provided a forum for many literature extension projects. For example, the groups might collaborate on plays to recreate a book they read, write commercials to sell the book to the class, or plan book posters. These projects were an outgrowth of genuine enthusiasm, not mandated assignments.

None of this happened magically or overnight. My reading workshop is the product of much teacher reading, preparation, modeling, and revision. This structure is one that has worked for me this year, but it is not written in stone. I always try to remain open to suggestions and modifications based on the unique needs of my students.

NEW APPROACH BEARS FRUIT

I believe very strongly in my new approach to reading instruction for two reasons: (1) It has had a very positive effect on my students, prompting them to see reading as a lifetime activity that is fun, exciting, and immeasurably rewarding, and (2) it works. My students are still required to take the *California Achievement Tests* given by the district. Each year I hold my breath and wonder how they will do on such a decontextualized, fragmented assessment of reading skills and abilities, but each year they come through very well. There is no significant difference on the test between my class and those that have been doing drill-and-practice activities all year. The only real difference I see is in the attitudes of the students. The way my students now view the process of reading is very different from that of my students in years past.

In preparation for writing about my reading program, I asked my students to tell me how they learned to read and what we do in reading class. The following are some of their exact responses to the question, "How did you learn to read?"

> We learned to read by having Mrs. Mulcahy read to us every day. She shows us how it's done and then she lets us practice ourselves. She always has good books around so there are lots of things for us to read.
>
> I learned to read by practicing every day. The more I practiced the more I could read harder books.
>
> When you learn to read, you need to use your whole brain. You have to think before you start, think about the title, think about the pictures, think about the author. This will help you read the words and understand the story better.
>
> Mrs. Mulcahy helps us learn to read by teaching us to think. She also lets us help each other when we come to hard words or she tells us to skip the hard words and go on. Most of the time you can still understand the story.

Their responses strongly suggest the importance of incorporating many reading strategies in the reading process. There isn't one key that unlocks the door to reading success for everyone. Providing time for sustained practice was also seen as very important to my students.

In responding to the question, "What do we do in reading class?" they clearly linked reading and writing together.

> I write books and read books and sometimes we get together and tell about what we are reading.
>
> I read books and write letters to people like friends and authors about the books. I also write about stories I read.

The students have made a very strong connection between reading and writing. They view this connection as the essential element of their reading class.

THE JOURNEY CONTINUES

During the last few years I have learned the value of reading extensively about the changes I anticipate making and adjusting what others have found successful to the specific needs of my students. As a result, the changes I have made have been more lasting and more successful. I began this chapter by describing teaching as a pilgrimage, and myself as a pilgrim. This metaphor continues to ring true for me. My journey is not over and perhaps will never be, for each new group of students brings with it new ideas, new challenges, new directions, and new paths that may be taken.

REFERENCES

Becoming a nation of readers: The report of the commission on reading. (1985). Washington, DC: National Institute of Education, the National Academy of Education.

Hansen, J. (1987). *When writers read.* Portsmouth, NH: Heinemann Educational Books.

Westerhoff, J. H. (1987). The teacher as pilgrim. In F. S. Bolin & J. M. Falk (Eds.), *Teacher renewal: Professional issues, personal choices* (pp. 190–201). New York: Teachers College Press.

CHAPTER 3

Reading, Writing, and Literature in a Harlem Second Grade

DAWN HARRIS-MARTINE
Mahalia Jackson Elementary School, New York City

A visitor to my second grade classroom, filled with 28 lively 6- and 7-year-old children, might initially experience a bit of uneasiness about the wide variety of activities going on at once. A closer look would reassure our visitor that, in this classroom, children are actively engaged in making critical reading/writing connections: writing or revising stories, conducting research on a subject of interest to them, discussing the illustrations in a favorite book, writing important ideas in their journals, playing a game in one of the learning centers, drawing, sharing a joke or riddle, or quietly reading a book.

My classroom is located in Mahalia Jackson Elementary School, P.S. 123, in New York City's Harlem. Most of the students live in public housing projects close to the school. Some are bussed in from Spanish Harlem, where the schools are overcrowded. Almost all of them participate in the free-lunch program. According to prevailing criteria for school success, my students are considered "at risk." Yet I find them to be eager, active learners in all they set out to do.

When I began teaching 5 years ago, my idea of a smoothly functioning classroom was one in which I directed the entire class from one activity to another. Personalized instruction took the form of my periodically darting around the room to assist those who needed help. After observing a primary grade, process writing classroom, my ideas gradually began to change. I was amazed at what these young children were accomplishing, how self-directed they were, and how their teacher appeared to assume a role much different from what I had always envisioned the teacher's role to be. Today, after attending many workshops, reading countless professional journals and books, observing many process classrooms, engaging in my own teacher research, and participating in numerous discussions with colleagues, I continue to examine my teaching and expand my understandings of how children learn. My teaching has changed and so have I. I now take great pleasure in sharing the ideas that have helped me to create a community of readers and writers with my second graders in Harlem.

GETTING STARTED

Getting started actually begins the spring before new students arrive in my classroom. I visit with the first-grade teacher who is currently teaching most of the children I expect to receive. During my scheduled preparation time, when my current students are involved with various instructional specialists or resource teachers, I arrange to observe my future students at work. I make notes about them on index cards, especially on their work habits and interactions during reading and writing. I invite small groups of children at a time to visit my classroom. They participate during the read-aloud time and get a sense of what my classroom is like. Toward the middle of June, I switch classes with the first-grade teacher for an afternoon. My current students always enjoy returning to first grade and reminiscing about what it was like. The two classes may take a joint trip to the library or the local park as a special activity. With the help of the first-grade teacher, I see to it that each child has a library card, a list of summer reading, and a personal letter and questionnaire from me to take home. The brief questionnaire enables me to get to know each child better and permits me to begin planning for next September with my future second graders in mind.

When school begins in the fall, I am always reminded of an anecdote told by the famous children's author and illustrator, Tomie dePaola, about his own childhood. He recalls that on his first day of kindergarten, he was told that he must wait until first grade to learn to read. dePaola remembers replying, "O.K., I'll be back next year!" With this in mind, I ask my students what they expect to learn in second grade. I want to know what their expectations are and I use their responses as a base for getting started.

I also ask students to share what they are expert in. We make a list of their responses. Jonathan is a good artist. Sean can count money very well. Simiko likes to clean and organize things. Damian knows how to take care of turtles. Those who have never thought of themselves as being experts at anything need a little help initially. With a little prodding and discussion, however, we soon move into a discussion of how they can share their expertise and use it to help others.

I like to start the year with a unit on dinosaurs. The very fact that it is both a familiar and a popular topic makes it a good one for observing how my new students approach learning. Over a period of days, I share a number of books about dinosaurs. I use this as a basis for introducing the unit and as a way of helping children distinguish between fiction and nonfiction. After each book is read we discuss its content and then I ask, "Do you think this really happened?" "Why or why not?" As we go along, I make two piles of books and label them "fiction" and "nonfiction."

After the topic is introduced, I allow each child to select one of several favorite dinosaurs to research. Each signs his or her name on a sheet of paper headed with the name of a favorite dinosaur. The names on each list constitute a research group. I model the generation of research questions by having the children form a big circle on the floor with one research group in the middle. I act as recorder as we discuss what they want to know about their dinosaur. Each day the children are given time to pore through the many books I have collected on the topic. They read with each other, discuss pictures, and write their own dinosaur books. Children are asked to find out two or three facts about the dinosaur they have selected for their nonfiction writing, but they are also encouraged to write fictional stories if they wish.

ORGANIZING FOR AN INTEGRATED DAY

Our day is organized to allow as much undisturbed time for reading and writing as possible. Over the years, I have learned to "chunk" various curriculum areas together to teach them in an integrated way. For example, we start the day by generating a class morning message. The children dictate personal news and various activities we have planned for the day. As they dictate, I model the writing process and call attention to aspects of grammar and various writing conventions: "How do you think we should end this sentence?" "Do I need to put an apostrophe here? Why?" "What do you think we should write next?" "How can we say that better?" When our message is complete, we reread it and edit where necessary. The message is then copied by the children as a handwriting exercise. They are urged to add a personal sentence or two about their special plans for the day. During the day, the message may be further augmented by each child. It is then taken home as a report to parents about our day's activities.

Science and social studies are always chunked with reading and writing. Research groups such as those described in the dinosaur unit are constantly being formed for both long- and short-term investigations. Sometimes two or three children are selected to look up a question posed by the group. This may be done in the classroom or at the library. In every case, the investigation will involve posing questions, searching for information, recording it, and sharing it with others. Before they go off to work independently, we work as a group, modeling how to pose questions and investigate them. We ask ourselves: What do we want to know? Where do we think we can find out? What kinds of books should we look for? How can we save (or record) the information? How can we share what we know? A large collection of easy-to-read informational books is always available so that children can browse through them, read as partners or in small groups, and select the information they think is relevant. Reporting back to the whole group may take the form of a brief oral report, a captioned picture, an informational book, or any other form of expression that children wish to use. My concern is for getting them into the process of asking questions, seeking information, and sharing it with others. Often we find that the process leads to more questions and the circle of inquiry begins once again.

My children love to learn. They are fascinated by bizarre, humorous, and unusual facts and they love to share them with the group. One important outcome of the inquiry process is the sense of control that children feel over their learning. Even though I carefully guide them in the background, they are the ones generating the questions and seeking the answers, and they are the experts. They learn that even experts may need to return to their sources to check certain facts or to get more information.

Sharing Responsibilities

The underlying structure in my classroom is highly organized. As we move into the year, more and more of the responsibility for classroom chores is shifted to the children. They take attendance, distribute and collect materials, monitor supplies, and generally care for the day-to-day housekeeping chores associated with classroom life. They also become responsible for instructional tasks such as holding reading and writing conferences with one another, teaching a new game, or acting as expert to arbitrate a rule disagreement during a game. All of this takes time to gradually work into our program, and not all children are equally prepared or capable of participating in the same way at the same time. I am convinced, however, that giving a child even the smallest task says, "You are worthy and you can learn." Students are made to feel that they are contributing members of the classroom community, and I am freed to help give individual and small-group attention to as many children as possible.

The Classroom Environment

I spend a great deal of time planning and working toward a truly print-rich classroom environment. Opportunities for reading and writing are virtually everywhere. Books are displayed in learning centers, on the chalkboard ledge, and in and on top of bookcases. Included are storybooks, social studies and science books, encyclopedias, dictionaries, spellers, and basal readers. I try to include a range of reading levels and a variety of genres and topics: poetry, folktales, cookbooks, math books, and sports stories, among others. If we are involved in an author or genre study, I display a collection of related books. Children's magazines and newspaper articles that I think will be of interest are also available.

I keep a number of card and board games available as well. Games such as *Candyland, Concentration*, chess, and *Uno* are fun, yet require thinking, attending to rules, turn taking, and a spirit of cooperation. Puzzles and other manipulatives are also available.

The writing center is located in one corner of my room. It includes a round table, several chairs, and an open metal bookcase containing dictionaries, writing utensils of all types, tape, a stapler, hole punchers, envelopes, and an assortment of other supplies. A rack filled with a variety of writing paper and construction paper is kept on top of the bookcase. At any given time there will be an assortment of postcards, stickers and stamps from junk mail, and other items of interest, to use in conjunction with their writing. Immediately beside the paper rack is a box containing the children's writing folders for work in progress. These are simply manila folders, labeled with each child's name. Another box, located on a lower shelf, contains work ready for final editing and publishing.

The writing center is accessible to children during our reading/writing workshops or at any time they have completed their other work. During workshops in which everyone writes, the children may select where and with whom they work. Our room is not very large, but we have two large tables and two small round ones, a small conference area, and some small rugs that may be placed around the room for children who wish to stretch out on the floor. Some days the room is so quiet that I can play a soothing FM station. On other days the energy level is high and the hum of the classroom provides its own kind of background "music." When children complain about the noise level, I try to place them in the conference area. When this doesn't work, we stop a minute and resolve to keep our voices down.

Scheduling

In my classroom, although reading and writing literally go on all day, I do schedule three large chunks of time each week for a process reading/writing workshop. After the entire group is seated on the floor, we begin with shared reading. This may take many forms. I may read aloud a story, poem, or short article. Sometimes I include a selection written by a child. Only those already shared by the child and included in our class library would be used for this purpose. This gives validity to their work as a part of our read-aloud repertoire and provides an adult rendering of the piece.

Shared reading is followed by a minilesson, which involves brief direct instruction on a specific concept or skill. Frequently, we return to some element from the literature read during shared reading. For example, I might use some elements from the stories to talk about action words, leads, or other interesting language. Then I will encourage the students to look for the same elements in their reading and to try and include them in their writing. Since these are very young children, I don't expect immediate transfer. My primary purpose is to strengthen their sensitivity to storybook language and the conventions of written language. As the year goes by, I begin to see the pay-off in their reading and their writing.

Often, the minilesson will focus on some problem that seems to be widespread across the group. If so, I will use work samples from the group to illustrate the problem. For example, one common problem among second graders is the repeated use of the same rather flat, monotonous sentence structure: "I went to school," "I saw Justin," "I gave him my book," and so on. Examples are read from children's work or put on the board, and we discuss how the story might be made more interesting.

After the minilesson, I spend a short period of time planning the remainder of the workshop activity time with the children. Sometimes the children work in small groups. They may read the same book or story silently and then discuss it, or they may take turns reading orally. Either way, one child acts as group leader and another records ideas from the discussion. Later, the ideas are shared with the entire group. Sometimes, the children work alone or in pairs. Some method of written response, no matter how brief, is always kept so it can be shared at some later time. The room is apt to get a bit noisy, but the children tend to remain on task throughout.

Writing is carried on in much the same way. Children may obtain their writing folders with the intention of starting a new story or continuing where they left off. Individuals may confer with one another or with me. Throughout the activity time, I work with both individuals and small groups.

Grouping and Personalizing Instruction

Groups are varied and ever-changing in my room. In the beginning of the year, I simply try to seat children together who get along. For our unit work, such as the dinosaur unit, they work with children of similar interests. I do very little ability grouping. For reading, I most often use multiple copies of good literature that I have already read to the children. Then I group them heterogeneously for small-group reading, making sure that there are one or two strong readers in the group. As with the writing, most reading is done independently, with children coming together to share what they have read with one another.

The "survivor's club" is a special group of youngsters with whom I meet on a regular basis. These are children who need something extra in the way of coping skills. I help them learn how to look out for themselves and other siblings as well. Each morning, I check to see that they have had breakfast, whether they are dressed appropriately, and whether they have any medical problems. Once a week, we have lunch together. We discuss various survival skills such as whom to contact in an emergency, how to use the laundromat, how to count change and buy wisely, what to eat when you are alone at home and hungry, fire safety, home safety, dealing with strangers, and keeping away from drugs. We also discuss what to do when you are locked out of the house, and whom to call and where to go if there is no heat. These are real issues for all of my students, but for the survivor's club they are critical daily concerns. Many of these children have adult responsibilities. Not only do they need coping skills, they need to know that there is someone who understands and empathizes with them. I treat grouping in my classroom much like everything else. I try to be open and flexible and, most of all, responsive to the needs of my students.

MORE STRATEGIES FOR READING AND WRITING

Library Visits

Every Thursday afternoon we visit our neighborhood public library. The librarian always has something new and wonderful to show us. It may be a film, a new book, a storyteller, or a puppet show. We have the entire children's section, the whole second floor of the library, to ourselves. Our time at the library follows a predictable pattern. The librarian makes a presentation first. Then the children research and read with assistance from myself, the librarian, and her assistant. Then we select books to take home. One afternoon we had a library scavenger hunt. I formed four teams, gave each team a list of books to find, and monitored how long it took each team to find them. The team that located the most in the least amount of time was allowed first pick from the newest books in the library.

Writing Notebooks

Each child keeps a writing notebook. In it is kept ideas for stories and poems, words or sentences they want to remember, or any other things they wish to include. It is not a journal in the sense that it records ideas day-by-day, but a place for them to put down thoughts for future writing or simply store memories of things they don't want to forget. For example, Douvone wrote his remembrances of a trip to his grandmother's house. Later, he made a copy of it and sent it to her as a gift.

Learning to Interview

I want my students to know that there are many ways to get information. Books and other reference materials are important resources, but so are people. During a social studies unit on community helpers, we decided to interview some community helpers in our neighborhood. We discussed some of the questions we might ask, and I modeled the process by role-playing an interview with a fellow teacher in front of them. Then the children practiced interviewing each other and members of their family. Finally they were assigned to teams in order to interview people in the community. They took notes, wrote brief reports, and reported what they learned to the entire group.

Writing Letters

Letter writing is a very important part of our reading and writing program. We are always on the lookout for authentic opportunities to write letters. I encourage the children to write letters to parents, grandparents, and other relatives regularly. They simply share with them the special things that are going on in their lives, both inside and outside the classroom. Often, they like to share their personal letters with the group before taking them home. During an autumn hot spell, the water in the class was turned off because of a leak in the sink. It was not turned on again until we wrote a letter to the custodian telling him how inconvenient it was not to have water in our classroom. The letter was signed by each member of our

class. Chantee wrote a letter to Vera B. Williams, the author, after she
noticed the inscription she had written in our class copy of her book, *A
Chair for My Mother* (New York: Greenwillow, 1982). Chantee wrote:

> Dear Vera B. Williams,
>   Did you really sign the book that is in my class? When did you
> come? Do you like my teacher? I do. Will you come again? I love the
> pictures you draw and the beautiful frames you put around them. I
> do that myself sometimes. Ms. Martine told me that you like nick-
> names, my mother calls me 'Skooter.'
>
>   Love,
>   Chantee

Sharing Memories

One day Ifora brought in a picture of herself, taken when she was a
small baby. I decided that this was a great time to introduce memoir, the
opportunity to reflect on your lifetime. What significance does this have to
a 7-year-old? A connection to the past. A promise of a future.

I asked everyone to bring in a baby picture. I mounted them on a
bulletin board with the caption, *Do You Know Who These Babies Are?*
Numbers were placed next to each name and the bulletin board was covered with acetate. This bulletin board was at eye level, making the pictures
easy to observe. A small table had paper and pencils for children to list the
numbers and place next to each one the name of the person that they
thought was in each picture. A box with a slit in it was available for them
to place their guesses. They had great fun trying to determine who those
babies were. They used every means available to them — direct inquiry, the
process of elimination, even cornering a parent for questioning whenever
possible. All of the pictures were identified except one, mine. One child
said, "I didn't know you were a baby."

Storytelling was an important part of our memoir activities. I asked
the children to have their parents tell them stories about when they were
babies. I told them stories that my mother had told me about when I was a
baby. We had fun sharing our stories. The children began to collect their
stories in their writing notebooks. When Tiffany's Mom told her about an
incident that Tiffany remembered differently, we had an opportunity to
talk about point of view. I asked other children to think about the stories
their parents had told them and reflect on whether or not they remembered it differently.

I read stories about family relationships and remembrances. Eloise
Greenfield, James Stevenson, and Cynthia Rylant are a few of the authors

that we read and discussed. Finally, we wrote our own personal memoirs and placed them in our class library of family books.

REFLECTIONS

As I reflect on what I do, I think that my most important task is to create an environment that says to the children that they are special and that I have high expectations of them. I want them to realize that each of them has a special talent and that it must be nurtured and shared. Making the most of those naturally occurring moments that allow me to get to know my students, I help them determine what they know and what they want to know, and I guide them in the process of finding out. Together, we become a community of learners.

CHAPTER 4

Learning to Read Through Literature: An Administrator's Perspective

FREDERICK R. BURTON
Wright Elementary School, Dublin, OH

The speaker finished and the host gave the nod of approval signaling to the audience that questions would be taken. I stood up from my chair in the back row and began my question: "As a principal. . . . " That did it. At the word "principal," heads turned. Some eyebrows went up; some eyebrows went down. This was, afterall, a conference of the National Council of *Teachers* of English. As I sat back down, someone leaned over and quietly whispered "More principals need to be here to learn about literature-based reading; otherwise, how can they support and help teachers?"

Indeed, how *can* principals — most of whom possess far less practical and theoretical knowledge about the reading process than the teachers they work with — help and support both teachers in transition as well as the experienced whole-language practitioners?

Reflecting on my experiences (including the abysmal failures) as an elementary teacher and my current position as an elementary school principal, I offer the following advice to administrators desiring to create conditions favorable for classroom reading programs such as those described by teachers in the preceding chapters. Grounded in the best language learning theory and research, these literature-based programs deserve support. While some of the advice is conceptual and deals with changing "worldviews," I've tried to give practical examples in each case regarding what it means in relation to the teaching of reading in elementary classrooms.

DUMP THE "GREAT PERSON" THEORY OF LEADERSHIP

In the last decade, there has been an enormous amount of research on "effective" schools and principals. However, while principals and schools may be "effective," it does not necessarily follow that they are *good*. Whenever I read the effective principal research, I feel grossly inadequate. This research inevitably points to the principal as a Great Person — someone like Ghandi or Joan of Arc — who possesses *extraordinary* vision, drive, power, and knowledge. This research conjures up images of a person who knows all of the answers, acts decisively, and, through sheer will and charisma, brings along the masses to his or her point of view. It is, as Murphy (1988) points out, a poorly conceived view of the leader as "lion" rather than a "lamb."

Such a view of leadership creates unrealistic expectations and anxiety on the part of principals. If one accepts "the Leader as Great Person" point of view, then knowledgeable whole-language teachers act as a threat to principals who would feel inadequate not having answers.

Knowing that they can never be that Great Person, principals understandably retreat. They stay with the known. How can one have all of the answers when there are teachers whose knowledge far exceeds that of the principal? Of course, teachers also fall prey to the Great Person complex as well. Sadly, there are people who would and could do perfectly well at teaching reading through literature and providing integrative language experiences for children, but who never take the risk, believing that they can never be the superteacher that they know, or have at least been led to believe, exists.

In the everyday world of public and private education, there are very, very few extraordinary principals or teachers. Yet, there are many, many good ones. And so, what are the good principals to do?

First, they can begin to adopt the position of "servant leadership" (Greenleaf, 1977). Rather than wield power, they share it. Rather than always answering questions, they sometimes raise them. Servant leaders are responsible for creating *shared* visions. Ordinary people with good intentions and reasonable "human skills" can do this.

Good principals — ones not stymied by the expectations that they have to be omnipotent and omniscient in all circumstances — can create organizational structures that promote what I call a *professional quest*. Such a quest should be thought of as an "adventurous expedition." A climate of professional questing is evident in schools where a community of learners exists. Such a community is a place where adults as well as children can raise questions that perplex them and passionately pursue courses of action that lead them forward. An example of how such a "quest" might look follows.

The Professional Quest

Although I am an advocate of teachers doing action research, I am personally finding the notion of a "quest" to have more power than "research." While research and quests have much in common, the latter term is more evocative. A quest conjures up an image of active seeking, personal struggle, and adventure found in great works of literature such as the Arthurian Legends or the Chronicles of Prydain.

In the spring, teachers in our school begin formulating a dimension of teaching and learning worthy of a quest the following year. All individual quests are compiled and published for the staff to discuss in small groups. Next, items on the list are clarified, revised, and formulated as questions. For example, one might ask: "How can I better communicate a child's growth to parents in a literature-based reading program?" More often than not, teachers from across various grade levels learn that they have similar quests or find the quest of a colleague to be of interest to them as well.

Once the various "quests" have been framed as questions, small groups of teachers meet to begin formulating plans of action to answer these questions systematically. Some make summer plans that relate to their quest, such as to pursue course work, review professional readings, travel, and contact colleagues/speakers that might help them. Others simply file away their question with the knowledge and satisfaction that they have a tentative professional path they can follow the next school year.

The groups meet the following year to deliberate about their chosen "quest-tions" with others, forming small circles of learning. Staff meetings, then, can be used as opportunities to get together.

The principal's role in creating the professional quest is to:

- Facilitate and participate in the spring meetings
- Meet with teachers individually to question and clarify the quests as well as assist in developing the plans of action in the spring and confirming and/or revising them again early on in the following school year
- Help to form groups or small circles of learning (which, because of similar quests, may be self-selected)
- Turn staff meetings into settings for groups to discuss their professional quests in a systematic way; articles on "action research" may

provide helpful frameworks for pursuing questions systematically (see, e.g., Strickland, 1988)

Finally, the principal may develop formats for bringing closure to the professional quest. Teachers may choose to write about their quest, video- or audiotape their findings, create an archive or portfolio of their journey, or devise some other way to share and express their knowledge. Of course, one year's quest may provide the foundation for the next year. Questions sometimes lead to more questions!

THINK OF THE SCHOOL AS A "COMMUNITY OF LEARNERS"

Organizational charts are fine, but they do not begin to reflect the rich complexity of the school culture. Schools are much more than a set of hierarchical schematic drawings. Instead, principals, parents, teachers, and children are "culture makers" every day of the school year. Cultures are made and sustained as the participants share experiences, question and challenge each other, and develop a common language.

What might the principal do to promote a "community of literacy learners" in a school? In my first year as principal of Wright Elementary School, I was faced with the challenge of opening a brand new school building with children and teachers coming from five different attendance areas. How could I create a community of literacy learners?

After a little thought and a lot of panic, I decided to try three strategies that would help create cohesiveness. First, I eliminated the schedule for ringing bells in our building. Secondly, I vowed never to use the intercom system. These two strategies helped preserve the "community" of literacy learners in each of the classrooms by greatly reducing the number of outside interruptions. However, nothing moved our entire school toward a sense of community more than the third strategy—establishing school Town Meetings.

The Town Meeting As Community Builder

Town Meetings are weekly all-school meetings that last from 20 to 25 minutes. The purpose of the Town Meeting is to celebrate children and adults as learners. Every Friday, children, teachers, custodians, and the secretary gather in our Commons, a large tiled area in our school. The format varies little from week to week. I begin each meeting with a few announcements that deal with the more mundane aspects of administration (e.g., comments on the fire drill, clarifications about playground safety, etc.) We usually end the meetings with a song. For example, I might talk about Peter Spier's *Erie Canal* and then sing the song with everyone. But it is the *middle* portion of the meeting that has best served to build a community of literacy learners in our school. Examples of events that have occurred during the middle portion of meetings include:

- A first grader recites his first dinosaur poem.
- Children in Reading Recovery do a choral reading of *The Very Hungry Caterpillar* (see Chapter 13 for more on Reading Recovery).
- A fourth-grade girl reflects and talks with the school about learning the piano prior to playing for everyone.
- About the time when the World Series takes place, 25 second graders dramatize "Casey at the Bat."
- A teacher recites an original poem and talks with the school about her composing process.
- Another teacher shares some facts from an information book on bats (on the same day that a bat had been discovered outside and had been observed by many of the children).
- Two fifth-grade boys perform a "rap" they have written based on their reading of Scott O'Dell's *Island of the Blue Dolphins*.

These are a few examples of what turns up at Town Meetings. Other literacy events might include a student "position paper" on the inhumane treatment of animal experimentation followed by another student reading a rebuttal. Parents might bring toddlers and grandparents to share their literacy stories. Children's literature is continually being shared, re-enacted, written about, and read.

While the Town Meeting is a rather dramatic example (yet in reality a simple thing to do), there are other effective ways to build a community of literacy learners, including:

- School newspapers
- Buddy Reading: Older children read with, read to, and listen to younger children reading (see Chapter 12 for an example)
- Family Sleep-Ins: A school slumber party in which families read together and participate in other literacy events
- Asking children to submit photos and captions of school events for the local media

The International Reading Association and National Council of Teachers of English have publications that can be helpful. I'd also recommend Heald-Taylor's (1989) *The Administrator's Guide to Whole Language*.

THE ROLE OF PROFESSIONAL PLEASURE

Sitting in my office one day, my thoughts drifted over the following: The superintendent was visiting our school, and he might not be happy about the mud on the carpet; the cooks had reminded me again that they definitely needed a phone in the kitchen; the custodians were less than thrilled that a teacher had tried to put plaster down the classroom sink; a parent had called last week and was not pleased that her child was not getting enough phonics instruction; legislators in Ohio were requiring every teacher to teach phonics, yet many teachers thought that *too* much phonics was already being taught; three teachers wanted to know what I was going to do about their paint orders that had not arrived yet; a child had brought a toy (yet very real looking) gun to school yesterday and I had been asked to see him about this today; the school secretary was ill and would not be here; our copy machine wasn't working; if the spring school tax levy didn't pass this time, then what?; and, lest I forget, a parent had informed me that I would probably be subpoenaed to testify in a divorce case.

All of this and the school day hadn't even started yet!

However, it wasn't all gloom and doom. The following also happened: A kindergarten child came into my office to share a book that she had written—I immediately phoned the surprised yet pleased parent and shared the good news; a third-grade child brought in a poem he had written, and I asked to hang it in my office; I ran upstairs just in time to relax in a dark classroom of fifth graders sprawled out on the floor listening to an audiotape of Shel Silverstein reading his poetry; I read aloud Remy Charlip's picture storybook, *Fortunately*, to a first-grade class that had been discussing the "good news/bad news" theme in another story their teacher had read; I smiled as a second-grade teacher who was moving away from using a basal excitedly described how well her children had responded to children's literature through a writing activity.

Pleasure and fun are two words you will rarely, if ever, see in scholarly journals and academic course work—especially *administrative* journals and academic course work. Synthesizing the latest research in medicine, brain research, and psychology, Ornstein and Sobel (1989) have made a powerful case for the role pleasure plays in our ability to sustain ourselves and others. Yet pleasure and joy are often seen as "frills." Perhaps it is time to recover this important dimension of learning.

FINAL NOTE

In the previous chapters, we have outstanding examples of teachers who have artistically created highly interactive and engaging literacy environments. These are classrooms where inquiry, community, and joy are present. We know that reading for pleasure is why children learn to read. Isn't it reasonable to assume that the principals who find joy in learning about literature-based reading and helping children and teachers become more engaged in such programs will also be the same principals who will be *supportive* of teachers and children? Principals often find themselves removed from the joy and intimacy of the classroom. It is essential that they seek out and share in such experiences — for themselves and for the school culture they are continually helping to create every day.

REFERENCES

Greenleaf, R. K. (1977). *Servant leadership*. New York: Paulist Press.

Heald-Taylor, G. (1989). *The administrator's guide to whole language*. Katonah, NY: Richard C. Owen Publishers.

Murphy, J. T. (1988). The unheroic side of leadership: Notes from the swamp. *Phi Delta Kappan, 69*, 654–659.

Ornstein, R., & Sobel, D. (1989). *Healthy pleasures*. New York: Addison-Wesley.

Strickland, D. (1988). The teacher as researcher: Toward the extended professional. *Language Arts, 65*, 754–764.

Part II

THE MIDDLE ELEMENTARY YEARS

JOAN T. FEELEY
William Paterson College

"Why did the farmer name his hog Ink?"
"Because he kept running out of the pen."

"Knock, knock."
"Who's there?"
"Duane."
"Duane who?"
"Duane the tub, I'm drowning." (Schickedanz, Hansen, & Forsyth, 1990, p. 487).

Anyone who spends time with children in the middle-elementary grades knows about the riddles and "Knock, knock" jokes they like to tell. Because they have developed metalinguistic awareness — the ability to pay attention to the syntax used to convey meaning, instead of just the surface meaning itself — they can play games with language, trying to outwit listeners with their tricky punchlines (Schickedanz, Hansen, & Forsyth, 1990).

This section deals with children in middle childhood, those 8 to 10 years old who typically are in Grades 3 through 5 and sometimes called "school-age" children. Although children this age are highly visible in our society — on the playground, in the school bus, in the local stores and pizza shops — they often don't receive the adult attention paid to children in infancy, early childhood, and adolescence (Collins, 1984). One reason for this could be that, for the first time, school and friends take up much of their time, and another could be that the physical and psychological changes during this "latency" period are more gradual and not as obvious as those that take place during the other developmental stages (Shonkoff, 1984).

However, even though gradual, many changes do take place during this period. Besides adjusting to the shift to more formal classroom instruction, school-age children are introduced to new social rules and are challenged to expand their world beyond their immediate neighborhoods. They are required to make important changes in the way they think about the world and relate their own experiences to those of others. Knowing about these changes is important to those involved in helping children to grow in literacy. After a brief sketch of the physical, cognitive, and social-emotional growth of children in middle childhood, this overview will describe these children as writers and readers, concluding with implications for teaching and an introduction to the chapters to follow.

THE MID-ELEMENTARY SCHOOL CHILD

It is not unusual to see school-age children riding bikes and playing games requiring throwing, hitting, and kicking. Although physical development in middle childhood is less apparent than in the earlier years, school-age children rapidly acquire many gross and fine motor skills that enable them to engage in sports, games, and activities that require coordination. In general, they are taller, slimmer, and stronger than they were during early childhood, and they like to engage in a wide range of physical activities, from frisbee throwing in the park to long bike rides and extended hikes in the woods (Papalia & Olds, 1990).

During these years, children make dramatic gains in cognitive skills. Their thinking has been labeled by Piaget (1955) as "concrete operational," meaning that they can think logically as long as they can see and interact with what is to be learned. They begin to operate on the basis of rules and can use mental operations to solve problems. Children in middle childhood start to mobilize their knowledge to target problems and arrive at solutions. Metacognition, the ability to think about thinking, begins to develop. This is why they can play with language and enjoy corny jokes; also, they can begin to monitor their understanding of what they read and hear and develop increasingly more sophisticated mental strategies to help them study (Schickedanz et al., 1990).

The ability to remember is related to schemata: the knowledge, experiences, and concepts available to help one organize what is learned. According to Zigler and Finn-Stevenson (1987), during middle childhood, children begin to see hierarchical relationships between subordinate and superordinate classes, for example, that Terriers, Collies, and Great Danes belong to a subordinate class of dogs and a superordinate class of animals. As schemata become increasingly more complex, memory improves greatly. Also, because memory capacity increases rapidly, children become more adept at using mnemonic strategies such as rehearsal, categorization, and elaboration (Papalia & Olds, 1990).

Because of their growing ability to put themselves in someone else's shoes, school-age children acquire important social understandings. They become aware of others' thoughts, feelings, and intentions, and develop a sense of "right" and "wrong." As they experience self-awareness through interaction with peers and adults outside the family, they become increasingly aware of how others will react to their actions and ideas. Zigler and Finn-Stevenson (1987) say that when children are able to understand the perceptions of others, they become more empathic and better able to communicate, since effective communication depends on sensing what people know and need to know. Also, self-concept, based on one's perception of self, develops dramatically in middle childhood. As they internalize social values and the views of others, children begin to compare the real self with the ideal self. Whether positive or negative, self-concept is greatly influenced by their relationships with family, friends, peers, teachers, and other significant adults in their lives.

WRITING DURING THE MID-ELEMENTARY YEARS

Teaching writing as a process (Calkins, 1986; Graves, 1983; Hansen, 1987) appears to be exactly right for the mid-elementary school years when children are experiencing self-awareness and forming their concept of self. As they engage in writing personal narrative and specialty reports with feedback from teachers and peers, they gain more and more control over their own lives and over written language. Their writing undergoes noticeable changes during these years.

Perhaps because of their growing control over the mechanics of written language from having learned to read, third graders seem to be preoccupied with conventions and correctness (Calkins, 1986). Selecting broad topics and writing events in a chain-like manner, they enjoy showing what they know. For example, once a convention like writing dialogue or using exclamation points is learned, it tends to be used profusely.

Demonstrating Piagetian concrete operational thinking, 8-year-olds do not mull over alternatives before writing; rather, they put down everything they may want to use — for example, drafting three leads or endings to choose from and revising by copying over with very few changes. Bereiter and Scardamalia (1982) say that young children lack a central executive function that allows them to go back and forth between talking, listening, writing, and reading. They tend to write short pieces that are technically correct but which often lack "voice" (Calkins, 1986).

From Grade 4 on, children begin to reread to revise, especially if they are in workshop situations in which they can get responses from others during conferences. They soon move toward "holding their own internal conferences," reflecting Vygotsky's "zone of proximal learning theory," which posits that what children do today with others, they can do alone tomorrow. As they develop metalinguistic ability, children learn to use more representational thought and "just think about" alternatives rather than writing everything out. More and more, writing becomes a means of thinking and rethinking (Calkins, 1983, 1986).

By the age of 10, children can view their writing through the eyes of a reader. Experimenting in their minds, they can go back and forth from writing to reading. As they gain more control over mechanics and content, they can shift between narration and description and narration and dialogue in one piece. While younger children favor writing personal narrative and stories that reflect exactly what happened, older children can weave together truth and fiction, using their craft of writing to please an audience. They can take on the voice of a third person as they move from writing personal narrative to writing in many genres.

READING DURING THE MID-ELEMENTARY YEARS

Because of wide differences in abilities and experiences and the idiosyncratic nature of literacy development, describing readers in the middle-elementary grades is difficult. Most third graders can integrate all the cue systems (semantic, syntactic, graphophonic, and schematic) to "figure things out" for themselves. Regarding print as literal truth, they think that "what the book says is right." They enjoy reading orally for an audience and silently for pleasure and information. From their exposure to books and reading, they have internalized print grammars or structures, both narrative and expository, to help them make sense of written language within their experiential backgrounds (Cochrane, Cochrane, Scalena, & Buchanan, 1984). Even though narrative is the mainstay of the primary grades, Langer (1986) found that 8-year-olds have a good knowledge of exposition. They can talk about the differences between stories and reports and know they are used in different ways.

As they move through the grades, children's ability to comprehend text is limited only by their prior knowledge in general and their knowledge of text structures specifically (Mason & Au, 1990). According to schema theory, reading is the interaction between the reader and the text. Readers are actively constructing meaning, based on their own schemata and what the author has written. Readers' schemata help them to make inferences, summarize, remember, add new knowledge, and make decisions about what is important in a text (McNeil, 1987).

Frank Smith (1985) says that reading comprehension is raising questions about a text and finding answers. Children in the middle-elementary years are active readers who can ask questions as they read rather than read just to answer questions raised by others (Palincsar & Brown, 1984; Singer, 1978; Stauffer, 1975). Besides being active, questioning readers, they are strategic readers. As metacognitive thinking develops, they learn about and use a variety of reading strategies (Meyers & Paris, 1978).

Vocabulary grows in leaps and bounds during the elementary years. Nagy and Anderson (1984) found that books read in the elementary grades contain approximately 90,000 different words. Nagy, Anderson, and Herman (1987) reported that, beginning about third grade, the major determining factor to vocabulary growth is the amount of free reading. Students seem to be able to learn words at a rapid rate, perhaps 3,000 words or more per year. The amount of vocabulary learned depends on three factors: the amount of written language children are exposed to; the quality of the text; and the students' ability to remember the meanings of new words when encountered again. While children learn about 200–300 words per year through direct instruction (Durkin, 1979; Jenkins & Dixon, 1983), they pick up thousands of words incidentally, within the context of their reading. Besides school texts, trade books, and their own writing, school-age children read newspapers, magazines, comics, hobby books, TV listings, video games, directories, baseball and bubblegum cards, and a host of other print materials that may be part of their environments.

When it comes to reading interests, strong sex differences begin to emerge by grade 4. Girls read fiction more than do boys, selecting social empathy, fantasy, and mystery-adventure. While expressing some interest in fiction, especially mysteries, adventure, and science fiction, boys show more preference for non-fiction categories like sports, history, biography, and science (Feeley, 1981; Graham, 1986; Wolfson, Manning & Manning, 1984).

In her ChildRead survey, Burgess (1985) found that children from Grade 4 up selected books on the basis of appearance, author, and recommendations of peers and adults. While parents and librarians were frequently mentioned as resources for recreational reading, teachers, unfortunately, were not viewed in this capacity. Burgess also found support for the research on interests cited above: Most children did show a preference for one kind of reading, yet were willing to sample a wide variety of materials.

A new area of general interest was the nonfiction category "technology," which Burgess attributes to the current focus on computers. Interestingly, some are using nonfiction collections heavily for recreational reading. All children surveyed reported having at least one favorite book that they had re-read several times.

Toward the end of the elementary school years, as they move from concrete thinking to more formal operational thought, able readers can process materials further and further removed from their own experiences, and reading provides a major source for continued schema development and refinement (Cochrane et al., 1984).

IMPLICATIONS FOR THE CLASSROOM

In her study of school-age children from 8 years of age and up, Langer (1986) found the dominant concern was with the meanings they were developing while reading and writing. When reading, they focused on specific content, validating the "text world that was being developed." When writing, they took more control over the process, focusing on ways to create their meanings. "In each case, the children relied upon operations that helped them to make sense—either of their own or someone else's ideas" (p. 139). Accordingly, reading and writing programs in the middle-elementary years should center around meaning-making. Strickland and Feeley (1991) offer the recommendations that follow:

• Reading and writing should be taught through a process approach (Calkins, 1986; Graves, 1983; Hansen, 1987). The conference aspect, in which others provide the external executive function needed by children still mainly in the concrete operational stage, works well for both reading and writing. The authors in this section started teaching writing as a process and then moved to teaching reading in a similar manner. More and more, they found themselves using trade books as models for children's writing, and it seemed only sensible that they should offer children the opportunity to read good literature rather than basal readers. They eventually abandoned the basal systems that restricted their focus on the process of meaning-making for self.

• Children should be encouraged to engage in schema activation before reading and writing so that they can make use of what they already know to aid understanding. Langer (1984) used a Pre-Reading Plan (PREP) to assess children's text-specific background knowledge before reading and found that the process significantly improved their comprehension. McNeil (1987) suggests that webbing, semantic mapping, and other background-generating and organizing activities be modeled and demonstrated. Note that Ziegler, Klika, and Stampa in the chapter to follow show their students how to create webs as they read and write nonfiction.

• Teachers should give increasing attention to expanding children's knowledge about text structures. Although 8-year-olds understand exposition, they tend to use mainly description or fact collections when they write reports (Langer, 1986). In her chapter on using reading-writing process within the context of a social studies unit, Pilchman (Chapter 7) opens her students to many varied ways of reporting information, such as letter exchanges, newspaper eye-witness accounts, and historical fiction. Ziegler, Klika, and Stampa (Chapter 5) read exemplary nonfiction trade books to their children as models for writing informational pieces.

• Vocabulary should be expanded within the context of real reading and writing. Nagy, Anderson, and Herman (1987) have determined that the most effective way to increase vocabulary is to have students do lots of reading. While Mezynski's review (1983) concluded that vocabulary training had little effect on reading comprehension, Gipe (1978–1979) found that an interactive context method was superior to other methods (including the time-worn dictionary approach) for developing vocabulary and comprehension among third and fifth graders. Maureen Armour (Chapter 6) used a contextual approach with her fourth graders as they read trade books in small groups. Most of the time, the children could come up with precise meanings of unusual words because they "figured them out" together within the context of a developing text. In reading workshop approaches such as those described in this section, children read a great many books of high literary quality, two of the factors mentioned by Nagy, Anderson, and Herman (1987) as being crucial to vocabulary growth.

• Children in the middle-elementary grades, who are naturally developing metacognitive abilities, should be encouraged to step back and monitor their attempts at meaning-making. Stevens, Madden, Slavin, and Farnish (1987) taught third and fourth graders metacomprehension activities in a cooperative learning approach and found significant effects on several measures of literacy achievement. Paris, Cross, and Lipson (1984) successfully taught third and fifth graders to monitor their reading. Students learned to plan, evaluate, and regulate their own comprehension, becoming significantly more aware of reading strategies while improving their comprehension. In the classrooms described in this section, children work cooperatively as they read and write; they are encouraged to think about what makes sense and help each other to achieve meaning. The emphasis is on cooperation rather than competition in the pursuit of learning and learning how to learn.

• Reading and writing across the curriculum, through a cooperative workshop approach, should be emphasized to enhance learning in the content areas. Langer (1986) found that children were more able to talk about what strategies they had used and how their knowledge had changed after writing than after just reading. She says that writing seems to be useful in helping children gain a real understanding of subject matter. In Chapter 6, Pilchman describes how her fifth graders read biography and historical fiction besides factual sources to learn about the American Revolution. To share their learnings, they wrote in a variety of genres such as historical fiction, informational picture books, and newspaper reports. Her account is an excellent example of reading and writing to learn in a content area.

THE CHAPTERS THAT FOLLOW

It is obvious that the educators in this section are aware of the characteristics, needs, and interests of children in the mid-elementary years. All use a workshop approach in developing readers and writers. All use literature as the basis for their literacy programs. Reading and writing are learned together as children pursue their own interests in writing nonfiction, reading favorite authors and genres, and learning history.

Edie Ziegler, Marilyn Stampa, and Jim Klika, known as "Team C" in their suburban New Jersey elementary school, teach cross-graded groups of second, third, and fourth graders. In their chapter, they describe how they organize for nonfiction reading and writing. Beginning by describing how they read exemplary nonfiction books to the children, they move on to how they deal with topic selection and then to how they encourage research methods that involve the home, community, and library, as well as the school.

When Maureen Armour taught fourth graders, she first introduced the writing workshop and then experimented with teaching reading in a similar way. Poetry helped her make the connection. She describes how she replaced her basals with multiple copies of paperbacks and organized her reading workshops to develop reading skills and strategies while allowing for personal response.

Because Bev Pilchman found teaching reading and writing as processes so successful, she extended the approach to social studies. To find time for an in-depth, yet personalized, study of a unit on the American Revolution, she combined time allocated to reading, writing, and social studies into one focused workshop. From 9:00 A.M. to 11:00 A.M., four days a week, her students were immersed in reading, writing, listening, and talking about the events that led up to and occurred during the American Revolution. After being exposed to much background information through reading and listening, they chose topics to explore, research, and present in very innovative ways, from letters between John Adams and his wife to the publication of an early American newspaper.

The final chapter in this section is a report about an urban elementary school in the process of change from a traditional, basal-reader, skills-driven reading program to a process-oriented, reading-writing workshop approach. Change came about through a combination of grass-roots interest on the part of teachers who had been experimenting with writing workshop and using more literature in their classrooms and the fortuitous arrival of administrators who promoted the movement toward a process approach in developing literacy. Administrators and teachers worked together to achieve this transition, which is still in progress.

As you read these chapters, you will note the similarities and idiosyncrasies of these educators and their approaches to teaching reading and writing through real situations and authentic texts. In general, they got caught up in the writing process movement of the 1980s and then moved naturally from developing writers through a process approach to developing readers in the same manner.

REFERENCES

Bereiter, C., & Scardamalia, M. (1982). From conversation to composition: The role of instruction in a developmental process. In R. Glaser (Ed.), *Advances in instructional psychology* (Vol. 2, pp. 1–64). Hillsdale, NJ: Erlbaum.

Burgess, S. A. (1985). Reading but not literate: The ChildRead survey. *School Library Journal, 31*, 27–30.

Calkins, L. (1983). *Lessons from a child.* Portsmouth, NH: Heinemann.

Calkins, L. (1986). *The art of teaching writing.* Portsmouth, NH: Heinemann.

Cochrane, O., Cochrane, D., Scalena, S., & Buchanan, E. (1984). *Reading, writing, and caring.* New York: Richard C. Owen.

Collins, W. A. (1984). Conclusion: The status of basic research on middle childhood. In W. A. Collins (Ed.), *Development during middle childhood: The years from six to twelve* (pp. 94–109). Washington, DC: National Academy Press.

Durkin, D. (1979). What classroom observation reveals about reading instruction. *Reading Research Quarterly, 24*, 174–187.

Feeley, J. T. (1981). What do our children like to read? *NJEA Review, 54*(8), 26–27.

Gipe, J. P. (1978–1979). Investigating techniques for teaching word meanings. *Reading Research Quarterly, 14*, 624–644.

Graham, S. (1986). Assessing reading preferences: A new approach. *New England Reading Association Journal, 21*(1), 8–11.

Graves, D. L. (1983). *Writing: Teachers and children at work*. Portsmouth, NH: Heinemann.

Hansen, J. (1987). *When writers read*. Portsmouth, NH: Heinemann.

Jenkins, J., & Dixon, R. (1983). Vocabulary learning. *Contemporary Educational Psychology, 8*, 237–260.

Langer, J. A. (1984). Examining background knowledge and text comprehension. *Reading Research Quarterly, 19*, 468–481.

Langer, J. A. (1986). *Children reading and writing*. Norwood, NJ: Ablex Publishing.

Mason, J., & Au K. H. (1990). *Reading instruction for today*. Glenview, IL: Scott Foresman.

McNeil, J. (1987). *Reading comprehension: New directions for classroom practice* (3rd ed.). Glenview, IL: Scott Foresman.

Meyers, M., & Paris, S. G. (1978). Children's metacognitive knowledge about reading. *Journal of Educational Psychology, 70*, 680–690.

Mezynski, K. (1983). Issues concerning the acquisition of knowledge: Effect of vocabulary training on reading comprehension. *Review of Educational Research, 53*, 253–279.

Nagy, W. E., & Anderson, R. C. (1984). How many words are there in printed school English? *Reading Research Quarterly, 19*, 304–330.

Nagy, W. E., Anderson, R. C., & Herman, P. A. (1987). Learning word meanings from context during normal reading. *American Educational Research Journal, 24*, 237–270.

Palinscar, A. M., & Brown, A. (1984). Reciprocal teaching of comprehension. *Cognition and Instruction, 1*, 117–175.

Papalia, D. E., & Olds, S. W. (1990). *A child's world*. New York: McGraw-Hill.

Paris, S. G., Cross, D. R., & Lipson, M. Y. (1984). Informed strategies for learning: A program to improve children's reading awareness and comprehension. *Journal of Educational Psychology, 76*, 239–242.

Piaget, J. (1955). *The language and thought of the child*. New York: Meridian Books.

Schickedanz, J. A., Hansen, K., & Forsyth, P. D. (1990). *Understanding children*. Mountain View, CA: Mayfield Publishing.

Shonkoff, J. P. (1984). The biological substrate and physical health in middle childhood. In W. A. Collins (Ed.), *Development during middle childhood: The years from six to twelve* (pp. 213–254). Washington, DC: National Academy Press.

Singer, H. (1978). Active comprehension. *The Reading Teacher, 31*, 901–908.

Smith, F. (1985). *Reading without nonsense*. New York: Teachers College Press.

Stauffer, R. G. (1975). *Directing the reading-thinking process*. New York: Harper and Row.

Stevens, R. J., Madden, N. A., Slavin, R. E., & Farnish, A. M. (1987). Cooperative integrated reading and composition. *Reading Research Quarterly, 22*, 433–454.

Strickland, D. S., & Feeley, J. T. (1991). Research on language learners: Development in the elementary school years. In J. Flood, J. Jensen, D. Lapp, & J. R.

Squire (Eds.), *Handbook of research on teaching the English language arts* (pp. 286–302). New York: Macmillan.

Wolfson, B. J., Manning, G., & Manning, M. (1984). Revisiting what children say their reading interests are. *Reading World, 24*(2), 4–10.

Zigler, E. F., & Finn-Stevenson, M. (1987). *Children: Development and social issues*. Lexington, MA: D. C. Heath.

CHAPTER 5

Triskaidekaphobia and Other Uncommon Nonfiction Interests

EDITH R. ZIEGLER, JAMES KLIKA, MARILYN STAMPA
Tenakill School, Closter, NJ

Poor Tommy. He represents our students who are interested in and know something about a subject, but who are never given an opportunity to pursue it further or share what they know with others. His school probably demands certain material be "covered" without respect to Tommy's passions. If we were to continue this scenario (and it would no longer be comical) Tommy would be assigned a topic to research. He would probably go to the public library after school and copy information from an encyclopedia. He would then draw or cut out a few pictures to supplement the text, make a cover, and hand in his completed assignment. Newkirk (1989), discusses the misuse of written sources in informational writing and points out that plagiarism is tempting because "the sources provide the information so well that any change in the language seems like a degradation" (p. 86). If there were another cartoon strip of this character, we would see him deliver a tiresome, voiceless report, crammed with information organized in predictable patterns. None of it would reflect his thinking or understanding. The last panel would surely show ZZZZZZZ's coming from classmates and teachers alike. As teachers, we see this all too often.

THE STORY OF TEAM C

Team C, as our optional program is called, is led by three teachers and populated by 60 heterogeneously grouped suburban children in Grades 2 through 4. Parents have the choice of enrolling their children in this multi-aged educational alternative. In this team-teaching mode, we work to build a community of independent, self-directed learners who become "confident respondents" and experts at reading and writing nonfiction (Graves, 1983). What we strive to achieve is a way to connect nonfiction reading and report writing with the natural interests and excitement of children. Students select topics and become actively involved in reading and writing about a wide variety of subjects. We help children transform the information they acquire into picture books of their own that accommodate their interests, language, and thinking.

Because of our own experiences in teaching/learning, we understand how powerful reading and sharing can be. It can challenge or reinforce beliefs, expand and update what we know, and help us probe our own thinking. Children, with a little help from teachers and parents, can feel the excitement that studying a topic in depth can bring.

In *The Art of Teaching Writing*, Lucy Calkins (1986) quotes Erik Erikson in her discussion of report writing:

> We are the teaching species. Not only do the young need adults, but adults also need the young. . . . Human beings need to teach not only for the sake of those who need to be taught, but for the fulfillment of our identities and because facts are kept alive by being shared, truths by being professed. (p. 271)

TAPPING WHAT CHILDREN KNOW

Consider this lively scene of a diverse group of students exchanging ideas around the classroom conference table. Deborah is leafing through a collection of brochures and magazine articles on sculpture. Timothy is gathering information on gerbils from the latest edition of *Ranger Rick*, a children's nature magazine, and from the pamphlets Mr. Brown, the local pet store owner, had given him. Brande is reading from *National Geo-*

graphic's detailed explanation of turning cocoa beans into chocolate. She is trying to supplement the information she had received while on a tour of Critchley's Chocolate plant. All three are preparing to write about their chosen topics and are sharing their information and discussing their problems. All three are in the process of connecting their interests with reading, organizing, writing, and learning.

These children are claiming, developing, and sharing what they know. As students in a nonfiction reading/writing workshop, they are invited to become teachers, while we, in turn, learn from our students. We have learned much from our second, third, and fourth graders, including how to prepare and enter a cat in a cat show, how the ancient Egyptians created mummies, how ducklings dabble, how lizards and newts differ, and how basketball originated.

Children learn from resources beyond the classroom. Victor, an 8-year-old who recently arrived from Sweden, was busy making a long list in his notebook one day as one of us approached his desk for a conference.

> TEACHER: Hi, Victor. What are you working on?
>
> VICTOR: This is a list of airlines I know.
>
> TEACHER: Airlines?
>
> VICTOR: Yes, I know the names of a lot of airlines, and whenever I look up into the sky and see an airplane, I write the name of it down here in my notebook.
>
> TEACHER: (*amazed at the length of the list and somewhat incredulous*) Victor, you just see an airplane flying and you can tell what kind it is?
>
> VICTOR: Yup, that's correct.
>
> TEACHER: You mean, like when I see a car on the street, I can tell whether it's a Subaru or a Jaguar?
>
> VICTOR: Yes, but this is MUCH HARDER!

Victor went on to research the safety records of many airlines before writing a piece telling his choices for flying and made us all more aware of the next plane we saw.

LAUNCHING THE NONFICTION GENRE

We believe reading and writing go hand in hand to support what the children already know and what it is they need to learn. Our challenge and responsibility is to demythologize "the report" as a rite of passage (something children do as their siblings did when they reached fourth grade) and instead look at what real researchers do.

Before the topic choice is made, we begin reading aloud the best in children's nonfiction literature. Some examples are: *The Popcorn Book*, by Tomie dePaola (1978); *The Lady and the Spider* by Faith McNulty (1986); and *Once There Was a Tree* by Natalia Romanova (1985). The books we choose serve as models for children to present their own data. These books are engaging, colorful, and rich in information without being overwhelming. We continue our daily read-aloud, asking upon completion, "What did the author need to know?" and "How do you think the author got the information?" By doing this we are trying to strengthen the need to read, to observe closely, and to interview experts.

Well in advance of the starting date for beginning nonfiction studies, the team gathers, and we teachers model for the children what they will be doing. We talk as if we are on a TV talk show, giving examples of our interests. Edie explains what she knows about dreams. Lynn speaks of travel in Italy, and Jim describes how he makes bread. First we reveal what we know about our topics and then raise questions that we want answered.

All students are then asked to brainstorm possibilities for study. One group came up with the following list of diverse topics:

rabbits	Arbor Day	monkeys
horses	Walt Disney	animals in winter
flowers	zoos	oil/gas stations
bears	pandas	Olympics
computers	sea creatures	turtles
moon	space	snow
eagles	Mother's Day	Father's Day
New Orleans	boy scouts	Disney World
animals	Epcot Center	turkeys
queens	Caldecott Medal	explorers
airports	dinosaurs	living in space
tornadoes	Yugoslavia	Colorado
stars	transportation	ships
oceans	telephones	India

No one is held to a topic at this point, but each is directed to think more about the choices and to narrow them down to one or two that can be "lived with" for the next seven weeks. Most importantly, students have to choose a topic that can be studied up close through observation, interview, or firsthand experience.

Although this requirement might eliminate some suggestions from the original list, still enough topics remain to be explored. Interviews could be conducted with experts in the child's field of choice, and observations could be made through visits to museums, galleries, zoos, or aquariums.

Watching a video on the topic of choice is considered another important way to collect information.

Involving Parents

Parent cooperation is enlisted through the letter shown in Figure 5.1. The letter provides a meaningful link between what parents can arrange on the outside and what the children are reading about in school.

During our research cycle, a high level of parent involvement exists.

FIGURE 5.1. Letter to parents enlisting help

Dear Team C Families:

Team C is about to embark on its third reading/writing workshop cycle. Beginning May 1, our new groups will focus on research. Since the children will be required to work on their topics for the next seven weeks, it should be something they can live with for that time. Please help them narrow their choices with these criteria in mind:

1. a topic your child is familiar with, but would like to know more about, and
2. a topic that can be looked at closely through interviews, observations, and firsthand information, as well as print resources.

It would help if you would work with your child in filling out the attached sheet, making a minimum of two choices. There are three columns to be completed. The first should tell what your child already knows about the topic. The second should list what he/she wants to find out about the topic, and the third contains the ideas for resources that might be used throughout the research. Attached is an example of a filled-out sheet. There is also a blank sheet that should be completed and returned to school by Tuesday, April 25.

NOTE: If your child should choose a topic such as a wild animal or the planet Jupiter, ask yourself if it is possible for you to provide a trip to the zoo or planetarium.

Sincerely,

Edith R. Zief
James G. Kuhn
Lynne Stampe
Team C Teachers

"Homework" takes on new dimensions when a family goes on a whale watch, visits the Museum of Natural History, or invites a friend who is working with chimpanzees to the house. The idea to be imparted is that good writing comes from real information that you possess. One cannot just write writing; there must be some content to it.

Figure 5.2 shows a form that goes home to parents. There are three columns, each headed with a question: What Do I Know? What Do I Want To Know? and How Can I Find Out? We can see that 7-year-old Amy's topic choice was "Triskaidekaphobia" (fear of the number thirteen). Eight-year-old Kara was torn between "Ducks" or "Puffins." After filling our her form, Kara decided to study "Ducks," perhaps because she found she already knew so much and wanted to become a super expert.

It is obvious these children have something to say, because they know something about their topics. They each have many questions stimulating them to gather more information from printed matter as well as from people and from their own observations. The need to find out more connected these children to the classroom library, school library, home library,

FIGURE 5.2. Choosing a research topic

Amy: The number 13

WHAT DO I KNOW?	WHAT DO I WANT TO KNOW?	HOW CAN I FIND OUT?
Some people are afraid of it. That is called Triskaidekaphobia.	Where did this superstition originate?	Ask people what they think about the number 13.
They don't put 13 on elevators. They put 12A instead.	Why do some people have this disease?	Read books on Triskaidekaphobia and the number 13.
Some people think if you are born on Friday the 13th you will have bad luck for life.	Why doesn't a clock go up to 13?	
It's a number after 12 and before 14.		
It's the first teen number.		

and town library with no coaxing from anyone. Often, parents become partners in the project, helping children to find resources.

This need to know also justifies all the saving we teachers do. As ideas for topics are being explored, our closets, which had been filled with collections of nonfiction literature, magazine articles, charts, pictures, and file folders bulging with "stuff," begin to empty.

Narrowing The Topic

The process of topic selection continues as children share their early interests both in school and at home. Finally, children are asked to write about their topic choices in an effort to narrow them down. We ask children to think on paper. Figure 5.3 shows the thinking of 8-year-old Fred, who has narrowed his topic down to mantises because of the accessibility of information, and Kristen, age 7, who has chosen whales, because her family has recently made plans to go on a whale watch.

In *When Writers Read*, Jane Hansen (1987) reminds us that children read to learn and learn to read at the same time. She writes:

> Print had to make sense. They knew those marks were someone's attempt to
> tell them something and they wanted to find out what it was. They read to

FIGURE 5.3. Fred's and Kristen's topics

FRED

My two topics are hamburgers or mantises. I like both topics, but I think mantises is more accessible because I could get info at the Closter Nature Center. I could buy them at the store that sells garden supplies. And I also know alot about them anyway.

KRISTEN

I'm going to write about whales. Cause it seems to be much more interesting then diamonds. Since I already found books and articles on it and none on diamonds, and I like whales better.

I'm going to do whales. Sometimes I see shows on whales or when my parents are watching the news the talk is about whales.

One time we had an assembly on whales. And also we adopted a whale so I can find out something on whales.

---

learn. This drove their desire to learn to read. When I studied reading in graduate school, I learned that children first learned to read and then read to learn, but these little children turned that notion of reading upside down. They were writers, and writers write information. Thus, when they read, they read for an author's information. This insistence on meaning helped them learn to read. (p. 146)

THE NONFICTION READING/WRITING WORKSHOP

Each day's reading/writing workshop follows the same basic structure, even though children's work progresses at different rates. Each mini-lesson is designed to teach specific skills and strategies pertinent to the nonfiction genre. We model reading and note-taking so children can see what is expected. Guided practice is provided in finding important parts of the paragraph to paraphrase or to transcribe onto note cards. We teach children how to use key words and phrases, abbreviations, and symbols, the same strategies many adult researchers use for note-taking. We also model techniques such as interviewing people, using an index and a table of contents, and organizing a bibliography. The bulk of each workshop accommodates children's need to read, to confer about their reading, and to begin note-taking. We teachers listen, guide, and address specific problems.

Subsequently, children read silently or to each other and note pages important to them. Some are using their newly acquired note-taking skills and adding to the pile of index cards they have already filled. A few children exchange materials, since in a community of readers and writers, each person in the room knows what the others are looking for. A chart on the bulletin board lists the children's names along side the topic being researched.

When students have finished reading and researching, they need to organize their information. Once the teacher has demonstrated a technique called "mapping" or "webbing," which chunks the bits and pieces collected, children can begin to develop their own webs, helping each other before coming to the teacher for a final check. Figure 5.4 shows a sample web about whales by Kristen, a second grader.

Sharing, the wrap-up section of each day's workshop, highlights new and interesting information discovered by resident experts. It is also a chance for children to present any difficulties they may be having and to ask for help. The original questions from "What do I want to know?" are often discarded for more pressing areas of concern. As the research progresses, children find they have new information and new questions.

FIGURE 5.4. A web on whales by Kristen

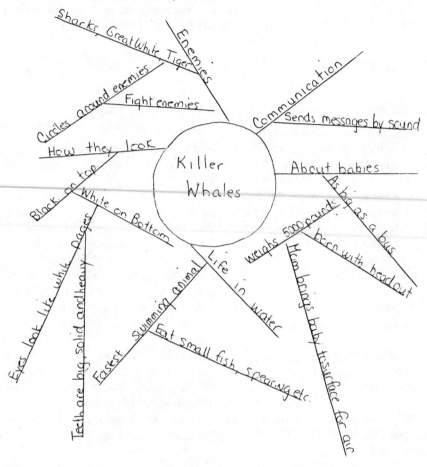

Drafting Begins

Once children become filled up with ideas about their topics through reading, talking, observing, and sharing, (this phase can take 3 or 4 weeks), it is time to reflect on what has been learned and to decide how it can be presented in written form.

At times, during the process described, we go back to the authors of books we have already read aloud to focus on their styles of presentation. For example, Natalia Romanova, in *Once There Was a Tree* (1985), uses a romantic, yet realistic text in describing the ecology of her subject — the tree. Tomie dePaola, in *The Popcorn Book* (1978), weaves scientific, historic, and legendary information into the conversation of the two main characters. Faith McNulty, in *The Lady and the Spider* (1986), tells the story of a spider's very important life in the garden of a lady who unknowingly chooses the spider's haven for her lunchtime salad. Filled with details about spiders and their habits, and with a healthy respect for even a tiny life, the book provides a suspenseful, informative story.

Children also need to explore ways to finally package all they have researched over a 3- to 5-week period. Leigh, a fourth-grade student, uses a family visit to Mount Vernon as the basis for a book. She retells one experience from her trip by providing characters and dialogue as the family is given a guided tour through Mount Vernon. She then creates a classroom situation in which students are studying George Washington. As the students and teacher discuss life in the 1770s, they share information learned from the tour. Again, through character and dialogue, the "facts" she has gathered come alive.

Sandy, a third grader, uses her pet newt, Patches, as the subject for her firsthand observations and study (Figure 5.5). Her report speaks in the voice of the animal to inform the reader of everything he or she would ever want to know about newts.

Crystal, a 9-year-old devotee of Jean Craighead George, spins a true-to-life tale of two gray wolves who meet, mate, and raise their young (Figure 5.6).

Choices are the children's to make, right down to the final decisions

FIGURE 5.5. Excerpts from Sandy's piece on her pet newt

.... Do you know me? I am not what you may think I am. You may think I'm a lizard, but you'll be surprised. I'm a newt, a four toed friendly amphibian that makes a great pet.

I'm most active at night and love to eat insects, fish and other tiny pond creatures.

I'm a really lucky guy, hardly anything will eat me because my skin is irritating and toxic to them. Don't worry I wont hurt you. But, you might hurt me by holding me too long or too much. Ouch! It's from the salt on your hands! My skin is really fragile. Salt burns it easily. I could die from that and believe me, that's not fun.

About my babies, first our eggs are laid. We lay several hundred of them. Bet that's more than you! Most eggs are laid in water, but some of us lay our eggs on land like my cousin the four toed Salamander.

FIGURE 5.6. Excerpts from Crystal's story about gray wolves

    Somewhere in the coldest part of Alaska a wolf lurks
hunting for deer or game birds. When the Gray Wolf comes
back from hunting he is dripping perspiration from the
glands in his mouth. Then after theGray Wolf cools off by
rolling in the mud hole he starts eating his dinner.
    When he just finished dinner he heard a wolf cry. He
knew he had to leave for his pack. Just as he got to his
pack he saw a different wolf. The wolf was a stranger to
him. It was a female wolf. He could tell by the smell of the
wolf. When they rubbed noses they smelled each other.
    Then the female wolf ran off into the woods. The Gray
Wolf followed. They met again....

---

about pictures, layouts, cover designs, dedications, and acknowledgments. It seems like an involved process, and it is. But it is a time when the children are so involved that they hate to miss even one day of school. Unlike Tommy, they read about airplanes and how they work, or whatever else interests them, and find out how worthwhile their passions can be.

REFERENCES

Calkins, L. M. (1986). *The art of teaching writing*. Portsmouth, NH: Heinemann.
dePaola, T. (1978). *The popcorn book*. New York: Scholastic Inc.
Graves, D. (1983). *Writing: Teachers and children at work*. Portsmouth, NH: Heinemann.
Hansen, J. (1987). *When writers read*. Portsmouth, NH: Heinemann.
McNulty, F. (1986). *The lady and the spider*. New York: Harper and Row.
Newkirk, Thomas (1989). *More than stories: The range of children's writing*. Portsmouth, NH: Heinemann.
Romanova, Natalia (1985). *Once there was a tree*. New York: E. P. Dutton.

CHAPTER 6

Organizing for Reading and Writing Workshops in Grade 4

MAUREEN W. ARMOUR
University of South Florida

The inescapable logic of the writing process burst upon education like a nova: The idea had been there for years, but the light took a long time to reach the classroom. When it arrived, I wondered how we could have stumbled about in the dark for so long. Eight years of teaching writing and reading workshops have made the endless workbooks, lock-step readers, and fill-in-the-blanks "writing" exercises seem as obsolete as the Edsel, but I still remember the dissatisfaction and frustration they produced.

A New Jersey Writing Project summer workshop provided the information and confidence I needed to begin teaching writing as a process, but with the anticipation came a fair amount of worry. How and where could I fit 45 minutes of writing into an already crowded school day? Would this new group of 9-year-olds know what a marvelous experience they were embarking on and immediately begin turning out pages of great stuff, or would they ask for last year's workbooks back? What would my principal say? What would I say? I felt as if I were standing at the end of a pier, looking at water that was far over my head.

On the first day, I took a deep breath and, figuratively speaking, jumped in. "Now we're going to write," I said, beaming. I saw on that small sea of young faces an assortment of responses: expectancy, impassivity, wariness, but no outright rejection. Encouraged, I proceeded to launch my first writing workshop.

It's very difficult for a classroom teacher to try anything new without administrative support and almost impossible to succeed without it. Fortunately, my principal agreed that teaching writing as a process was an idea whose time had come and was an invaluable help in the ensuing months of trial and error.

UNEXPECTED CHANGES

Three years of writing workshop with two classes of fourth graders produced unanticipated changes. Instead of teaching formal lessons, I was using teachable moments, conferences, and minilessons to deal with children's needs as they became evident. It seemed too casual and natural to be considered serious teaching, but I eventually recognized that it worked better than the old model and stopped worrying.

Often the teaching came from the children. Mike startled me by producing a second draft before I had mentioned revision. Delighted, I asked him to tell us how he'd done it, and his strategies became a minilesson. Days later, as chalkboard space filled up with revision guidelines, Carla said, "Why don't we copy that down and staple the paper to our writing folders? Then you could erase the board," and thus was born the "How to Revise" page that became an integral part of the writing folder.

The central, essential change taking place was in the fundamental relationship between the students and me. The authoritarian teacher role, never a favorite, was gone. With more freedom to make choices, the children were taking more responsibility for their learning. But I worried about possible chaos and "wasted" time; I was constantly striving to find an acceptable balance. Walking that tightrope required multiple roles: a lecturer in minilessons, an editor in conferences, and something akin to a talk-show host in group-sharing sessions. Gradually the children and I developed a kind of editor-writer relationship. They trusted me not to get dictatorial and I trusted them to do authentic work, to write as authors and not as teacher-pleasers.

But learning is a rocky road. When things went smoothly I savored the moment, knowing it was fleeting. Before long, a topic bank came up empty, an epidemic of pencil-sharpening struck, or the twenty-seventh bed-to-bed travelogue to and from Disney Land took the entire sharing time. Whole-class sharing was often a mixed blessing. Almost always we enjoyed the story its author read to us, but sometimes a piece was ignored, criticized, or overpraised according to the writer's social status rather than its merits. Violence and slapstick humor were always great crowd-pleasers, independent of telling details, strong verbs, or careful revision. But the thoughtful, effective pieces that were greeted by sincere responses and insightful suggestions kept us sane and hopeful.

POETRY MAKES THE CONNECTION

Our first poetry workshop unexpectedly created our first reading/ writing connection. While planning the workshop, I talked to teachers who taught poetry and learned that they usually began by reading poems (often unrhyming) to the children. After telling my class that we were going to be writing poetry for the next few weeks, I read several of Valerie Worth's delightful small poems (1972). Then we went outside to find small objects — a leaf, stone, scrap of foil, bit of glass — to write poems about. It worked like magic, which poetry is, and in a few weeks we published an anthology, heralded by a wildly popular Poetry Publishing Party.

During the workshop, I continued to read published poems to them and they read their own to me, each other, the whole class, and anyone else who was available. One day Grant asked if he could take the poetry book to his table to read. I almost said, "No, this is writing class," but caught myself in time and handed it to him. A day or two later the librarian mentioned that my kids were taking out books of poetry — not a usual choice for fourth graders. Sharon brought in her father's copy of Robert Louis Stevenson's *A Child's Garden of Verses* (1885/1950) and we enjoyed "The Land of Counterpane." Where poetry was concerned, reading and writing were firmly connected.

MOVING FROM BASALS TO PAPERBACKS

Still, the poetry workshop was different from reading class, where we worked in ability groups with basal readers, workbooks, and skill-sheets. Once planted in a reading series, especially one laden with sequential skills instruction, it was very difficult for a child to escape the cycle and move into a different group. Each new workbook required the student to know the terms and formats used in the previous one. Yet in our writing workshop, budding novelists and children with learning difficulties were developing skills and sharing ideas through the written word without the social stigma of grouping.

My classes were doing real writing, not what James Britton (1970) calls "dummy runs." Why couldn't they do real reading too, with real books? Our classroom library held a collection amassed from years of paperback book clubs and book fairs, but the children seldom had time to enjoy it. I wondered if, and how, this could become the core of a reading program that would somehow connect with writing.

Although I knew teachers who completely individualized their reading programs, the prospect of each child reading a different book was daunting; two classes could require a dizzying 45 titles a week. With enrollment in the low twenties and several children who had reading instruction elsewhere, I could have four groups of five or six children per class, each group reading its own book. Eight books I could handle, especially since most of them would already be familiar.

Looking through catalogs of paperbacks, I was amazed to discover that several of them could be bought for the price of one basal reader. For a modest investment, my classroom library could be turned into twenty sets of books, six copies each, enough to begin with in the fall. I knew I was going to be investing a great deal of time and thought in this project; the financial part of it belonged in the school budget. I approached my principal with a proposal to teach reading with children's books instead of basals, and to connect it with writing. The writing workshops had been going well for about 3 years, and she was supportive. Yes, I could order the paperbacks and use them to teach reading, but since the basal was board-adopted, I'd have to cover that too.

Years ago during a lecture on motivation, I heard a psychology professor proclaim, with emphasis, "Time drives." That pithy statement certainly applies to the classroom. How could the crowded school day hold both reading workshop and basal readers? I began to think about how teaching reading groups used up time. There were the instructional charts, the presentation of skills and vocabulary, introduction to the story, silent reading, questions to check comprehension, oral reading, worksheets, workbook pages that had to be done and then corrected, tests that showed which skills needed to be retaught, and worksheets to reteach them.

If we pared to the bone and used only the hard-cover books and workbooks, the basal could be covered on Fridays or when a group finished their paperback book earlier than expected. The children would read the hard-cover books and do workbook pages on their own. Once a week, I would record the pages each child was on, help anyone who was stuck, and oversee parent aides who would help children check their workbooks.

Getting Organized

Now I had four periods a week, about 50 minutes each, for reading workshop. Lucy Calkins's (1986) advice that since the process is unpredictable, the structure should be kept predictable, had proved true in writing workshop, so I began to organize our reading workshop with zest. Day 1 would be used for silent reading, Day 2 for written responses and vocabulary work, Day 3 for oral reading, and Day 4 for a small-group conference with me. Somehow I believed that the groups' progression through the sequence could be staggered so that on each day a different group would be ready for the conference when we would discuss what they had written and thought about that week's pages. Of course, real life is not that tidy; as the system went into effect, I was usually the one who was staggered.

While organization is a virtue, its dark side can be an overemphasis on control. I know teachers who employ a looser structure in their reading workshops with great success. From the time the program began, I was often aware of the need to loosen the reins in order not to tie us so tightly to the system that its real purpose was poorly served. A difficult question was whether or not to limit the number of pages to be read each time. I wanted the kids to be able to read for the whole period and so did they, but if they did, some would be far ahead and others would never catch up. For the children to work together and thereby learn from each other, everyone in the group needed to be familiar with the same material. I decided to assign sections of anywhere from 10 to 25 pages, depending on the book. But what would the fast-finishers do while the rest of the group was still reading? Obviously, they would go on to write their responses. Already the neat 4-day plan was getting ragged around the edges.

Grouping

It was exhilarating to work out all these subsystems, but every solution produced new problems. How would the groups be formed? And how would they choose their books? Even the lottery has better odds than the chance of four 9-year-olds wanting to read the same book at the same time. Assigning them was out of the question: choice was essential. Still, I thought, how often does life let us have our *first* choices? Maybe they could each choose five or so books they'd like to read . . . and then I realized that this could be a way of forming the groups as well. With wish lists from the kids, I could assemble groups that looked promising.

I briefly considered letting them choose their own groups, but remembered what often happened when they did that for project work. The chooser acquired the power of an absolute ruler; some choosees were satisfied, some were not and therefore disinclined to the project, and some were reminded yet again that nobody ever chose them first for anything. Furthermore, boys almost never chose girls and vice versa, and I wanted the groups to be integrated. Never mind the trendy issue of sexism; girls and boys benefit from hearing each other's points of view. Student-selected groups can be effective in many circumstances, but they hadn't worked well for me in a fourth-grade instructional setting. I decided to act the benevolent despot and assign groups, keeping the children's needs and personalities in mind.

An unavoidable question concerned reading ability. Suppose a "bottom-group" child and a "top-group" child both wanted to read the same book? Of course the difficulty of the book would have a bearing on the answer. But readability formulas based on word and sentence length don't always work. Children with a burning interest in the subject matter can read books beyond their measured reading-level abilities, particularly if they have a foundation of information about the subject. And then there was the back-up insurance of book choice: few children, knowing that they were going to spend several days reading a book with a group of peers, would choose one that clearly was too difficult to read successfully. I decided to risk new problems rather than let a child's purported reading level determine grouping or limit book choices.

As our reading workshops continued over time, experience almost always supported that decision. For example, a group who had chosen a book about whales because of their interest in the topic came to me and asked if they could "quit the book." When I asked why, the spokesperson said, "It gives us so much information there isn't room for it all in our heads!"

Only twice in 4 years did a member of a group have to change books because of difficulty level. Heterogeneous groups became the norm, and that did a great deal for the children's self-esteem and my peace of mind. Interestingly, achievement test scores for these classes were comparable to those of classes I had taught using only basals.

Vocabulary

When I began to think about vocabulary work and realized I had no word lists, I almost felt nostalgia for the basal until I remembered that when "new" words were presented to a reading group, most of them were already known by most of the children. Why not let the kids find their own words? Surely they were the best judges of which ones they didn't already know.

Experience later showed that it was too much to ask 9-year-olds who are reading a good book to hold in mind the task of flagging unknown words (sometimes they didn't know they were unknown), stop reading, and write down the word and its page number. We tried going back and skimming to find them, but that dragged out the process painfully. It worked better if I did the skimming and chose about ten words that best fit the criteria of being unknown and worth knowing. These I printed on an index card in the order they appeared in the text and identified the card by book title and page numbers of the section.

Working together, each group would skim their book's pages to locate the word and read the sentence it was in. Standard procedure called for them to look the word up in the dictionary, but when I recalled how that process had worked in the past, I was doubtful. Sometimes the definition was as puzzling to young readers as the unknown word. Even when they understood the definition, they often struggled heroically but unsuccessfully to fit it into the text so it made sense.

Instead, they could use contextual clues. When they had located the word in the book, they were to discuss its possible meanings. Democratically they would thrash out the best definition, test it by inserting it into the sentence in place of the unknown word, and write it down on the vocabulary form I provided (see Figure 6.1). When we met, I would quickly review their choices, commend the appropriate ones, and either explain the others or choose one or two for the group to look up in the dictionary.

Oral Reading

The idea of including rehearsal and oral reading came from the kids. I thought they viewed reading aloud as a chore and wouldn't miss it until I asked them to write about it. Two boys wrote, "It's fun to read out loud." Others said it was exciting and wrote, "I especially like it when it's my turn to read," and "I like it when I am reading because I like it when everyone listens to me." I had to agree with them. For years I read C. S. Lewis's *The Lion, the Witch and the Wardrobe* (1986) to my classes and had developed

FIGURE 6.1. Vocabulary form

Title: The Twits (Roald Dahl)   Date:

Vocabulary

	Word	P#	Meaning	Name
1.	giddy	70	dizzy, sick, confused	Cathy
2.	beastly	50	terrible, frightening	Topal
3.	grandly	43	proudly, importantly	Stella
4.	perch	43	sit-upon	RJ
5.	fearsome	66	scary, terrifying	Roy
6.	clambered	49	climbed-upon	Cathy
7.	scampered	53	ran quickly	Topal
8.	shudders	54	the chills	Stella
9.	frenzy	55	Hyper mood	RJ
10.	gaping	55	with mouth open	Roy
11.	hoisted	63	brought, carried up	Cathy
12.	thrashing	74	kicking rambunctiously	Topal

a repertory of voices. I looked forward to reading as much as the children enjoyed hearing the story. Objective support came from research that says repeated reading can produce "marked improvement in speed, accuracy and expression during oral reading of new selections and, more important, improvement in comprehension during silent reading" (Anderson, Hiebert, Scott, & Wilkinson, 1985, p. 54).

The positive feeling toward oral reading wasn't unanimous, however. Patty wrote, "I hated to read out loud 'cause I would always get interrupted by one of the boys." How could I guard against unfortunate events? I would be deep in conference with another group while the oral-reading group, tucked away in a corner to minimize its distraction of others, would be on its own. The ready solution was a tape recorder. Not only would it convince any doubters of the importance of their work, but later they would be able to listen to themselves read, an irresistible lure for most kids. I made a simple form each group could use to keep track of who would read what with book title, date, page number, and a place for the child's name beside the section each chose to read. Children found corners or carrels in which to practice before they met as a group to record their reading. Occasionally the better readers acted as coaches, which was especially helpful for children who were bilingual. I listened to the tapes at my leisure and shared my responses during the group meeting.

FROM WRITING TO READING

The next question was how to connect reading class with writing workshop as a usual routine. Minilessons, a way to get information to the whole class, seemed a natural transfer. They could be used to establish procedures in the beginning, present strategies for effective reading, and relate what we were doing in writing classes to the reading process. And reading could bounce back to our writing workshop minilessons by my reading aloud passages from the paperbacks that illustrated a useful writing strategy. For example, the main character in Beverly Cleary's *Dear Mr. Henshaw* (1984) gives wonderful advice to his young correspondent.

I also wanted to provide something comparable to whole-group sharing time, and decided on book shows. After finishing a book, each group would choose some way to share it with the rest of the class. The shows could be drawings, constructions, oral reading of particularly good parts, or a small play. Writing came into the picture here when the children wrote plans for these activities. Along with the forms the children used in every part of the program, these plans became part of my record keeping.

READING WORKSHOP

After a spring and summer of planning, it was time for another launch. On the first day each class came in for reading, they found a large table covered with colorful paperback books. I showed each one briefly and enthusiastically and said these were going to be our reading books, so they needed to preview them to find out which ones they wanted to read. That is, they were to pick up books at random, take them back to their seats, look them over, read a few lines, list chosen titles, write why they wanted to read those books, and number them in their order of preference. After the first time of trying to make sense of a considerable variety of shapes and sizes of these written responses, I produced yet another form, which made the process easier for all of us (see Figure 6.2).

As soon as I could fit it in, I read to the children Margaret Embry's *Mr. Blue* (1963), a short, delightful book about a cat that adopts a third-grade class. This led to the first minilesson on responding to literature. At good places in the story, I stopped, gave a short response of my own, and asked the class what they thought or felt. On the chalkboard, I quickly wrote their names and abbreviated versions of what they said, and went back to reading. I hoped that later, when it was time to talk about or write their responses to what they were reading, this modeling process would serve as a guide.

FIGURE 6.2. Preview form used to help in forming groups around titles of books

Book Choices

Name: Dorothy   Date:

Preview the books on the six shelves in the corner and in the boxes on the blue shelf. Choose the five that you would most like to read next. Write the title of each and tell why it seems like a good book to you. After you've done that for all five, number them in the order of your preference (1 is the one you most want to read, etc.).

Title

Charlotte's Web	I always get to the second page and then never finish.	1
Sadako	It sounds great.	2
Dinner at Alberta's	I liked the book show.	3
Dad lives in a Downtown Hotel.	It makes me wonder what will happen.	5
Owls in the Family	It sounds interesting.	4

Homework

Assigning homework, a policy of the school board and a desire of many parents, was required of each teacher. Writing and reading were the only subjects I taught every day, and writing workshops offered no opportunities for regular homework assignments. Nancie Atwell's (1987) work with middle schoolers and their written responses to reading sounded wonderful. Perhaps I could adapt some of these ideas for fourth grade and satisfy the homework requirement at the same time.

I gave each child a composition book (the kind with the marbled black and white cover), which we called a reading log. The homework assignment would be the same, Monday through Thursday: Read a self-selected book for at least 20 minutes, record the starting and stopping times and pages, have it initialed by an adult (so parents would have some contact with the homework), and write a brief response. I told the children I was looking forward to reading what they wrote and would write back to them; it would be like writing letters about the books we were reading. On the same day I sent home with them a letter to their parents explaining the procedure.

Reading the logs was a delight. Children chose books I never dreamed they would and their responses ran the gamut: hilarious, sophisticated, dull, poignant, puzzling. When Michiko was reading *James and the Giant Peach* (Dahl, 1961), she speculated about the earthworm's fear of being used as seagull bait. She wrote, "Being eaten by a shark is fast, you didn't have to feel the hurtness but when you are eaten by a seagull it hurts because when it pecks you, you feel the hateness in you." Richard liked historical books and wrote, "I thought the first Congress was very small. It seemed like a little league baseball team compared to today's Congress." At the end of one log entry Robby wrote, "I know how bad it felt to be ignored because everybody does it to me in school."

An abiding problem was finding the time to write responses in 45 reading logs. As the year went on and time demands grew, I felt lucky to be able to write in each log twice a week, but the children took me to task severely for not writing back to them every day. The following year, I told the classes I would read their logs every day and write in them as often as I could, and they were more patient with me.

The Process Becomes Easier

Although establishing and maintaining reading workshop took a lot of time, it required less as we progressed. After the first September when I read 15 children's books in 2 days, the new ones came one at a time, and they were short and fun to read. Skimming for vocabulary words went faster. Once when I had forgotten to prepare the list for a new section of pages, I gave the group their first word and managed to select the other nine before they had settled on the first definition.

The hardest part was learning to juggle the groups. When we sat down for a meeting to talk about a chapter, we got so involved that soon the period was over and I hadn't checked someone else's vocabulary page or been available to deal with unexpected questions or concerns. And the long years of using basal readers had programmed me more firmly than I realized. For each meeting, I was preparing sets of questions that covered literal comprehension, inference, prediction, main idea — a miniteacher's edition for each paperback. It gradually became clear that if I asked one or two general questions and then let the children talk about what they'd read, they'd demonstrate all the skills that the questions in the teacher's manual were designed to test. These "book talks" went faster, were more fun, and allowed for unexpected and deeper learnings.

Developing a planbook page format that fit what I was doing helped keep the workshops organized. I made a planning page for each day of the week and ran off enough copies for the year. Trying to make sure necessary areas of writing instruction such as mechanics and organization would get regular attention, I wrote in a different category of minilesson (ML) for each day, but was flexible about substituting topics that were more pressing than the one on my plan. I wrote in GS to remind me to include group sharing at the end of each writing period. Since I had four groups, each reading a different book, I made four boxes on the planning form for the reading plans, each having space for the day's minilesson and the book titles and page numbers we were on. When I wrote in my plans, I numbered each box to show which group I wanted to see when.

Teaching reading this way still took longer than reading a prepared script from a teacher's manual, but the benefits I had hoped for — increased enthusiasm for reading; opportunities to read, write, and talk about good books; freedom from the emotionally and socially stultifying effect of ability grouping — showed in the children's faces and behavior every day. They exhibited impressive comprehension skills and an awareness of what real reading is, a recognition of their own processes. When I asked them to write about what you have to do to be a good reader, Mark wrote, "You have to experience another world, and even concentrate hard when you read." According to Russ, "You must also like the book you read. Don't just read any book that the audience likes!" Marshall was given the dramatic hyperbole: "You have to be continuously reading one book after another. It gives you great practice. If you keep this up, you could read

War and Peace in the time it used to take you to read *A B C, One, Two, Three!*"

   War and Peace wasn't on our growing list of books that groups chose to read, but children's classics were well represented. Beverly Cleary's works were consistently popular; our set of *Beezus and Ramona* (1955) had to be reordered after 2 years because the children literally read the covers off. Roald Dahl's *The Twits* (1981), irreverent and outrageous, was always in use, as were *Charlotte's Web* (White, 1952), *From the Mixed-up Files of Mrs. Basil E. Frankweiler* (Konigsburg, 1967), and *Dinner at Alberta's* (Hoban, 1975). Each year I added a few sets of new titles and occasionally sent to the storeroom books that were never chosen or didn't live up to expectations. And each year, as the kids and I muddled along together, we revised our procedures, trying to find better ways to make our reading workshop a place in which children could function as autonomous, involved learners.

   Reading and writing became inextricably connected. In addition to their reading-log homework, the children wrote summaries of chapters or entire books, scripts for their book shows, responses to books (which included their own questions, criticisms, and speculations), reasons for wanting (or not wanting) to read a particular book, and answers to questions I asked or they asked each other. Questions included the following: Who are the characters? What are they like? Could this story have happened in a different time or place? Why? What words or ideas puzzled you? What questions would you ask the author if you could?

   I often asked the whole class to write the answer to a question about their own reading and writing. In response to "How does reading help you with writing?" George wrote, "Reading helps me with writing by the more I read the more I have to write." Beth understood that writers inspire each other: "Reading helps me in one way like if I read a good book I get a good idea from the book and I want to write about it even though the idea isn't exactly the same as the idea in the book." A child for whom English was a second language wrote, "The reading helps me with writing. It helps me at punctuations, pronunciations, spelling, and other things. I can write stories better if I read more stories."

   Some novels provided an easy lead into research. After reading *Sadako and the Thousand Paper Cranes* (Coerr, 1977), children investigated Japanese customs, World War II, and nuclear warfare. This book also led to the expression of some deeply felt thoughts about death. Katie wrote, "I think Sadako was good the way she pulled through all that pain. When she went through that there was no more pain. She just died. And she was such a good person. Sometimes when people die I go out of hand. People should just cry and get it over in a few weeks, but sometimes they don't. Well it is all right to cry and let it all out."

REVISION NEVER ENDS

One spring afternoon when the children had gone home, I found myself evaluating reading workshops for next year, in spite of knowing I would be moving away from my district. I looked around the room at the physical evidence of the system. A row of boxes on a shelf held sets of books and the folders that contained vocabulary cards, questions, and student papers. A section of the chalkboard was dedicated to the current book titles (four per class), page assignments, and the part of the process each group was on. Large charts on the walls gave guidelines for silent reading, oral reading, or vocabulary. My plans, written records, and copies of the books rested on the rolling cart that I trundled from table to table as I met with one group for a book talk, sat in on a vocabulary discussion, or started a group on the new book they had chosen.

Because two or more groups seldom finished their books on the same day, the one that finished first waited until another group or two was also ready for a new book so that we could form new groups. Usually those who had to wait worked independently in their basal readers. For "next year" I wanted to assemble a collection of magazines, library books, reference works — anything that was interesting and not a part of the paperback collection — for the children to choose among and read until the new groups were formed, perhaps reading for the first part of the period and sharing for the last 10 or 15 minutes.

The vocabulary segment of the process worked well. Hammering out definitions that fit the context engaged the children intensely in discussions that were often heated. Testing tentative meanings by inserting them into the context usually produced reasonable definitions. What was missing was transfer: How could I get the kids to use more of these new words in writing workshop? Maybe if each child had made and kept a copy of the words and meanings instead of the group handing in a single copy, the new words would have been more accessible. And maybe I should have made the expectation more explicit to them: "Try to use new reading words in your writing whenever you can, and be sure to tell me about it when you do."

For oral reading the children read the whole section, which took too long and lacked variety. "Next year" I would have given options: Select the funniest (or saddest or most exciting or most beautiful or disgusting, etc.)

part and practice reading it aloud before reading it to the group; or choose the part of the chapter that the story just couldn't do without; or find the paragraph that you most wish you could have written. Any of these choices would have involved the children in thinking critically about what they had read instead of just choosing a set of pages to read aloud.

Above all I would have had a whole-class sharing session at least once a week. Book shows only came when a book was finished; often a group found something exciting or funny or curious as they were reading that deserved to be shared with the class. What better way to foster children's love of reading than by encouraging them to talk often with their peers about the wonderful ideas they discovered in books and in themselves?

FINAL COMMENT

When I asked children to write about what reading meant to them, many said it was fun or interesting or helped them learn. They also wrote that it took them to another world where they felt free and forgot everything around them. A boy who was usually at odds with the school establishment wrote, "Reading means to read or to speak in a different world, like you feel calm and get to control everything." Teaching in ways that help children read for their own purposes means giving up the kind of control we as teachers sometimes wish for. But when children use reading and writing to make sense of their own worlds, our world of teaching becomes an exciting, rewarding place to be.

REFERENCES

Anderson, R. C., Hiebert, E. H., Scott, J. A., & Wilkinson, I. A. G. (1985). *Becoming a nation of readers: The report of the commission on reading.* Washington, DC: The National Institute of Education.

Atwell, N. (1987). *In the middle.* Portsmouth, NH: Heinemann.

Britton, J. (1970). *Language and learning.* London: Penguin Books.

Calkins, L. M. (1986). *The art of teaching writing.* Portsmouth, NH: Heinemann.

Cleary, B. (1955). *Beezus and Ramona.* New York: Scholastic.

Cleary, B. (1984). *Dear Mr. Henshaw.* New York: Dell.

Coerr, E. (1977). *Sadako and the thousand paper cranes.* New York: Dell Yearling.

Dahl, R. (1961). *James and the giant peach.* New York: Knopf.

Dahl, R. (1981). *The Twits.* New York: Bantam Skylark.

Embry, M. (1963). *Mr. Blue.* New York: Holiday House.

Hoban, R. (1975). *Dinner at Alberta's.* New York: Dell.

Konigsburg, E. (1967). *From the mixed-up files of Mrs. Basil E. Frankweiler*. New York: Dell.

Lewis, C. S. (1986). *The lion, the witch and the wardrobe*. New York: Macmillan.

Stevenson, R. L. (1950). *A child's garden of verses*. New York: Penguin Books. (Original work published in 1885)

White, E. B. (1952). *Charlotte's web*. New York: Scholastic.

Worth, V. (1972). *Small poems*. New York: Farrar, Straus & Giroux.

CHAPTER 7

Extending Reading and Writing Process to the Teaching of Social Studies

BEVERLY PILCHMAN
Tuscan School, Maplewood, NJ

My fifth-grade students were gathered on the rug after having read and discussed in small groups the novel *Island of the Blue Dolphins* (O'Dell, 1960). "Is it ever okay to break the law, and if so, under what circumstances?" My question was a relevant one; the main character Karana was the only remaining person left on the island after her tribe was killed. She was thus forced to break taboos about women's behavior in order to survive.

Sean reasoned this way, "Karana wasn't really breaking the law. The law was the law of Karana's tribe, and the tribe didn't exist any more."

But not everyone agreed. For some students, the law was the law. It remained even if the tribe didn't.

Groups in which such questions are discussed are the heart of the reading model in my class. This model evolved as I came to see learning as a process for myself as well as for my students. The classroom gave me the opportunity to research how students could best learn to be active and involved in their study of literature as well as in other subjects. The contributions the students made to how their learning could be improved were also included in the formation of literature study groups.

LITERARY STUDY GROUPS

The literature period often begins with a short teacher-directed lesson. I might ask students to focus on how the setting of a story informs the reader about the story's events or how an author weaves actual historical

88

events and people into a fictional story. A 20-minute reading time follows in which students are free to read alone or with partners and to respond in their reading logs. Responses include both commentary about the text and questions that will be raised within students' small groups.

While students read, I confer with individuals in much the same way in which I confer about students' writing. I might ask a student to explain a log comment. A student may ask a question about confusing text. I sometimes ask students to make a prediction.

When reading time is over, small, heterogeneous discussion groups meet for 10 to 15 minutes. Students rotate the role of notetaker; this person keeps notes about the content and process of the group's discussion. These groups were born when a former student suggested that it would be easier to start discussing each reading assignment in smaller groups first. I began by inviting children to list two classmates with whom they would most like to work and to list another three students who would be acceptable to them. I now form literature study groups using such student suggestions. There is real power when students have a say in how they will learn. Sometimes, students can choose with whom they will work; at other times, they have a voice in what book they will read, and their learning partners are those who have made the same choice.

As students proceed with their discussion, I visit with groups, listening to suggestions, asking questions, and sometimes joining the discussion. I spend about 5 minutes with each group, meeting with three small groups a day.

I have found it useful to keep my own journal-style notebook in which I record my mental image of what the class will learn, but I try to keep it flexible enough so that I can take advantage of spontaneous developments. My journal enables me to examine my own thinking about teaching and also to remember students' comments.

The value of these small groups has become clear because of comments like Sharon's: "It's nice to have small groups because if you're afraid to say something or [you want to] have something cleared up you don't have to say it in front of the whole class." Sharon's remark made me remember the feeling of fear of exposure in front of a large group.

After small-group discussion time, we assemble on the rug. As class reporter, I let the whole class in on the content and processes (e.g., students shared responses, raised questions, or asked for clarification) that I noticed during my time spent among the groups. Student notetakers then report on what their groups discovered. Students may ask questions, discuss characters' viewpoints, share journal responses, or perhaps read favorite passages. Students' responses usually are focused and interesting because topics for reading responses already have been generated by the class. This year's list is as follows: (a) character development and change, (b) point of view, (c) author's style, (d) how your book is connected to what you already know, (e) what life was like at the time in which the book was set, (f) puzzling parts, (g) predictions, and (h) anything that has meaning. "I like the big groups at the end because you get to hear other groups' perspectives and points they might have made," Terence said.

AUTHENTIC LEARNING

When I think about the evolution of teaching reading as a process in my classroom, I am struck by the authenticity of students' learning. Students challenge their reading, comparing it to their own ideas and to other reading, and they elaborate on the text. They think deeply and they write deeply. Students are driven to understand, interact, and question, alone and with each other. Aiyanna wrote that what she enjoyed about responding was that "you were allowed to write and talk like you really felt, that when you read from textbooks they put questions that seem like they're trying to put certain words in your mouth." Paul really captured the essence of students' collaboration in learning: "Not only did I learn about reading, I learned how to work with the kids in my group. I learned how they think. I learned a new style."

INTEGRATION OF SOCIAL STUDIES AND READING

Because of the successes with writing workshops and literature study groups, it seemed quite natural for social studies to be included within our reading and writing workshops. By integrating literature, social studies, and writing for an entire morning or afternoon, I would not have to clock-watch and move students from one subject to another. Yet wanting to be free of artificial time constraints made me even more eager to make better use of learning time. Lucy Calkins (1986) described how our society emphasizes quick and easy solutions and that little time is permitted for sustained effort. Teachers often make and hear comments such as: "There is so much to cover in the curriculum, I'll never finish by June!" My school district is no different from many others in that more and more has been added to the curriculum with little ever being taken away. Time has become the enemy of learning. I remembered the voice of a colleague: "Teaching is like a garden where more and more is planted, but nothing is ever weeded." My own metaphor for the fragmented curriculum is "smorgasbord teaching" — a little of this and a little of that. I wanted to pause so that my students and I could savor the flavors.

One goal for the integration of social studies, reading, and writing in a unit on the American Revolution was to have students use multiple resources — not just a textbook — to learn about this period. I also wanted students to be involved in authentic age-appropriate research in an environment where they would be able to learn from one another. Most importantly, I wanted students to be able to set their own learning goals. Thus, I invited them to identify a topic to learn in depth and to publish their expert knowledge in a format of their choice. I knew that they understood this goal because they already were published experts and readers of each others' stories on "Hamsters As Pets," "Camp Gray Glen," and "How The Earth Got Rain."

The first step was deciding which lessons, activities, or textbook readings were necessary. It was the first time I gave myself permission to weed. I knew I couldn't simply add historical fiction and biographies of American patriots; I had to provide time to read and respond within the classroom. In deciding what to keep, I also had to decide what to leave out — for example, information on "The Europeans Before Columbus," "Early Immigration," and "The Westward Movement." This decision was based partly on the availability of multiple copies of Jean Fritz's American patriots' biographies. I knew that my students would enjoy seeing Sam Adams as a man who refused to ride a horse, John Hancock as someone who had a reason for signing the Declaration as boldly as he did, and Patrick Henry as a late bloomer. I also worked closely with Shelah Fried, Library Media Specialist at my school, to develop a booklist of rich historical fiction appropriate for a wide range of students. These books became the literature core for the unit. We tried to include at least two copies of a title to ensure that students would have the opportunity for paired interaction.

To bring the class together to model discussion, encourage inquiry, and foster comparisons, I selected two read-aloud books: *King George's Head was Made of Lead* by F. N. Monjo (1974) and Jean Fritz's *Can't You Make Them Behave, King George?* (1977).

In order for students to construct meaning for themselves as they read, students wrote in reading logs. Here is one example of how Matt used his writing to learn a life lesson for himself from the story *Early Thunder* (Fritz, 1967):

> The main character is Daniel West and his biggest problem is himself. In other words he doesn't know if he is a whig or a tory and is also very mad at the whig and tory conflict that is splitting Salem in half.
>
> This book taught me an important lesson and that is that running away from your problems only makes them grow.

Reading logs forced my students to record their thoughts before being influenced by others' ideas. Fifth graders understood the Bill of Rights better because they were first asked to write their thoughts about the meaning of the amendments. Sharon's response embedded her interpretations of the amendments in assertions about her rights:

> The Sixth Amendment: If you don't have a lawyer you'll blow the case for yourself. If you have a lawyer then you'll do the case right. But if you say one false word you'll blow the case for yourself too.
>
> The Fourth Amendment: I would not like people to search my house without permission. If they went through my personal things, I'd get mad. They don't have the right.

Brian considered the following possibility after learning about the signers of the Declaration of Independence:

> I think those men were very brave to sign the Declaration of Independence because if America would have lost the war to England then the signers probably would have been killed. I would have been really scared!

Terence speculated on why, if the British had the finest army, they lost the war:

> If the redcoats were an excellent fighting machine, how come they lost the war to farmers? If the redcoats were the best how come they didn't think of not wearing a bright color? They were easy targets. It does seem impossible for the British who were supposed to be warriors to get beaten by farmers.

Laura used her own experience to try to understand King George's resistance to listening to the American point of view: "King George seems so obnoxious and stubborn. It seemed so simple—just to have a meeting and talk."

WRITING FOR A REAL AUDIENCE

Adults choose to write when they have a real purpose for doing so, and students are no different. I learned that my students appreciated a real task as much as adults would. One such task was writing a book review so that next year's fifth-grade class would be able to make good choices when studying the American Revolution.

Planning to Write

Using the framework of a Critical Review Think Sheet (Troyano, 1989) designed by a colleague, students considered what is important for a reviewer to tell. I read *The New York Times* children's book reviews to the class, and together we analyzed what was included to encourage or discourage readers' book selections. Since the class had been writing book reviews for the whole year, they were ready to progress to writing thoughtful and convincing reviews. For example, Katie's appreciation of fine writing led her to conclude:

> Esther Forbes is a very talented writer because it is difficult to think that Johnny and Rab weren't really living in 1773. I especially like the way that Esther Forbes makes Johnny one of the main reasons the Boston Tea Party and Paul Revere's ride were successful. She writes as if these events could not have happened without Johnny.

Katie also learned a life lesson that she passes along to the reader: "Johnny Tremain shows you how sometimes you have to face yourself and accept the way you are before anyone will accept you."

Matt engages the reader with this lead: "*Early Thunder* gets its title from flashes of violence that occur between whigs and tories in Salem, Massachusetts just before the Revolutionary War." Sarah and Erica, even more critical book reviewers, knew how to illustrate their dissatisfaction as readers of *The Mystery Candlestick* (Bothwell, 1970):

> We thought that the idea of the story was great but it needed more demonstration. The book could have been better if the author expressed the main point of the story with more incidents of secret messages being hidden and sent to people working toward the cause of freedom.

Identifying a Topic

As apprentice writers, young people need an environment that encourages them to go beyond reacting to a single book to the more complex task of developing and answering research questions and organizing the information into a meaningful format. Following a format developed with our librarian (Fried & Pilchman, 1987), I assigned research reports after the class had been immersed in studying a larger topic for some time; then students could identify specific topics each wanted to know more about. This identification takes time. Students' emerging knowledge about this historical period, along with having been asked to consider topic choices, gave them possibilities to think about. During a brainstorming session, I recorded topics offered by the students. At this point, since topics were not yet selected, students had time to reflect on choices. Before selecting a topic, students agreed that everyone should be an individual researcher, and they understood that the group would be enriched by the diversity of topics.

One year, three students were interested in becoming researchers on George Washington. Knowing that it would be difficult to be an expert on Washington's entire life, I suggested they research different aspects of his life. One chose to concentrate on Washington's boyhood, one decided to focus on his life as a military leader, and one student researched Washington as president.

Carefully delimiting topics kept students interested and kept them from being overwhelmed. Topic selections often took several days and initial choices often changed during this time. When the students were secure in their choices, I began our writing workshop by having students write down everything that they knew or thought they knew about their topics. When students finished writing, they were asked to generate a list of questions about what else they would like to know. Some students were already able to write quite a bit, while others could only list their questions.

Each student started at a different place. Chris, who wanted to know why Paul Revere is famous, first made a list of what he already knew: (a) he's famous, (b) he helped organize the Boston Tea Party, (c) he moved to Charleston, (d) the British captured Paul, (e) he had five kids, (f) Paul Jr. helped dump the tea, (g) he was a Sons of Liberty leader, (h) Paul was very helpful in the war, (i) he was a silversmith, and (j) he knew where he wanted to go.

Chris's interest in Paul Revere began when he read *Mr. Revere and I* (Lawson, 1953), and this interest flourished during his research. Consider the ending to Chris's report on Paul Revere as a Son of Liberty:

> I didn't write about all of Paul Revere's life because I thought it
> would get boring, so I just wrote about when Paul Revere was a Son
> of Liberty. I learned a lot about him and I think he would be
> a neat person to meet. He sounds reasonable and very interesting
> to talk to.

Organizing for Research and Reporting

Once students selected report topics, I created a visual scheme showing how different topics related to each other and fit into the larger whole.

From that visual scheme, writing groups were formed. For example, under the heading of Battles and Military Leaders, students whose individual topics were related met as small writing groups. Some of the related topics might be: the Battle of Lexington and Concord, the Battle of Bunker Hill, The Boston Massacre, General Thomas Gage, and General George Washington. The purpose of the writing groups was for members to meet daily to offer suggestions, ask for clarification, confirm ideas, and help writers become aware of their audiences. These small writing groups functioned in much the same way as sharing with the whole class during a writing workshop where individual students discuss any part of their writing before the class. These writing groups remained together throughout the entire process, from developing questions through research to final publication.

When students felt they had done sufficient research and had their information noted on 5 × 7 cards, I met with them to help prepare oral reports that were given before any writing was begun. Talking about a topic before beginning to write helps students organize their thinking and also reveals whether they are ready to write.

Modeling in front of the entire class with a student who felt he was ready to write, I encouraged this student to talk about what he wanted to say first and had him write key words or phrases on a notecard. We continued this process until the student was comfortable that all the important information would be cued by his one notecard. This process helped students develop an outline for the written report. After I modeled this procedure with several students, most were ready to begin to help each other with this task within their writing groups.

After students shared their oral reports in the writing group, the other members decided whether that student was ready to begin writing. Each topic was put on separate draft paper so that the writing order didn't matter; the parts could be properly sequenced later.

Ryan helped me understand why an oral report before a written report is so valuable for young writers when he remarked, "Oral reporting helped me organize my thinking so everything wasn't so scrambled in my mind." Also, in his journal, Ryan showed that he had learned an important lesson as a researcher:

> I learned that you don't have to suffer to do research on something because a lot of books have the same information so you don't have to read so many books. If some books have different information you don't have to read the whole book because you're only looking for certain information. I grew as a learner because I knew how to get what I wanted to know.

Not every student was ready to begin writing after an oral report was given. Oral reporting often revealed the need for further research. Students needed to know that this was a necessary part of the process, but it was equally important to set deadlines and teach students to be realistic about holding themselves to a time frame.

Using their simple outlines and brief notes, the students wrote. Their heads were bursting with information. I found that it is important to stop the writing before students want to stop because it keeps the energy level high and encourages decision-making about what to include.

Managing Time

During the time that social studies was integrated with reading and writing, whole mornings or afternoons were spent doing research. The library became the center of student activity. Students also were encouraged to interview experts when topics lent themselves to this approach. One year, a student who was researching colonial homes interviewed a staff member who happened to be a volunteer tour guide at a historical home.

During our scheduled weekly sessions, Shelah Fried and I worked with students in the library to help them understand the material they were reading. This sometimes meant reading difficult material aloud, paraphrasing technical vocabulary, providing background information, or showing students how they might read only part of a text.

In the classroom, I listened and conferred with whole groups or with individuals. Students also kept daily logs in which they catalogued what they accomplished each day and what they planned to do during their next session. Students could visit the library independently and seek assistance from the librarian.

During the research phase, students' writing was limited to taking notes about statistics, names, key words, and bibliographic information. Students answered their own questions as simply as possible. Students learned how to do a bibliography appropriate for their grade level and how to list their resources on a large manila envelope in which they also kept all of their writing.

Our writing workshop had thus become integrated with reading. Students knew that when they were reading, their pencils should not be in their hands. If they wanted to take notes, they knew to turn their books over. In this way, students learned to write about what they had come to know and not merely what they could copy. They became immersed in their research as they answered questions, eliminated questions, and developed new questions.

Planning for Presentation

From the beginning, students understood that the format for their research was a personal choice. Some children wrote historical fiction, some wrote question-and-answer books, and some wrote newspapers reflective of the time period. There were also picture books written for younger readers and expository reports that were rich with students' voices. After Stephanie completed her research on the marriage of Abigail and John Adams, she decided to publish a series of letters as she took on Abigail Adam's voice writing to her husband John (see Figure 7.1).

My research model is more than the reordering of facts. Youngsters who become researchers are proud of their writing. Lucy Calkins (1986) stated that the purpose of report writing is for students to develop areas of expertise, to synthesize and organize information, and to teach others what they know and what they think. In the process of developing expertise on a chosen subject to share and teach others, the students needed to use reference books, the card catalog, indexes, and magazines. They needed to scan, take notes, question, synthesize, deduce, and organize. Students' research stimulated better answers to better questions for themselves and their peers. The result of authentic research shouted, "I have learned something important that I need to write about. What I write is important, and so am I!"

Marcella's research topic was the Battle of Bunker Hill. She had a list of twelve questions, and except for one question about women's participation in the battle, she was able to answer her questions through her reading. What became apparent to the young researchers was that it is possible to have good questions to which there aren't always answers. Marcella wrote about herself as a researcher:

FIGURE 7.1. One of Stephanie's letters

```
                                             June 14, 1766

Dear John,

       How are you doing?  Is your job going well?  I hope
it is fine because I know how you like everything to go
your own way.  Sometimes I wish you didn't have to work
so far away but it will probably pay off.  I really want
you to go to Philadelphia so that you can do what you do
so well, which is writing laws, and to be happy.  But it
it is so hard for me to let go.  I never know if that
will be the last time I ever see you again...
```

I liked the way we could pick our own topics and the way we found out what we wanted to know. I couldn't find out everything that I needed to know such as if there were any women involved in the battle. The thing that made my research most difficult was that some books told me one thing and other books told me just the opposite.

I learned that I don't have to read encyclopedias and copy out of them to write a report, and the form could be a newspaper or a picture book; you can write something original on your own.

I know Marcella has become not only a fine researcher but a lifelong learner because she knows what she wants to know and is willing to search for it.

REFERENCES

Bothwell, J. (1970). *The mystery candlestick*. New York: Dial Press.

Calkins, L. (1986). *The art of teaching writing*. Portsmouth, NH: Heinemann.

Forbes, E. (1943). *Johnny Tremain*. Boston: Houghton Mifflin.

Fried, S., & Pilchman, B. (1987). *The process of writing: Research reports across the curriculum*. Unpublished manuscript, School District of South Orange and Maplewood, Maplewood, NJ.

Fritz, J. (1967). *Early thunder*. New York: Coward McCann.

Fritz, J. (1977). *Can't you make them behave, King George?* New York: Coward McCann.

Lawson, R. (1953). *Mr. Revere and I*. Boston: Little Brown.

Monjo, F. N. (1974). *King George's head was made of lead*. New York: Coward McCann.

O'Dell, S. (1960). *Island of the blue dolphins*. Boston: Houghton Mifflin.

Troyano, T. (1989). Idea exchange: Writing book reviews. *The Reading Instruction Journal, 32*(3), 67–68.

CHAPTER 8

An Urban School Becomes a Community of Readers and Writers: Administrators Lead the Way

JOAN T. FEELEY
William Paterson College

The day I visited P. S. 321 in Brooklyn, New York, the school lobby was set up to "celebrate writing." Children's work was displayed on all available walls, and a microphone stood in one corner. By appointment, classes came to the lobby to hear student authors read their pieces. At 11:00 A.M. I came upon second graders reading for fourth graders. ("This took courage," I thought, "but writing has always been risky business.")

Parents and passing school personnel stood around the periphery, listening intently as the 7- and 8-year-olds read their fairy tales, personal narratives, and poems into the mike. Some fourth graders also shared their pieces; for example, Joey Castillo read "Tiglon" (about an imaginary animal that was a combination tiger and lion) and Terrence G. offered "He's Gone" (about his father, who had died recently). Everyone clapped politely for each author, and a feeling of mutual respect permeated the event. Forty to fifty children were seated on the stone floor, and there was practically no need for teachers to remind them about behavior. This was truly a self-disciplined group. Remarkable!

Throughout the day, teachers and children alike were abuzz about the impending visit of Jean Craighead George. Authors themselves, they were looking forward to sharing literary adventures with this famous author of books they enjoyed reading. Any casual visitor could see that this was a community of readers and writers who took their work seriously.

How did this literate community develop in this mid-sized, urban school in a landmark-restored neighborhood that serves a diverse population of children from all socioeconomic levels and many ethnic backgrounds? It appears that a series of fortuitous events occurred that brought "the right people at the right time" together in an environment ripe for change. Having been introduced to process writing in the early 1980s through staff development provided by the Teachers College (TC), Columbia University, Writing Project, the primary teachers and some of the middle-grade teachers had warmly embraced teaching writing through a process approach. But they hung on to entrenched reading systems like DISTAR in the primary grades and various basals in the others. Change came with the arrival of a new assistant principal, Aida Montero, who had been a teacher/staff developer for bilingual programs and a specialist in process reading and writing. In her first year, the new administrator gave in-service workshops, modeling for the staff by teaching small groups of children. During these sessions, she introduced "big books" with sets of little books and demonstrated the language experience and shared reading activities that had worked so well in bilingual programs. Within three years, all the primary teachers were using these whole-language techniques, and DISTAR gave way to a literature-based reading program characterized by materials from publishers such as The Wright Group, Rigby, and Scholastic.

Still, only a third of the middle-grade teachers, sustained by their own network, were holding writing workshops, and just a few were using a literature approach for reading. Again, a new administrator came along who was a perfect match for the school's needs. Steeped in the process movement from his involvement with the TC Writing Project, Principal Peter Heaney arrived from the South Bronx where he had served as a teacher, early childhood coordinator, and staff developer in process writing. Since Aida Montero had already successfully brought about change in kindergarten through Grade 2, Heaney decided to concentrate on Grades 3 through 5 in this K–5 elementary school.

INITIATING CHANGE IN THE MIDDLE GRADES

Soon after his arrival at P.S. 321 a year and a half ago, Heaney sought advice on what needed immediate attention from the upper-level Program Improvement Committee, a 4-year-old school-based management team made up of teachers, parents, and administrators. The response was in-service training for teachers who were not well versed in process writing. A consultant was brought in to work with those teachers in their classrooms, and the need was met within the fall term.

Next came fourth-grade teacher Laura Kotch with an article by Cora Five in *The New Advocate* (1988) that described how Five had replaced her basals with trade books after experiencing success with her fifth-grade writing workshop. Like Cora Five, Kotch had been using trade books with good results for her reading-writing program and wanted to help colleagues who were trying to make a change. She thought the new principal could use her experience and the article to get things going. Not wanting to impose this new integrated approach in a top-down fashion, Heaney invited all teachers of Grades 3 through 5 to bi-monthly noontime meetings (he supplied lunch) to discuss what changes they might want to make and how to go about them. All 21 teachers attended regularly, and a continuous, fruitful dialogue took place during that first spring term.

In discussing goals for their literacy program, the teachers agreed that they wanted to develop students who were real readers, who read both at home and in school, and who could speak and write about how books reflected their lives and the worlds they knew. All were pleased with the way their writing workshops were going. They saw their students writing regularly, revising, sharing, and publishing in various forms; growth was evident. But most were not happy with their traditional basal reading program.

To get a profile on how their students thought about reading, Heaney suggested that the teachers give their students Nancie Atwell's Reading Survey (1987, p. 271). The results were telling. Although they had always done well on standardized tests, these students were not very interested in reading and could not list very many books and authors that they read and enjoyed. It became obvious that the school reading program was not leading to the teachers' instructional goals, and they were ready to change, to follow Laura Kotch whose students outshone the rest with their interest in reading and their ability to talk about books and authors.

Heaney asked his middle-grade teachers to plan their new literature-based reading program with him during those luncheon meetings, inviting them to bring in favorite books to share. Then he set up the meetings in workshop fashion. Before each meeting, teachers received a letter from him in which he would focus on one issue, for example, selecting books or starting reading logs. This issue would serve as the minilesson, and teachers would break into groups, distributed by grade level and interest, to respond to the letter. Finally, groups would share at the end of the session. Working in this fashion helped to alleviate fears and concerns.

Finding that some teachers really weren't very familiar with children's books, Heaney had the librarian and resource center consultant introduce books at each session. To provide a common experience with a piece of literature and to have a model that could be used to demonstrate how to teach with trade books, together they read Roald Dahl's *The Witches* (1983). Through minilessons, the participants developed webs, story maps, character profiles, and post-reading activities, all based on *The Witches*. Through the book talks and their own response logs, they were enjoying real literary experiences and learning teaching techniques at the same time.

Of course, there were many issues to grapple with, such as how they would teach skills and where they would get the books. Drawing on the Atwell (1987) model, Laura Kotch and Leslie Zackman, the teacher resource center consultant, volunteered to write a guide that would show how all the goals for New York City's language arts curriculum (*Essential Learning Outcomes: The Communication Arts*, 1988) could be met through a reading-writing workshop program. The resulting *Handbook for Literature-Based Reading* contained many of the strategies developed in the luncheon sessions along with ideas Kotch and Zackman (1989) had gleaned from reading the literature, going to conferences, and experimenting in real classrooms.

Although Heaney offered to purchase *Bridges*, Scholastic's literature program for those teachers who wanted more structure, even the most skeptical decided they could go with only the handbook, which they had seen take shape throughout that spring. They were getting more and more comfortable with the language arts workshop concept as they shared their own journals, visited each other's classrooms, read some wonderful children's books, and continued their explorations during the lunchtime meetings. Given the opportunity to change from using traditional basals, all teachers in Grades 3 to 5 opted to go for a literature-based program.

As for books, Heaney said they could use their New York State Textbook Levy (NYSTL) money to buy multiple copies of trade books. Locating a local vendor who carried a large inventory of children's paperbacks with reinforced covers, he arranged for the teachers to browse through the book warehouse to select titles they wanted to read with their students. By the end of May, they had spent $10,000 and had dozens of sets of wonderful children's books in their school, ready to be used in reading-writing workshops.

KEEPING THE MOMENTUM GOING

As they moved into their first full year of literature-based reading, Heaney and his staff had to deal with issues ranging from grouping practices to additional staff development. Although for years their classes had been grouped heterogeneously, they had been regrouping for math and reading. Now they elected to keep their classes intact for an hour and a half of reading-writing workshop first thing each day. Some started with the whole class reading a selected novel. This allowed them to demonstrate many of the new techniques learned in the in-service workshops, such as webbing the characters' traits or following the story structure graphically. Then some moved to having three or four groups of children each reading the same book or books by the same author. Others started with a completely individualized approach, with students selecting their own books, and interspersed this mode with a class novel or an author study. Although multiple copies of books are stored in classroom libraries, an inventory of where all the books are at any given time is kept in the principal's office so that teachers can plan together when they want to use certain titles or authors.

The staff knew they were going to need continued staff development to implement the new program and especially to be able to deal with the wide range of abilities the new grouping plan posed. Heaney arranged for their resident expert, Laura Kotch, to be released from her fourth-grade class for three periods a day, during which she worked with teachers in their classrooms, demonstrating, planning, helping out with literature groups, and troubleshooting in general. Instead of the bi-monthly sessions, the teachers held grade level meetings every three weeks, led by Kotch and teacher consultant Leslie Zackman. Teachers brought in their day-to-day problems, and Laura and Leslie added to the agenda, often spotting problems that needed to be addressed during classroom visits. Leslie also added that important dimension, the latest in "book talk" about what's going on in the world of children's literature, augmenting the spirit of the "literate community." Besides helping the staff to select tradebooks for their next big annual order ($14,000), she also helped implement the "Meet the Writers" program, funded by joint parent-teacher projects, to bring authors such as Jean Craighead George to the school. At these grade-level meetings they began to develop thematic units for the three levels to avoid undue repetition of titles. This staff definitely appeared to be moving toward its goal of developing readers who read and enjoy the best in children's literature.

A TYPICAL DAY

I visited early in the spring semester of this first year of implementation and was really impressed with what I saw. From 9:00 A.M. to 10:30 A.M., all classes were reading and writing. In one fourth grade the teacher was giving a minilesson on the importance of careful observation in gathering information for the children's pieces about a family member. "Writers are spies," he told them, "who look for the special little things about their subjects that would make their pieces interesting." He added that they could end up writing straight, factual reports or fictionalized sketches of their subjects. Skimming through their reading journals, I saw that they were responding to four specific elements as they read their Roald Dahl books: leads, character descriptions, settings, and conflicts. One boy, who was reading *Mathilda*, had focused his most recent entry on the main character, and the teacher had written an empathetic response, keeping the dialogue open.

As I walked through the halls of the middle-grade wing, I saw children reading real books—silent sustained reading for sure! I dropped in on one class, assembled on a rug in a corner of the room, that was discussing what authors do to hold a reader's attention, since this had been the focus of their minilesson at the beginning of class. A girl who was reading *The Great Gilly Hopkins* thought that Katherine Paterson (1978) creates suspense by having Gilly move from place to place, adding, "You keep wondering what will happen to Gilly next."

Another girl noted that Paula Danziger in *There's a Bat in Bunk Five* (1980) talks to her readers directly to keep them on track. Mentioning *The Twits* (1981), *Charlie and the Chocolate Factory* (1964), and *The Witches* (1983), a boy thought Roald Dahl kept readers in suspense by raising the same implicit questions throughout his books. "There are lots of little problems that eventually solve the big problem," he explained.

While one child remarked that *Mathilda* (Dahl, 1988) was "not realistic because *no one* could have parents that horrible," another said she thought Dahl did have a good fix on life because *her* parents were not very nice. "I never see my dad, and my mom doesn't really care about me," she confided. Philosophically she added, "In life you don't always get what you deserve."

When you hear thoughtful discussions like these and see hallway bulletin boards full of reading-writing connections such as child-composed character "webs" of subjects about which they are writing juxtaposed against sketches of characters from books they are reading, you know that these teachers are getting what they deserve: tangible proof that their integrated, literature-based approach is leading toward their goal to develop reflective readers and writers who can and do read, who can and do write, for a myriad of personal, social, and educational reasons.

Even the special education teacher for the 10-, 11-, and 12-year-olds is using literature in her reading program. Caught up with the rest of the staff, she showed me 30 picture books she had just gotten out of the library for her students to read. She found that they enjoyed and, because of the rich pictorial context, could easily read books by Tomie dePaola, William Stieg, and Ezra Jack Keats. Because she had read *The Witches* (1983) and

Fantastic Mr. Fox (1970) to them, they could discuss Roald Dahl along with the other middle-graders.

REMAINING ISSUES

After spending the morning watching children read and listening to them discuss their reading and writing, I returned to chat with Peter Heaney. In response to my question about what issues remained, he discussed continuing staff development and evaluation. He wants to continue to support his staff with all the help they need, but he is concerned that the in-service has to take place after school. Knowing that his teachers are putting in many more hours of preparation to implement this program than they would if they were just using a basal reader with its scripted teacher's manual, he wishes that he could somehow provide more staff development during the day.

As for evaluation, Heaney said that the P.S. 321 second graders always did very well on the skills-oriented Metropolitan Achievement Tests (MAT) even though the primary program was essentially a whole language, integrated approach. Although they do not score as well as the second grades on the MAT, the middle grades have performed adequately on their standardized tests, the Degrees of Reading Power (DRP). Heaney is not sure how the new literature-based program will affect performance on the DRP in the future, predicting that they will probably do about the same or better. The best evaluation for him is empirical evidence: seeing room after room of children buried in books, reading at desks, in groups, or alone in comfortable reading areas and observing their enthusiasm for literature as they discuss authors' styles and their own writing. He has seen a decrease in discipline problems in this new community: "Problem" kids see that their writing, opinions, and book choices/responses are respected and they respond accordingly.

Reporting progress to parents has not been a problem. Teachers review their students' writing folders with parents. Together they monitor reading through the response logs and the quality of participation in the all-group sharing time that takes place after every reading session; teachers keep track of the number of books read over specified periods. The city report cards are vague (Satisfactory, Unsatisfactory, Needs Improvement), allowing teachers to be more detailed in anecdotal notes that they write on the back. Because parents were consulted and offered workshops on the new literature-based, reading-writing approach, they have been generally supportive.

A PHILOSOPHY TO SHARE

Peter Heaney feels that the communication arts are inseparable and should be taught in an integrated fashion. Citing Frank Smith (1985) as a source for his philosophy that children learn to read by reading and to write by writing, he says, "If they read as writers, this will have to impact on their writing and vice versa."

Along with his staff, he wants his students to value literacy and to be excited by reading and writing. He wants literacy learning to be enjoyable and something students look forward to. He wants his school to be a community of readers and writers.

To other principals who want to move into process reading and writing, he recommends the following:

1. Learn the theory first by reading books by people such as Atwell (1987), Calkins (1986), and Smith (1985) and journals such as *The Horn Book, Language Arts,* and *The New Advocate.*
2. Visit model process classrooms so that you can talk to children, teachers, and administrators to find out how they got started.
3. Talk to the students in your school to find out how they think about reading and writing. Interviews or surveys such as Atwell's (1987) work well to help you find out where they are and what they need.
4. Involve your staff from the beginning. Invite them to plan with you. Start with small circles and encourage risk-taking within small circles. Be ready to support with materials, staff development, and encouragement.

The really wonderful rewards that come from integrated, literature-based programs are individual student responses such as that found in Sara's letter to her fourth-grade teacher (as she wrote it):

Dear Mr. F,

The first thing that you must know is that I love to read. Reading is something you must do. It's like brushing your teeth. If I'm reading a book, and you try to speak to me Well, you might as well save your breath. I'm out of your world and into a book world. Just ask my mom.

Right now my favorite books are: Babysitter Club Books, Judy Blume Books, and Nancy Drew.

My first book was cat in the hat. I learned to read it in kindergarten. I learned to read through the writing process.

It is kind of hard to say: "My favorite place to read" Because I will read anywhere, In bed, In any chair, On the floor. Let's put it this way, Anywhere.

When I read a book I think about "My Book".

Sara

REFERENCES

Atwell, N. (1987). *In the middle: Writing, reading, and learning with adolescents.* Portsmouth, NH: Heinemann.

Calkins, L. M. (1986). *The art of teaching writing.* Portsmouth, NH: Heinemann.

Dahl, R. (1964). *Charlie and the chocolate factory.* New York: Bantam-Skylark.

Dahl, R. (1970). *Fantastic Mr. Fox.* New York: Knopf.

Dahl, R. (1981). *The Twits.* New York: Knopf.

Dahl, R. (1983). *The witches.* New York: Farrar.

Dahl, R. (1988). *Mathilda.* New York: Viking.

Danziger. P. (1980). *There's a bat in bunk five.* New York: Delacorte.

Essential learning outcomes: The communication arts. (1988). New York: Office of Curriculum Development and Support, New York City Board of Education.

Five, C. (1988). From workbook to workshop: Increasing children's involvement in the reading process. *The New Advocate, 1,* 103–113.

Kotch, L., & Zackman, L. (1989). *Handbook for literature-based reading.* P. S. 321, 180 Seventh Avenue, Brooklyn, NY 11215.

Paterson, K. (1978). *The great Gilly Hopkins.* New York: Crowell.

Smith, F. (1985). *Reading without nonsense.* New York: Teachers College Press.

Part III

THE "WONDER YEARS"
OF EARLY ADOLESCENCE

SHELLEY B. WEPNER
William Paterson College

As Kevin Arnold (Fred Savage) in "The Wonder Years" says about his 13-year-old existence, "Being self-conscious is a full-time job." The day he discovered his first facial "zit," he wanted to "bar the door and wait for adolescence to run its course." He knows that there's bound to be a few "bumps" along the uncertain road through adolescence, but he's not sure he can survive. His private adolescent pain of denial, anger, and depression is tempered only by his fantasies of adolescent paradise: pizza, movies, and girls. And he changes from moment to moment. One minute he feels that his life is complete, enjoying a dance with the perfect "woman" in the perfect place; the next minute he feels like "crawling into the punch bowl and pouring ice cubes over his head."

Kevin's mercurial day-to-day existence reflects early adolescents' changing behaviors everywhere. Emotionally armed to "seize the moment" in one instance, they're ready to withdraw into permanent seclusion with the very next situation. The middle school/junior high teachers in this section know this about the Kevins they teach. In their transition to process reading and writing teachers, they've learned about grabbing literary opportunities to channel their students' energies into productive reading and writing behaviors. Before letting go of their security with the status quo, they thought long and hard about ways to match the needs and interests of early adolescents with the demands and rewards of reading and writing instruction.

This overview presents information about early adolescents, what they are like as readers and writers, what is happening in middle school/junior high school, and what the authors in this section are doing to support early adolescents' literacy development.

WHAT ARE EARLY ADOLESCENT CHARACTERISTICS?

Students in Grades 6 through 8 are in a process of transition from childhood to adolescence. Often referred to as "preadolescents" (Bolden, 1982), "early adolescents," "pubescents" (Rogers, 1982), or "transescents" (Eichhorn, 1966), these students are undergoing rapid biological changes that climax with puberty, the onset of primary and secondary sex characteristics. These "in-betweeners" (Cunningham, Cunningham, & Arthur, 1981) are beginning to shift their allegiance away from the family and more towards their peer group, all the while testing their previously held beliefs and values (Bolden, 1982). Because of their questioning of authority and preoccupation with peers, they are volatile and confused (Atwell, 1987). They are trying to figure out who they are within the confines of their familial, academic, and social environments.

Intellectually, they process information flexibly, efficiently, and logically (Bolden, 1982). Because of their newfound ability to formulate and test hypotheses, they enjoy delving into ideas to test their thinking (Atwell, 1987; McCandless, 1970). Their ability to appreciate the subtlety and double entendres of our language buoys their spirit for self-expression and self-discovery. Equipped to think about the nuances of their existence, they challenge what is and explore what can be in order to take control in their lives.

What becomes obvious is that it's not easy to teach early adolescents. Having passed the stage of only seeking approval from authority figures, early adolescent students are not as susceptible as young learners to the "sit up and listen" routine. They're feisty, mercurial, and painfully candid about what they like and don't like. At the same time, they're private, enigmatic, and disappointingly withdrawn from the mainstream of adult expectations. Socially entangled with peer expectations, early adolescents often forfeit adult reinforcement for peer acceptance.

WHAT ABOUT EARLY ADOLESCENTS AND READING?

When it comes to reading, early adolescents yearn for quality adolescent literature to which they can relate. They want to read material that deals with their realistic concerns and interests so that they can "see themselves in the characters, plots, and themes of the books they read" (Reed, 1988, p. 8). They need to read information on topics they enjoy that may not necessarily be grounded in the school's curriculum (Bradburn, 1988; Reed, 1985). They need choices so that they feel ownership in what they are reading (Atwell, 1987; Cooter & Griffith, 1989).

Nancy Atwell believes that when early adolescents have time to read what they want, they do read. Research has shown that when these students are given opportunities to engage in sustained silent reading of materials that they choose, their attitudes toward reading improve; moreover, in many instances, their reading achievement scores are higher (Atwell, 1987; Hodges, 1988; Oberlin & Shugarman, 1989; O'Tuel & Holt, 1988).

Unfortunately, "by the time many students arrive at the middle school doors they are tuned out or turned off to reading" (Cooter & Griffith, 1989, p. 676). This problem is compounded by the kinds of materials early adolescents are expected to read. Books deemed classics by adults are foisted upon these students, books they are neither emotionally nor intellectually mature enough to appreciate (Reed, 1988). Furthermore, because they are capable of reading more complex material, these students are assigned sophisticated stories, poetry, and folklore as well as specialized texts in science, mathematics, and social studies (Conley, 1989).

Content-area reading can never be minimized; however, early adolescents need a chance to read material that communicates to them in a more personal way. The more they appreciate the aesthetic value of reading (Rosenblatt, 1978), the more committed they will be to expand their literary horizons.

WHAT ABOUT EARLY ADOLESCENTS AND WRITING?

As writers, early adolescents run the gamut from tackling serious personal and universal problems to trivializing everyday events. Students in the middle/junior high years will write when they know that their writing can be entrusted to those who care. Inasmuch as writing exposes an individual's personal feelings, ideas, and knowledge, early adolescents are by nature wary of revealing, lest their audience will not accept what they say and how they say it.

Sometimes early adolescents simply are afraid to write. When they have not had opportunities to develop as writers, they are ashamed and embarrassed by what they put to paper. "They cannot write without envisioning red marks taunting them from the margin sidelines" (Calkins, 1986, p. 106). Other times, when these students move beyond their fears of criticism, they are bold, insightful, and fluent with what they have to say. They challenge themselves to seek meaning in their writing. They like the voices that they hear when they listen to what they write. They write about connections that they see between their own lives and the lives of others (Calkins, 1986; Rief, 1989).

As with reading, though, writing needs time. Early adolescents need vast and varied opportunities to search for what they want to say. Curriculum-based writing assignments and glorified story starters don't allow early adolescents to emerge as writers. Reams of ditto sheets and dozens of textbook writing assignments stifle these students' desire to speak from within; in fact, students usually cringe at the thought of having to write for a grade.

When students in these middle grades can write about *what* they want *when* they want, they are freed from the pressure to conform to external forces. And when they know they have an audience receptive to their latest surges of creativity, they are energized to transform disconnected ideas into coherent pieces of writing.

WHAT ABOUT READING, WRITING AND THE SCHOOLS?

Students' ability to write is affected both by their amount of reading and by the types of material they read; conversely students' ability to read is facilitated by certain types of writing (Noyce & Christie, 1989). Even though there is not one single way to teach the writing and reading process (Atwell, 1987; Rodrigues & Rodrigues, 1986), there are nine essential elements that facilitate writing-reading connections, and vice versa:

1. Opportunities for students to self-select what they want to write
2. Time for sustained silent writing
3. Frequent opportunities for students to read more about what they are writing
4. Time to collaborate with significant others
5. A variety of good books
6. Opportunities for students to self-select what they want to read
7. Time for sustained silent reading
8. Time for students to discuss what they read
9. Frequent opportunities for students to respond to what they are reading

Most middle/junior high schools aren't structured to include these elements. Teachers and students usually have only 45 minutes together each day. Teachers, in feeling the pressure to follow the district's prescribed curriculum, become "lecturers, assignment-givers, test-makers, paper-correctors, and ditto-designers" (Atwell, 1987, p. 15). Students, in reluctantly acquiescing to the patterns of schooling, become passive listeners and assignment followers. Real writing and real reading aren't valued enough to seep into curricular cracks. Becker's (1990) national survey of 2,400 public school principals found that "drill-and-practice activities were about twice as frequent as reading and discussion" (p. 453). Irvin and Connors' (1989) survey of middle school reading instruction found that the materials used for developmental reading courses were primarily basals and skill-oriented books. They also discovered that when reading instruction was offered, it was "the sole responsibility of the reading teacher." Overall, they found that "reading practice seems to lag far behind current reading theory in the majority of American middle level schools" (p. 310).

If schools want early adolescents to immerse themselves willingly in writing and reading, teachers and administrators must creatively restructure the curriculum so that students have choices in what to write and read so they will feel the need to write and read (Atwell, 1987; Calkins, 1986; Cooter & Griffith, 1989; Smith, 1982).

One example of curricular revision is occurring in Dublin, Ohio. A literature-based program designed around themes (for example, journeys, survival and courage, problems of modern adolescence) is now used as the middle school curriculum. The middle school teachers work closely with their school librarians to identify literature to reflect each theme. Students get to preview an array of books before they select one that they would like to read; interest groups are formed accordingly. During and after the reading time frame for each book, usually one to three weeks, students engage in a variety of reading and writing activities that culminate with a group project about the book (Cooter & Griffith, 1989).

Successful curricular changes also are occurring for below-grade-level and learning disabled middle school students. In working with below-level seventh- and eighth-grade students in South Carolina, O'Tuel and Holt (1988) set up a program for sustained silent reading and writing. Students choose their own reading material, share what they read, and journal write to their teacher for an open-ended response.

Oberlin and Shugarman (1989), in working with learning disabled students, Grades 6–8, modeled their curricular revision around Nancie Atwell's Reading Workshop. Because Oberlin and Shugarman have supplanted isolated word recognition and comprehension drills with reading minilessons, sustained silent reading, and reader's dialogue journals, they are finding that their students have better attitudes toward reading and higher levels of book involvement than before they instituted the reading workshop.

However enticing, change at the middle school/junior high school level is not easy. At the very least, any innovative program requires administrative trust and support (Cooter & Griffith, 1989). Sometimes administrators need to initiate change and/or work closely with teachers who want to change (see Chapter 12 in this volume).

For example, Phil Caccavale, Supervisor of Reading of East Brunswick (New Jersey), Public Schools, believes the key to successful change is to start small. In his effort to assist teachers in using literature as part of their reading program, he has set a minimum district-wide standard of one novel per marking period. To encourage his teachers to take their first step, he has written literature-based study guides for teachers to use as a skeletal framework for their reading and writing activities. He also created an elective reading enrichment course at the middle school to encourage students to become lifetime readers. Students spend the year reading, writing, and talking about 6–10 books of different genres. Similar to Brennan's (1989) efforts in a middle school in Trumbull, Connecticut, he sponsored an author's day for these students so that they could come face-to-face with Jan Marino, the author of *Eighty-Eight Steps to September* (1989), a semiautobiographical story about the death of a sibling. After one year of offering this course, student enrollment quadrupled (P. Caccavale, personal communication, January 7, 1990).

These educators are trying to find what works while considering scheduling alternatives, curricular flexibility, and material availability. As with the authors in this section, literature is the focal point for creating reading-writing connections. They know reading, writing, and early adolescents; they also know about the need to take risks at the secondary level in order to create meaningful reading and writing situations.

ABOUT THE AUTHORS IN THIS SECTION

Four teachers and one administrator share their own interpretations of process teaching over time and for specific projects. Although the roots of their desire for change vary, their message is the same: Early adolescents need every opportunity to experience the rewards of literacy.

Sixth-grade teacher Marianne Marino begins this section by describing her "literature treasure hunt" strategy for enticing students from the outset to think about their literary "finds." While talking about her philosophical framework for using literature across the curriculum, she offers a tightly-woven model for organizing a process-oriented, self-contained, heterogeneously grouped classroom around books of different genres.

David Taylor, an inner-city seventh- and eighth-grade language arts teacher, poignantly reveals the power of students' thinking when unleashed from the strictures of basalized assignments. Literature letter-writing, collaborative analysis of class-shared texts, and writing for publication are the heart of Taylor's efforts to sensitize his students to the impact of written communication.

Eighth-grade teacher Ralph Gioseffi chronicles the ups and downs of his transition into a process-oriented teacher. Steeped in process writing at first, he shares how his linear-oriented approach to reading evolved into a reading workshop atmosphere with the use of logs to monitor students' comprehension of whole-class and self-selected texts.

Joseph Sanacore, district language arts administrator, and Al Alio, seventh- and eighth-grade English teacher, complete this section with a step-by-step guide for an innovative storytelling project for sixth-, seventh-, and eighth-grade students. After reading and discussing a variety of children's books, these students write and illustrate authentic children's stories and then learn storytelling techniques so that they can retell their own stories to preschool and kindergarten children.

As you read between the lines, you will notice that these veteran teachers' commitment to find a better way to reach out to their students paved the way for their move toward creating literature-based, process reading and writing classrooms.

REFERENCES

Atwell, N. (1987). *In the middle: Writing, reading, and learning with adolescents.* Portsmouth, NH: Heinemann.

Becker, H. J. (1990). Curriculum and instruction in middle-grade schools. *Phi Delta Kappan, 71,* 450–457.

Bolden, W. (1982). Preadolescent development. In H. E. Mitzel (Ed.), *Encyclopedia of educational research* (5th ed.; pp. 1431–1436). New York: The Free Press.

Bradburn, F. (1988). Pre-teens in the library: Middle readers' right to read. *Wilson Library Bulletin, 62*(7), 37–38, 40, 42–43.

Brennan, C. J. (1989). One of us. In N. Atwell (Ed.), *Workshop 1 by and for teachers* (pp. 120–126). Portsmouth, NH: Heinemann.

Calkins, L. M. (1986). *The art of teaching writing.* Portsmouth, NH: Heinemann.

Conley, M. W. (1989). Middle school and junior high reading programs. In S. B. Wepner, J. T. Feeley, & D. S. Strickland (Eds.), *The administration and supervision of reading programs* (pp. 76–92). New York: Teachers College Press.

Cooter, R. B., Jr., & Griffith, R. (1989). Thematic units for middle schools: An honorable seduction. *Journal of Reading, 32,* 676–681.

Cunningham, J. W., Cunningham, P. M., & Arthur, S. V. (1981). *Middle and secondary school reading.* New York: Longman.

Eichhorn, D. H. (1966). *The middle school.* New York: Center for Applied Research in Education. (ERIC Document Reproduction Service No. ED 032 623)

Hodges, C. A. (1988). Encouraging a community of readers in the middle school. *Reading Psychology, 9*(1), 63–72.

Irvin, J. L., & Connors, N. A. (1989). Reading instruction in middle level schools: Results of a U.S. survey. *Journal of Reading, 32,* 306–311.

Marino, J. (1989). *Eighty-eight steps to September.* Boston: Little, Brown.

McCandless, B. R. (1970). *Adolescents: Behavior and development.* Hinsdale, IL: The Dryden Press.

Noyce, R. M., & Christie, J. F. (1989). *Integrating reading and writing instruction in Grades K–8.* Boston: Allyn and Bacon.

Oberlin, K. J., & Shugarman, S. L. (1989). Implementing the reading workshop with middle school LD readers. *Journal of Reading, 32,* 682–687.

O'Tuel, F. S., & Holt, S. B. (1988). Sustained silent reading and writing. *Journal of Reading, 31,* 478–479.

Reed, A. J. S. (1985). *Reaching adolescents: The young adult book and the school.* New York: Holt, Rinehart and Winston.

Reed, A. J. S. (1988). *Comics to classics: A parent's guide to books for teens and preteens.* Newark, DE: International Reading Association.

Rief, L. (1989). Seeking diversity: Reading and writing from the middle to the edge. In N. Atwell (Ed.), *Workshop 1 by and for teachers* (pp. 13–24). Portsmouth, NH: Heinemann.

Rodrigues, D., & Rodrigues, R. J. (1986). *Teaching writing with a word processor, Grades 7–13.* Urbana, IL: ERIC Clearinghouse on Reading and Communication Skills and the National Council of Teachers of English.

Rogers, D. (1982). Adolescent development. In H. E. Mitzel (Ed.), *Encyclopedia of educational research* (5th ed.; pp. 67–76). New York: The Free Press.

Rosenblatt, L. (1978). *The reader, the text, the poem.* Carbondale: Southern Illinois University Press.

Smith, F. (1982). *Writing and the writer.* New York: Holt, Rinehart and Winston.

CHAPTER 9

Weaving the Threads: Creating a Tapestry for Learning Through Literature

MARIANNE MARINO
Glen Rock (NJ) Public Schools

The first day of school is an eye-opener for my sixth graders. When they walk into their classroom they are not greeted by freshly decorated bulletin boards or textbooks piled neatly on each row of desks. Instead their desks are in groups of six and newly purchased books are piled on the floor. Their faces have questioning looks as I tell them we are beginning the year with a "literature treasure hunt." I ask them to collaborate with the students in their cluster to find ways of categorizing some of the books to share with the rest of the class.

The energy builds in one group of students as Lauren reads a synopsis at the back of a book, and Cathy looks at the book covers for clues. In another group, Tim has found a book by C. S. Lewis and is looking for other books written by the same author. It seems to give him a safe feeling in this strange territory he is exploring. Other children like Tim's idea and look for familiar authors such as James Howe, Lois Lowry, or Susan Cooper. Eventually, the children return to their desks armed with all sorts of treasures. They share their "finds" with other children. This is where natural book talk begins. The door to the world of literature has opened a crack.

The next day we gather on a green rug in a corner of the room to share ways of choosing books. Cathy tells us that her older sister recommends books that she usually likes. Patrick enjoys fantasy and Brian loves a good mystery. Some children explain that they read a few pages and then decide, while others admit that they do choose a book by its cover. I ask them to find a book to read and many of them go toward a known author or a book they may have already read. I tell them to make themselves comfortable and read. Jill looks puzzled and in a low voice asks Matt, "Only read?" Since the answer is "Yes," they settle in, but still eye each other for reassurance. No one has the nerve at this point to raise his or her hand and ask, "When is school really going to begin?"

It takes time for the children to realize that this is learning. My classroom is a place where literature is an integral part of our daily lives as readers and writers. It is woven into our activities and is the fabric of our learning. I surround my students with good books and give them opportunities to experience them in diverse ways. I urge them to apprentice with good authors and give them time to read and work out their ideas and questions as they react and interact with each other about literature.

WHY I USE LITERATURE

Louise Rosenblatt (1978) theorizes that children bring all their past experiences to what they read and transact with the printed words in a unique way. She believes that they create the text along with the author, calling this transaction the "poem." When children understand this phenomenon, that they are composing and constructing a text with an author, they begin to feel the power to formulate opinions and take risks. Consistent time should be set aside for students to interact with ideas and reflect by writing in journals on what has been read. This time is crucial and makes students comfortable with authors and literature. The next step is to provide students daily opportunities to talk about their reading experiences in small and large groups. By allowing children to read, write, listen to, and talk about literature, teachers are creating a common ground in the classroom for the students to build relationships as learners and develop into a community where literature forms the beacon for all learning.

Literature also has the potential to become a powerful tool for inquiry in the classroom. It isn't merely the icing on the cake but instead is an integral part of learning. Just as the warp threads on a loom are essential to the weaver to form a framework for the weft, so literature creates a framework for meaningful learning and the building of special relationships among children.

HOW I USE LITERATURE

Creating an environment for literacy in the classroom takes time. I have found that it is an ongoing process and adventure for me and the students in my classroom.

My classroom literature collection began with about 15 books that were given to me by Dolly Cinquino, Glen Rock's Gifted and Talented Facilitator, 9 years ago. It now contains about 1,000 books. The accumulation of these books parallels my growth in understanding the power of literature to teach.

I began learning more about literature by attending workshops and summer institutes on writing and literature. I met other teachers with similar interests, and we began networking to share information and ideas. When I realized that children become comfortable with literature when they use it in the classroom, I began to find ways of building my collection. While reading professional journals, I became aware of the availability of grant money to purchase books. Because of several grant awards by the Writing Project under the direction of Lucy McCormick Calkins at Teachers College, Columbia University, and a sizable grant from the governor of New Jersey, my classroom library now has numerous class sets, small group sets, and individual copies of a great variety of books and literature resources.

I found that a literary environment is created by the combination of books and teacher's knowledge of the books used. I surround myself with literature in the same ways that I do for my students. Books have become a part of everything we do, whether it be language arts, science, social studies, or math. Books are highlighted in different areas of the room for different purposes.

Creating a Literary Environment

In our writing center, authors are in the spotlight on bulletin boards, and their works are readily available. This builds an atmosphere for "author studies," giving students incentives to learn about how authors write and why they use a certain style. I usually read aloud from the featured author's work and we talk about what is unique about it or how it compares with other writers' works. If Natalie Babbitt is featured, I might read aloud her haunting story, *Tuck Everlasting* (1975), and we would talk about what is unique in it, for example, how Babbitt handles setting compared to Lowry's vivid exposition in *Autumn Street* (1980). In addition to videotaping interviews with writers, I collect pictures and articles about writers and their writing. Because they have many opportunities to get to know authors and formulate opinions about them, students begin to see authors as real people who write from their experience and work hard at doing it. The writing center is a place to learn and gossip about authors, but most of all, it is a place to become aware of an author's craft.

Children also become more comfortable with literature through genre studies. In order to make appropriate choices, a student needs to be familiar with all kinds of literature. I begin the year with realistic fiction so that children can become comfortable with plot structure. We then study folklore, poetry, historical fiction, and short story.

One time, after we finished studying historical fiction, Cathy started reading several books in this genre, which not only made her our resident "expert" but also affected her writing. For example, she wrote several stories in journal form about children who moved during the period of westward expansion in this country and connected them to her own experiences of moving when she was in fourth grade. Reading and writing are so closely woven that one cannot help affecting the other.

Experiences in literature should also be creative and entertaining. Children of all ages love to play with words and need time to do this. Choral speaking, chants, and improvisational drama are as important to older children as they are to primary graders. Students get a feel for literature when they work together on a choral reading of a part of a book they're reading or improvise after studying Roald Dahl's (1961) characterizations in *James and the Giant Peach*. The classroom is a place where children can be actively involved in literacy activities, where teacher and students work toward deeper understanding of what literature is and what possibilities are inherent in it. The teacher, as role model, creates the structure and cheers the children on toward becoming critical readers who understand enough about writing and reading to ask the question, "Why?" Once the environment is in place, children need daily time to read, reflect on their reading in response journals, and talk about their ideas with other members of the class.

Interaction and Collaboration

During the first month of school, children grow in their familiarity with books and begin to see what language can do for them. This is the first step in experiencing language in a social and functional way. Halliday believes that children know what language is because they know what language does (Jaggar, 1985). Pinnell (1985) states that, "A functional view of language means focusing on how people use language in their everyday life, . . . how it functions in a world of people"; children learn that "language can be used to meet their needs and communicate with others" (p. 56). My classroom environment is based on the belief that reading, writing, listening, and speaking are necessary elements to help children construct their meaning of the world.

Because my classroom is self-contained and heterogeneously grouped, the children's reading levels can range from third grade to eighth grade.

But, it doesn't matter since we work together as a community of readers and writers who collaborate in a workshop atmosphere. My goal is to develop not only efferent readers who get information from the text, but aesthetic readers who don't simply extract information but respond to the story in a personal and cognitive way (Rosenblatt, 1978). The teacher plays an important role in this process.

Koeller (1988) states that the teacher occasionally provides frameworks and content, models and ideas, possibilities and speculations, encouragement and guidance. At other times she simply allows children to become familiar with literature in their own ways so they can predict what it does, comment on what they like and dislike, discuss how it changes, moves them, or disappoints them. From my experience, we encourage children to grow in literary response when we give them consistent opportunities to try. Students may not succeed at first, but through daily effort, they begin to sound like literary critics who are at home with and knowledgeable about writers and books.

I've come to realize that for learning to be meaningful, it needs to be a collaborative effort. We need to share our feelings, experiences, and ideas to bond as learners. We need to interact with other human beings in order to clarify and expand our understandings of the world. James Britton (1986) states that when people receive our utterances, we share a special bond with them, for it means that they are concerned with us as an individual: "Through such relationships we learn about the world and grow increasingly confident about our capacities to affect the future" (p. 3). Teacher demonstrations and whole-class literature experiences allow children to build a base that can become the foundation for future responses to the written word. Students don't begin the year with this critical ability, but through trial and error, they start making approximations of critical interactions with literature. By writing reflectively and testing ideas with classmates, students grow into readers who dig beneath the surface of the words.

Learning How to Choose Books

Modeling sets the stage for choice. Reading aloud helps the teacher demonstrate an appreciation for good literature. I read to my class daily. I begin with picture books that are good examples of writing style. After reading, I usually ask the children to look at the text of the story to discover the way that the author has written. It may be to find out how an author creates a mood or develops a character. Picture books afford endless opportunities for exploring the structure of literature. My class loves to be read to and looks forward to our special time each day. Children are also able to transact with literature as listeners and form a special bond with the person who reads. Once, I had read the book *Annie and the Old One* (Miles, 1972) and the next day showed a video of the same piece. I asked the children to compare the two experiences. Sean wrote in his journal: "Watching the video was just not the same because Mrs. Marino's voice was not there." I found that reading aloud is one way of building relationships with my students.

Children don't make appropriate choices for reading materials naturally, but develop this ability in a supportive environment. It is important for students to understand writing in order to make choices that will extend their world and, at the same time, evoke pleasure. There are several factors that affect choice: availability of books, demonstrations by teacher, author and genre studies, and most importantly, peer recommendations. Children influence each other tremendously. When students are in a literary environment, books are a natural subject of conversation. Last year, Alysa began reading *Julie of the Wolves* (George, 1972). Within a couple of days a few more children were reading it. Before I knew it, a group of children were engrossed in the story and formed a natural book talk group. I took advantage of the opportunity to share personal anecdotes I learned about the author at a day-long workshop at which she spoke. We searched for other books written by her and before we realized what was happening, one person's choice became the focus of a whole class's author and genre study.

Children grow in the ability to make appropriate choices when there are a great variety of titles and genres in the room. I also have multiple copies of certain books I believe to be strong examples of a certain genre of literature. My students aren't limited to books from the classroom but use the school and local library as well as books from home. It is important that children exercise the responsibility of deciding what and why they read, just as they do in writing.

A TYPICAL DAY IN OUR READING WORKSHOP

Our reading workshop has a predictable structure and follows a set pattern daily. The children choose a book and read at least 30 minutes a day. During this time, I walk around and chat with several children about their books. The conversation takes on the flavor of one reader to another, sharing joys and disappointments, discoveries and questions. This chat usually lasts 2 to 3 minutes and affords me an opportunity to help the children broaden their understanding of style and techniques. Since the children sit in groups, other children listen in and sometimes participate if they've read the book or have similar questions about another book they are reading. These few minutes are very influential because they continue to build on the foundation and provide another way of demonstrating how to talk about literature. Here is an example of a chat in which the student is focusing on personal relationships.

> TEACHER: How's it going?
> CHILD: Good, I just started this book yesterday and I really like it. It's interesting. It's about kids in a junior high and I can't relate to it because I am not in junior high, but I have friends who are. I guess that it's not that hard to relate to someone even though they are older than you.
> TEACHER: Why do you think age doesn't matter in relating to people?
> CHILD: Age doesn't determine their personality or anything. It just tells you their grade. It really doesn't matter.

This excerpt shows that the student focused the conversation and discovered something she hadn't thought about before she had the opportunity to talk to someone about it.

Journals

The transaction that takes place during reading affects the children's experiences with a book. Afterwards, they need time to reflect upon and respond to what was read. Journal writing is a powerful way for a child to think through, hypothesize, and speculate about a reading experience. "Journal writing works because every time a person writes an entry, instruction is individualized: the act of silent writing, even for five minutes, generates ideas, observations, and emotions. Such writing makes it harder for students to remain passive" (Fulwiler, 1982, p. 16). This is another way for students to be actively involved in meaning making.

In the beginning of the year, 5 minutes are set aside after individual reading for journal writing; this time is later increased to 10 minutes. The purpose of the response journal is to verbalize a reading experience and formulate a focus to be used in a small-group book talk. As the year goes on, children use their journals to help them make reading-writing connections. The children become personally involved in their reading, as is evidenced in the following entry.

> Paul Zindel is very corny. In *The Pigman* he wrote that John and Lorraine were eating chocolate-covered ants. Very weird. Another thing, I doubt that John and Lorraine would get away with telling the cops

that they were Mr. Pignati's kids and calling themselves Lorraine and John Pignati. Everything seems so unrealistic in this book yet it has so much seriousness. I think that is how Paul Zindel writes most of his books. It's not confusing either. I like it. I wonder if in real life he's actually done any of the things John and Lorraine did? Probably. He's also probably got a corny personality. But he changes his style so much when he writes with his wife.

This student has evidently read several Zindel books. He makes value judgments about parts of the book, the author's style, the author's experiences in life, and their possible effect on his writing. He completes the entry with a critical statement about Zindel's collaboration with his wife. He is comfortable with authors and sees them as real people. This is one entry and one type of response, but the kinds of responses are limitless.

While the response journal is a strong metacognitive tool, dialogue journals are quite dynamic and continue to strengthen the concept of a literate community. Writing to someone else about literature develops a different voice in the writer. It is like passing secrets to a friend. Children can build learning relationships and get to know students they wouldn't necessarily choose as friends. In this way literature has a social function, as can be seen in the correspondence between Marie and Alice.

Dear Marie,
    Today I am reading *A Gathering of Days* by Joan Blos. This is a journal written by a thirteen year old girl. I call it a journal but it's really just a story written from the girl's point of view. I think that it seems like a diary because it really tells how the main character, Catherine (the thirteen year old girl), feels. It really shows her feelings.
    If there is a sequel to this book, I think I will want to read it. I'll want to find out what would happen in the next book because I'm really enjoying this one. This book is mostly about a family who lived in New Hampshire in the 1890's. The chapters in this book move quickly because they are broken into journal entries.
    I think that you would like this book. You should read it some day. You and I usually like the same books so that is why I think that you should read *A Gathering of Days*.
                                                        Love,
                                                        Alice

Dear Alice,
    I read a book similar to *A Gathering of Days* except it was a diary. But the book seemed more like a made-up story put in diary form.

I think you'd like the book if you haven't already read it. The title is *Constance* by Patricia Clapp.

I would like to read *A Gathering of Days*.

Love,
Marie

These journals are an example of how children can understand each other's taste and influence each other's reading choices.

Group Sharing

Talking is a natural outgrowth of reading and writing in my classroom. We use talking to share ideas and build on what we know after we journal write. Sharing ideas in small and large groups is not only enjoyable but also a powerful instrument for developing critical thinking skills. When children take control of the substance and direction of the dialogue, they take control of their learning. J. T. Dillon (1981) believes that dialogue creates an atmosphere for more complex cognitive processes whereby students apply, imply, and interpret knowledge rather than recite it. Additionally, students actively focus on their responses to what they read, rather than on objective comprehension. One student, Lee, described the purpose of book talk when he told me, "A book is like a puzzle and we are taking the pieces apart to see how they fit."

Students have self-initiated book talks in the groups they are sitting in. It takes time for dialogue to develop. Children need to build trust in each other before they bond. Danielle expressed it best when she said, "I get to know how someone in my group thinks." I ask the groups to choose and build on a focus. After several minutes we meet on a carpet in the reading corner to expand the small-group focus. I act as facilitator of the group so I can confirm, clarify, and extend their understandings. I use their focus as an opportunity to build on their interests in minilessons.

Whole-group discussion occurs after small-group book talk and is a lively celebration of literacy. Children participate freely in a nonthreatening atmosphere. They are supportive and respectful of each other. The following is a short excerpt from a whole-group discussion that demonstrates how students piggyback ideas and take responsibility for getting back in focus.

CHILD 1: We talked about flashbacks in our small group today. I'm only on page 15 of the book I'm reading and there seems to be about three flashbacks.

CHILD 2: Is the flashback any help to you?

CHILD 1: Yes, she's talking about how her stepmother took her father
away from her.

CHILD 3: It's giving you the background information.

CHILD 1: There's one flashback that I'm in the middle of right now
about Thanksgiving with her stepmother. It makes you kind of
wonder about what is going to happen.

CHILD 4: With the flashback you can almost reach a conclusion about
what is going to happen at the end.

CHILD 2: It's probably just an easier way to make a prologue.

CHILD 5: Do you think that the flashback is totally necessary?

CHILD 1: Yes, it tells you how her stepmother took her father away.

CHILD 3: Do you think that when they tell you about how things used
to be with her father that there is a little bit of foreshadowing?

CHILD 1: Yes, the stepmother also has children and the father is going
to have to be nice to the other kids.

CHILD 5: Does she feel any competition with the kids?

CHILD 1: No, because one's four and one's three.

CHILD 3: So, in other words, it's going to be hard for her to get used
to all the new things.

CHILD 4: Getting back to Matt's question as to whether the flashback
is necessary, you can probably have a flashback in a different
way. It's just another way of saying something. A lot of times the
author could put it in a different way.

Whole-group discussions are the place where students confirm or re-
fute their hypotheses by talking about the ideas they have developed in
their journals. Even if some students don't participate in the discussion,
they learn from it; their prediction and communal confirmations are at the
heart of their learning process. Teachers play a crucial role in creating and
supporting this atmosphere.

TEACHER'S ROLE IN THE LITERATURE CLASSROOM

Books alone do not create a literacy environment. They are necessary
but not sufficient. The teacher's role is to lead from behind and follow her
students' interests and enthusiasms. The environment should build toward
a workshop atmosphere where child and teacher wonder at and share
responses to literature. The teacher gives the message that books are important. Once this message is communicated, children will feel comfortable
with getting to know and understand themselves as readers.

Another major condition for learning is modeling. When children are learning to talk, they draw from the models around them. They learn by hearing others speak in complete thoughts. Children do not merely imitate models, however; they use models as one source of language learning. So, too, with literature. As I look closely at my role in the classroom, I realize I model the reading process during the times when I read aloud, have book chats with individuals, and write back to children in dialogue journals. The best way to guarantee that we will raise a new generation of lifetime readers is to hope for literate home environments and to insure that children are part of classrooms with teachers who are readers.

Another kind of adult assistance to learning is *scaffolding*, which Bruner (1978) defines as the use of successful communication at one level to attempt at communication at a more adult level. According to Bruner, the adult should always take the child's ideas seriously, thinking through what the child is trying to communicate, allowing the child to move ahead when capable of doing so, and supporting the child only when the child seems to need help (cited in Goodman, 1985, p. 15). Halliday uses a similar notion of language learning in children, one that he calls *tracking*. He suggests that a teacher should take on a similar role to the caregiver (e.g., parent) by sharing in the language-creating process along with the child. The teacher should help the child find new ways to say things as children find new reasons to express themselves (Goodman, 1985).

EVALUATION

The classroom I have described creates readers who not only know themselves, but are very successful in standardized tests. The test results have been consistently strong in my classroom, with children at all reading levels showing growth. One year, the administration questioned me about using this approach with a group of children whose test scores had previously been of concern. The reading test scores at the end of the year for our sixth grade not only improved, they topped the sixth grades in our district.

To evaluate my program for the Governor's Grant, I used an instrument called the General Response to Literature, which had been used in the 1979–80 national assessment of reading. The results confirm my enthusiasm for this approach. According to Margaret Queenan, who helped in the evaluation, "The performance of the average 13-year-old in the national assessment was disappointing. The performance of Marianne Marino's sixth grade is not. Where the 13-year-olds could not carry on an extended written analysis of literature, Marino's students can. Where the 13 year-olds primarily summarize, Marino's students read for both enjoyment and information" (see evaluation by Queenan in Marino, 1986).

CONCLUSION

As Margaret Meek (1982) states, "Literature, not reading lessons, teaches children to read in ways that no basal reader can, because literature is read, if at all, with passion, with desire" (p. 290). Literature hooks us emotionally. The experience of reading a good book does not end with the book, but motivates children to look for more books to continue the joyful process. There is an Arabian proverb which states, "A novel is a garden carried in your pocket." By creating an atmosphere that allows children to participate in many, diverse language-based activities, we as teachers are enabling them to take the time to smell the roses.

REFERENCES

Babbitt, N. (1975). *Tuck everlasting*. New York: Farrar, Straus, Giroux.

Britton, J. (1986). *Prospect and retrospect*. Portsmouth, NH: Heinemann.

Bruner, J. (1978). The role of dialogue in language learning. In A. Sinclair, R. J. Jarvella, & W. J. M. Levelt (Eds.), *The child's conception of language*. Berlin: Springer-Verlag.

Dahl, R. (1961). *James and the giant peach*. New York: Alfred A. Knopf.

Dillon, J. T. (1981, September/October). To question and not to question during discussion: Non-questioning techniques. *Journal of Teacher Education, 32*, 15–20.

Fulwiler, T. (1982). The personal connection: Writing and reading across the curriculum. In T. Fulwiler & A. Young (Eds.), *Language connections: Writing and reading across the curriculum* (pp. 15–31). Urbana, IL: National Council of teachers of English.

George, G. C. (1972). *Julie of the wolves*. Boston: Little, Brown.

Goodman, Y. (1985). Kidwatching: Observing children in the classroom. In A. Jaggar & M. Smith-Burke (Eds.), *Observing the language learner* (pp. 9–18). Urbana, IL: International Reading Association/National Council of Teachers of English.

Jaggar, A. (1985). On observing the language learner: Introduction and overview. In A. Jaggar & M. Smith-Burke (Eds.), *Observing the language learner* (pp. 1–7). Urbana, IL: International Reading Association/National Council of Teachers of English.

Koeller, S. A. (1988). The child's voice: Literature conversations. *Children's Literature in Education, 19*, 3–16.

Lowry, L. (1980). *Autumn street*. New York: Dell.

Marino, M. (1986). *Reading process workshop: A literature-based whole language approach to reading*. Trenton: New Jersey State Department of Education.

Meek, M. (1982, Autumn). What counts as evidence in theories of children's literature? *Theory into Practice: Children's Literature, 21*, 284–292.

Miles, M. (1972). *Annie and the old one*. Boston: Little, Brown.

Pinnell, G. S. (1985). Ways to look at the functions of children's language. In A. Jaggar & M. Smith-Burke (Eds.), *Observing the language learner* (pp. 57–72). Urbana, IL: International Reading Association/National Council of Teachers of English.

Rosenblatt, L. M. (1978). *The reader, the text and the poem*. Carbondale: Southern Illinois University Press.

CHAPTER 10

Literature Letters and Narrative Response: Seventh and Eighth Graders Write About Their Reading

DAVID F. TAYLOR
Santa Barbara (CA) Junior High

A book is the electricity which turns the light in your brain on.

Anon. junior high author

I am thinking about Luis' mistake. After the first minilesson of the year on how to write "Literature Letters" about the self-selected books they were reading, the class settled down for 30 minutes of reading and writing about their books to me or to each other. Luis got it all wrong when he wrote to Rigel:

Dear Rigel,
    I like the story that you read of football. How you tackle 300 man and that you made 500 touchdowns. I also like how you put some action in your storys. Also how you discribe it very good. I also like the story about baseball. I like how you hit the ball for the homerun and how you got the ball when you jump. Well I hope you do another good story.

Sincerely, your friend right next to you,
Luis Guillen*

---

*All student writings are unedited first drafts.

Dear Luis,
I like your storyes becuse you put a lot of detail. I can't wate to
hear your next story abut football because it is my favorite sport.
Sincerely,
Rigel Boycan

As I read their exchange that afternoon, I first wondered where I'd
gone wrong. I envisioned myself patiently explaining to Luis that he was
supposed to write about the book he was reading, not about a story written
by a student. Luis was smart; he'd get the picture. And then, I got the
picture. After a couple of slaps on the forehead to shake out the afternoon
cobwebs, I whooped with pleasure, thanking the absent Luis for the
opportunity he'd sent my way. "Of course," I declared to the empty tables
and chairs, "We'll write to each other about our own writing."

I've had many people to thank these last three years. I don't even know
who it was who put a copy of Nancie Atwell's *In the Middle* (1987) on the
chalktray one afternoon during a South Coast Writing Project session at
the University of California at Santa Barbara. I got to it first. Atwell's book
introduced me to Donald Graves (1983), Donald Murray (1984), Lucy
McCormick Calkins (1986), Tom Romano (1987), Jane Hansen (1987), and
Frank Smith (1985).

I had always liked the idea of a community of writers and readers
working and sharing something beyond the boring, listless, step-by-step
learning bites offered by prepackaged basals and standardized test preparations. Agreeing with Frank Smith that these flashy, expensive packages at
once trivialize the richly complex nature of language and insult both students and teachers, I spent years piecing together open-ended curriculums
that, while more sensible than basals, lacked a superstructure to give me
and my students the kind of centering we needed to be liberated as active
thinkers and learners, readers and writers. So, I patched together one
clever assignment after another that kept me firmly entrenched at front
and center in the classroom.

Despite some recent efforts promoting heterogeneous grouping, the
Santa Barbara Junior High English department remains part of a five-
tiered academic tracking system: gifted and talented (GATE), honors,
average, chapter one (students who have scored two or more grades below
grade level on a battery of standardized tests), and special education. This
system at once denies and reveals the power of process/workshop education. Students, who are acutely aware of their academic segregation, have
commented to me that ability grouping is utterly unnecessary in the workshop classroom. I teach five periods a day of honors, average, and chapter
one classes. I am currently averaging a delightful 23 students per class. My

average class size will be about 26 next year and 29 the next. During class, students sit in groups of four at round tables or move about to areas designated for peer conferences and reading. We also have a section of the room open for "group share," a regular 10-minute meeting where we gather on the floor to listen and respond to each other's writing and reading.

Many new Reading Workshop students react with disbelief when I tell them that they get to choose what they will read. Others don't care one way or the other: They won't be reading under any circumstances. Curiously, some of these people were last week's most prolific writers. But the very thought of reading conjures up images of struggle and defeat, mispronunciations and failed quizzes, boring text and only one right answer — the teacher's. These abused readers have an unlearning process to go through until they begin to feel comfortable with an open book of their own in front of them.

LETTERS: STUDENT AUTHOR TO STUDENT AUTHOR

Luis and Rigel helped me open a door for many of these people to peek through. There aren't too many dictums in workshop education, but one is to always be ready to see when someone, anyone, is there with the light. That afternoon Luis was holding the light. Encouraged and enchanted by the seriousness with which they had responded to each other's writing, I began to see that the student anthologies we had published over the years could help bridge the gap between the writing and reading process, to help my students begin to read as writers and write as readers. We are now writing about our published stories. Students read an anthology until they find a story that speaks especially to them that day. Then the reader writes the author:

Dear Anabel,
     I liked your story called "The Green River Killer." I liked it because it is scary. I liked the part when your boss said that tomorrow you were going to work late. and when you couldin't find your keys and when the man grabbed you and said Do you want a ride home? I sure cant wait to read the other part of your story.
                                Bye,
                                Candy De Loera

Dear Candy,
     Well, I'm glad that you liked my story. I like scary stories too, and not everything in this story has happed to me only some of them.

But let me tell you that this story is about a real girls life. It's real sad what this girl goes through and I realy wish this wouldn't happen to no one.

Well, if you liked this story, wait till Part Two comes out. I think it will be better than Part One. Thanks for writing.

> Your Friend,
> Anabel Sanchez

Anabel and Candy don't know each other, but they have formed a bond as readers and writers that extends their literate community beyond the classroom. Anabel does not have a workshop class this year and is not writing much. She wrote Part One last spring. She told me that as a result of the letters she received she's going to write Part Two and wondered if it could be included in a publication even though she is no longer in my class. She doesn't want to disappoint her audience. After conferring at home with her sister, who is in workshop, she made arrangements to sit down with me for an editing conference before she writes her final draft. I'm sure her fans won't be disappointed.

Kai chose to respond to a piece written by a student who is now in high school:

Dear Rechelle,

The first thing that drew my attention to your story was the title, "Dear Diary." Also, the format was different from all the rest. I liked how you put the date on every one, and also how you show how you feel at the end of every letter like "Angry Becky". It was also like a real life situation, because you hear about a lot of dropouts who go to drugs. It also shows what happens when you mix with the wrong crowd. I like how you didn't make every letter too long but just long enough to show your feelings and whats going on.

> Sincerely,
> Kai Cogswell

Dear Kai,

I'm surprised that my title caught your eye. I didn't put much thought into it. It just seemed to fit. The reason I put the date on each entry was not only to make it more like a real diary, but to give the reader some sense of how much time passed between each stage of Becky's life. I thought that adding little hints of emotion at the end of each entry like "Angry Becky" made the entries a little more interesting. I'm glad you enjoyed them also. Yes, it does reflect "real life" situations. Every day hundreds, if not thousands, of teenagers contemplate or even attempt suicide. I'm glad that you enjoyed my story and I thank you for your comments.

Sincerely yours,

Rechelle Thorne

Rechelle wrote her piece when she was in the eighth grade. When I began the author-to-author project I hadn't considered that I might have to contact writers like Rechelle who had graduated. It has proven to be a less daunting task than I had first imagined, and we all wait with delight for the high school authors to respond.

It's a special pleasure for me to contact past students with the good news that they have joined our well-known authors' club. I wrote a cover letter to each ninth-grade writer and enclosed it with the letters from their admiring junior high fans:

Dear Rechelle,

In workshop this year we are writing Lit. Letters to students whose work was published last spring in "Let A Thousand Stories Bloom." I think it's wonderful that your story was chosen. It affirms your ability to engage readers with your voice, your language. It also helps these readers as writers; your piece became a part of topic-searching, a process with which you have struggled. I hope you are both pleased and encouraged as you read what I and your admiring readership at SBJH are sending you.

Would you consider responding soon to anyone who has written you? Please drop your letters off at the Reading Center or mail them to me.

Sincerely,

David Taylor

LITERATURE LETTERS: SELF-SELECTION AND BEGINNING LITERARY ANALYSIS

Using student writing is a natural part of making the transition from writing workshop to reading workshop and back again. There are plenty of student anthologies around the room, and letters may be written and placed in the author-to-author mailbox at anytime. Letter writing, in the form of "literature letters" (Atwell, 1987), is now a major part of my reading workshop program. I had believed that learning the hard work of rigorous literary analysis was either to be avoided altogether or could only happen when students read the books mandated for junior high and answered the multiple-choice questions at the end of each chapter. One of the first things I realized after reading *In the Middle* (Atwell, 1987) was that the junior high literature curriculum represented a rather narrow range of all the literary genres when compared to the diversity of authors and genres found in the index of student favorites. Reading lots of books was impressive, but I wondered how the students could know what to think about them unless I was prompting, wheedling, and cajoling at the front of the classroom?

Then I remembered that Frank Smith (1985) had said, "The distinguishable 'skills' of reading and writing are relatively superficial aspects of literacy. . . . To keep the two activities separate does more than deprive them of their basic sense, it impoverishes any learning that might take place" (p. 127). So we, the students and I, began to read and write together. I present minilessons about the many things that comprise the reading (and, inevitably, the writing) process: use of figurative language, interviews with authors, what I expect in a literature letter (remember Luis), genres of literature, hints for speeding up reading and comprehension, and lots of other good stuff that naturally comes up when people read and write together. And the students write to each other about the books they are reading:

Dear Erin,

   I am reading *The Call of the Wild* by Jack London. I really like this book because even though the author writes in the third person, and a little in the second, he tells the story through the dogs eye's, which makes you feel sorry for the dog rather than thinking of Buck as a rabid, fierce, and mean dog. This book takes place in the frozen wastelands of the Yukon. It is about a dog who is very brave and strong yet very intelligent, in a sense that he knows a lot, and figures out things he doesn't know.

   He is taken and beaten by cruel men which he thinks of as tormentors as they search for the gold of the Klondike. Jack London makes this book so that I can't put it down. This I think is the best dog story I have ever read, including *Old Yeller* and *Cujo*. Have you read it? If you haven't, I really suggest this book.

   I know a little bit about your book from what you read in Group Share, but not enough so tell me about your book when you write back.

                                        From,
                                        Nate

Nate,

I think I've read *The Call of the Wild* before. I'm not an animal
person so I wasn't as excited about it as you. But it was sad about all
the beatings.

I'm reading *Fire in the Heart* by Liz K. Murrow. It's called that
because Molly O'Conner, the main character is looking for information about her mother. The fire is a burning need about her
mother.

It's a pretty good book. If you like mysteries you might want to
read it.

Thanks for writing me!

Erin

There are no hard and fast rules about letter length. I do expect that
students will write thoughtfully, but lengths vary. Since they must initiate
two letters a week, one to me and one to a classmate, and respond to letters
sent to them, the responses are generally shorter than the original letter.
Thus, Erin's response to Nate is, proportionally, about average. Literature
letters don't have to be about specific books, they just have to be about
literature. For instance, one week Megan wrote:

Dear Mr. Taylor,

Hi! I'm not reading anything right now, so I will tell you why I
like humorous books. I've always liked funny books because they make
me feel good and happy not like sad books. When you read a sad book
you finish feeling sad or depressed. When you read a funny book you
finish feeling happy and recommend it to people. It also helps me
with my writing. I don't like to write serious or sad stories, I like to
write things that make people laugh or smile when they read it!
Humorous books make you feel good.

Love,
Megan

Dear Megan,

I enjoyed your thoughtful and informative letter. I'm pleased to
see you make the connection between your reading and your writing.
I enjoy a mix of genres, but overall I'd rather laugh than cry. Except,
there is a way in which a well-written sad story can make you feel
better. It's as if the story lets some of the sadness inside you leak out,
so you have a little less. Like helping someone, or some good cause,
makes room inside to help you feel as if you can make a difference. I
guess that's one reason some people write: to share a part of them-

selves with others. Thus, writing can be a very personal and powerful form of giving. Your writing does make me laugh and I appreciate the gift.

Sincerely,
Mr. Taylor

CLASS-SHARED TEXT: RESPONSE AND OWNERSHIP

Sometimes trade book authors make my job easy. In California, the state language arts framework calls for a core and supplemental curriculum literature list of books agreed upon by teachers at the district level. Several of my seventh graders this year wanted to read *The Outsiders* by S. E. Hinton (1967) as a class-shared text. This book is on the district list, but I had some vague, unsubstantiated hesitation about using it. Would this classic teenager-in-trouble paperback really offer enough for these youngsters to cut their analysis-of-literature milkteeth on? We'll see, I decided, and jumped in.

The day I handed out the class set, a colleague told me that she had just finished Hinton's (1988) new book, *Taming the Star Runner*. Aside from the fact that my students had decided on *The Outsiders* with no help from me, they were further entranced by the biographical information that Hinton had written this book as a teenager. It turns out that *Taming the Star Runner* is semi-autobiographical, with Travis, the familiar, troubled main character, as a closet writer who has sent a manuscript off for publication before the first chapter begins. What a tie in! And then, at the beginning of chapter two, Travis is writing his best friend and, as he rejects his first draft, I am provided with a natural minilesson on leads:

Dear Joe,
    It's okay here. My uncle seems to be okay. I started school. It's real small. Everything is okay.

    Travis broke off typing. Great literary merit in this letter, all right. What if someday, after he was famous, somebody published all the letters he'd ever written? Sometimes they did that with famous-author letters.

    He'd sure be proud of this one. He yanked it out of his typewriter and rolled in a new page.

Joe —
    I lived through the plane ride even tho we had to stop twice on the way. I thought I'd puke all over the dude sitting next to me, and it woulda served him right — I tried to get him to buy me a bourbon but he wouldn't go for it. (Hinton, 1988, p. 22)

It's a tight weave. After hearing this excerpt, they want me to read *Taming the Star Runner* aloud after we finish *The Outsiders*. Having the seventh graders in a double-language arts period gives me some luxurious latitude with them that I don't have in my other classes. We have been extending writing into period two and reading *The Outsiders* 20 minutes a day and for homework. Of course, not everyone is on the same page. I announce that we will do some oral and written response to the book the next day and that it's catch-up time. I'm anxious to see what they have to say about characterization, especially Ponyboy's point of view. We haven't had any class discussion, although I overhear snatches of book-centered conversation from time to time as we read.

As Ponyboy and Johnny hide in an abandoned church, they wake one morning to a beautiful sunrise. Ponyboy is moved to recite *Nothing Gold Can Stay*, a poem by Robert Frost that he learned in school. Frost describes nature's first greenery as "gold" and transient, lasting only an hour; just as the first golden shoot (a flower) gives way to green leaves, so golden dawn becomes a day that fades, hence the title, *Nothing Gold Can Stay*.

I asked them to read and reread this poem, which Frost wrote in 1923. In a recent article, my colleague, Sandra Robertson (1990), points out that "it has long been axiomatic among writing teachers that writing is rewriting" (p. 83). She then draws the logical parallel conclusion that thoughtful "reading is rereading" (p. 83). We look at the poem on the overhead and my students respond to the language that has drawn their attention by repeating those phrases or words aloud. I suggest that they then write about what Frost has to say to two frightened teenagers some 45 years later.

After $2^{1}/_{2}$ years of workshop, I still have to resist acting on the notion that I am the keeper of knowledge. When I first put the poem on the overhead screen, I had been tempted to offer the definitive answer. Then I'd just have them rework my answers in their own words and call it a day. Because I kept my mouth shut, I was privileged to share, once again, in their quiet excitement as they offered to each other and me rich and diverse responses. As we wrote, read, and discussed our responses, we discovered an expansive tapestry of student-owned interpretations:

> Ponyboy rembers this poem because he's growing and he's starting to notice how preshus nature can be when you want it to be. When nurture makes mountains, spring and brings a baby into this world this means nature's "first green." Its "gold" means its ment to be, its worth making, preshus.   — Monica Torres

> In the last part of the poem when it says "Nothing gold can stay" it

means nothing good will last forever because in the begining of the book Ponyboy walked out of the movie feeling pretty good about himself. Later in the book all of those feelings went away.

Johnny had the freedom to walk alone before and now he got jumped and he is afraid to walk alone and carrys a big knife. Ponyboy says that Johnny was a lot jumpier than usual, and Johnny had followed the law more than any one of the Greasers.   — Kevin Dunn

Students' interpretations of the interrelationship between a 70-year-old poem and a narrative of a modern teenager in trouble helped enrich my view of how a book can transmit important ideas. When I am willing to be bound and gagged through the process of student-owned response to literature, my students will show me how walls can become windows.

THE TEACHER ALSO WRITES TO BE READ

I'm not always bound and gagged. I write with my students and at home when I get the chance. They see me as a writer, which enhances my authority as a guide and a mentor of young writers. I read with them and write to them about my reading. They know I do what they do. I also read aloud from a variety of books. I often find out things about my writing just when they do. When I was reading a section from Eudora Welty's (1984) *One Writer's Beginnings* to the class, Teya broke in with, "Mr. Taylor, that part about the long train ride with her father sounds just like the dream part of your car ride in 'Grandpa Shoots a Chicken.'" She was right. And I had read Welty's autobiography before writing that autobiographical incident. We stopped and discussed once again that what we read often affects the style and content of our writing. Teya had shown me that I had topic searched without realizing it.

I publish a piece of my writing in each student anthology. The selections aren't long; a narrative piece or a poem is fine. I share my writing process in group share and ask for help with leads, imagery, conclusions — anything that may not be working just right for me. Invariably, I get real writer's help. But why should I expect less from the community of readers and writers of which I am privileged to be a part?

I also get an occasional piece of author-to-author mail. There's nothing like a nice letter from a fellow author to make the day:

Dear Mr. Taylor,

I just finished reading your poem "I Saw her on the TV News." I liked how you wrote the words the way she spoke. How you describes what she looks like. I thought it was pretty good because you can get a better idea of what she looks like.

> From,
> Maricela

Dear Maricela,

Thanks for the letter. Some people told me that running the words together made it hard to read, but, at the time, that was the best way I could think of to show how she sounded. And she was so thin, I thought she might fall over if a breeze came up. I guess I was topic searching as I watched TV and didn't even realize it.

> Sincerely,
> Mr. Taylor

Once a colleague, Davie Bregante, asked students to make a brief journal entry on their interpretation of this quote from Nancie Atwell, "Beyond all else, writing is thinking" (1987, p. 56). The next day she received this page:

> I think that what this states is that when you are writing you are thinking of what you are going to write next. The same go's for reading you don't notice it but you're un-trapping words and setting them free. There for, you are understanding what you are reading.
> — Jarom Kemp

I don't want to separate the writing/reading processes: They are integral, recursive parts of a whole. I encourage my students to write with a reader's eye and read with a writer's ear because I believe that, as they pay attention to how they see and hear, they will, to paraphrase Jarom, untrap the words and set them free. Written language begins in the mind. The writer hears the words and puts them on paper. The reader sees the words and sets them free by giving them meaning. The process is continuous, the relationship inseparable. As a teacher, I owe children the opportunity to discover the process for themselves and the time to pursue it for the pleasure and the power it can bring.

REFERENCES

Atwell, N. (1987). *In the middle: Writing, reading, and learning with adolescents.* Portsmouth, NH: Heinemann.

Calkins, L. M. (1986). *The art of teaching writing.* Portsmouth, NH: Heinemann.

Graves, D. H. (1983). *Writing: Teachers and children at work*. Portsmouth, NH: Heinemann.

Hansen, J. (1987). *When writers read*. Portsmouth, NH: Heinemann.

Hinton, S. E. (1967). *The outsiders*. New York: Dell.

Hinton, S. E. (1988). *Taming the star runner*. New York: Dell.

Murray, D. M. (1984). *Write to learn*. New York: Holt, Rinehart & Winston.

Robertson, S. L. (1990). Text rendering: Beginning literary response. *English Journal*, 79(1), 80–84.

Romano, T. (1987). *Clearing the way: Working with teenage writers*. Portsmouth, NH: Heinemann.

Smith, F. (1985). *Reading without nonsense*. New York: Teachers College Press.

Welty, E. (1984). *One writer's beginnings*. Cambridge, MA: Harvard University Press.

CHAPTER 11

Evolution Not Revolution:
Eighth Graders Really Read and Write

RALPH GIOSEFFI
Leonia (NJ) Public Schools

In 1980, my principal strolled into my classroom and said, "Ralph, you know the district has a writing committee which is in its third year. Well, one member has resigned and I wondered if you'd like to join." I did. I knew about the writing committee. What I didn't know was the committee was to become my first breakthrough to process teaching.

A year later, in 1981, another committee member and I attended a 2-day writing workshop at the National Council of Teachers of English Convention. This workshop was my second, but major, breakthrough.

Twenty-five K–5 students from Atkinson Academy in New Hampshire, where Donald Graves, Lucy Calkins, and Mary Ellen Giacobbi had been conducting research in the writing process, were the stars for these two days. The children, scattered by grade level around the perimeter of the room, formed little circles, stretched on the floor, and wrote. The other teachers and I walked from one group to another and observed what the children were doing. I couldn't believe what I saw and heard — children with three, four, and five drafts of a piece of writing who were conferring with one another about their writing. I thought about my eighth graders. I especially thought about Dave and Monica, students who never responded to anything in class. Would they do this? Never, I thought.

During the next year I spent my spare time reading Nancie Atwell, Lucy Calkins, Donald Murray, and Frank Smith. I also visited process classrooms to see what other teachers were doing. What I read and saw was what I wanted, but I did not believe it would appeal to my eighth graders. Dave and Monica still haunted me.

In May 1982, I took the plunge with one of my five eighth grade classes because they were the easiest to teach that year. I explained to them

I had learned many new things about writing and, though I still had a lot to learn, I wanted to try something different. After the students and I brainstormed about topics, I dropped the whole idea of writing like a hot potato. Three weeks later Suzy Klein, one of my eighth graders, tugged on my sleeve, cocked her head to one side and, inquired, "Mr. G., about three weeks ago we all decided on topics we wanted to write about. When are we going to write?" I rather embarrassingly responded, "Oh Suzie, it's almost June now, and you know how busy the end of the school year gets. We'll never have enough time to write." And that was that for writing.

It wasn't until I had my own writing experiences that summer at a beginner's writing workshop on Martha's Vineyard that I understood what I needed to do for my students. I learned how to step back and give kids ownership in their writing, and in their learning. As I observed Lucy Calkins and Mary Ellen Giacobbi, the teachers of that workshop, I began to learn how to coach. This is what I wanted my classroom to be.

That September I returned to school with the confidence I needed to begin. And a beginning it was. I logged everything I was learning as my classes and I labored. I sorted out and reflected on what was working and why, and on what was not. This was a far cry from the me who was always on automatic pilot. Finished product had always lodged uppermost in my mind. Writing process gradually changed all that. I had found a philosophy of teaching that suited me.

A PROCESS PHILOSOPHY

Concentration on process rather than final product could not stop with writing; it had to extend to reading. I get miffed when I give workshops and a doubting Thomas says this is a fad and like everything else in education, "This too shall pass." An emphasis on process is not a method of teaching. It is a philosophy — a philosophy of teaching and learning, not just a philosophy of writing and reading. Once embraced, this philosophy necessitates change. Gradually, everything I did in my classroom changed. And perhaps the biggest change came with reading.

I had always thought of reading as a nice set of skills packaged by a publisher and taught in a neat, linear fashion. Nancie Atwell (1987) talks about reading being "messy," but I didn't understand this at the time. I thought that I had to ask comprehension questions at the end of a reading, do workbook pages, and explain the themes, morals, and significance of everything read. I always aimed for doing things with the kids when they finished their books. "When you finish the book we'll have a test"; "You have three weeks to read this book"; "When you finish this book write a book report"; "How long did it take you to finish this book?" I was great at disengaging students in their learning. Now I say:

- While reading this book look for a part that surprises you and be ready to talk about it to the class.
- As you read, log your book (explained in detail later).
- When you're reading, and you come across something well written or whatever, turn to the person next to you and share it.
- If you have any questions that pop into your head as you're reading your books, ask someone in class about it — maybe they can answer it for you; or jot it down and we'll use it in our discussion about our readings.

READING WORKSHOP

When I conduct reading workshops and am asked how to start, I always respond by advising "nice 'n' easy." Involvement in reading process is not revolutionary, it is evolutionary. The change itself is a process that takes time. Embracing reading process upsets many conventions of teaching reading.

The class becomes a community of readers when process is emphasized. It is a place where we share as we read. It is a place where, for the most part, students will choose the books they want to read. In my class, there are two major components to our reading: whole-class, where everyone is reading the same book, and self-selected, where everyone is reading different books.

Whole-Class Reading

All eighth graders in my school are required to read certain books. One of these is *Anne Frank: The Diary of a Young Girl* (1952). I had permitted the kids to choose between reading the play or the actual diary. One year two girls said they were familiar with *Anne Frank Remembered* (1956), a version of the story by Miep Gies, the woman who helped hide the family. So this book became a choice, too.

Last year I asked the class how they wanted to tackle the reading. Some decided to read the play in groups, each taking a role with oral reading, while others chose to read the play silently. Two read Miep's version of Anne Frank. When things became too noisy for the silent readers, they read in the hall outside the class or went to the library.

Most days students are given half a period (25 minutes) to read and the other half to sit in a circle to talk about what they read. With some reading the play, others the diary, and still others Miep's version of Anne Frank, classroom atmosphere was ripe for discussion by these heterogeneously grouped 13-year-olds.

"I like the diary much more than the play," volunteered Beth. "As I listen to the people who read the play, I don't get the impression they learned much about Anne's thinking, but in the diary you do and I loved that about the diary." Amanda and Elliot nodded in agreement.

Ruth defended the play. "I liked the play because it moved very fast. You read nothing but action, what happened. I like that."

Michael interjected, "It's funny how in the beginning of the diary Anne wondered why she even bothered to keep a diary because no one would ever read it."

That was my cue to bring up irony. I teach the literary terms as they come up from the children. I follow Lucy Calkin's (1986) advice, "Don't front load the curriculum." That is, I don't introduce everything I must teach. I allow kids to introduce the curriculum. If they omit something I know must be taught, then I do the introducing. Usually, though, I don't have to do that because someone brings up what I wanted to talk about anyway. I am a participant in the discussions. I am a learner. And learn I do.

I use my district's teachers' guide as a framework for what I must teach or reinforce. As literary terms surface in discussions, I check them off. When the students don't bring up the terms, I contribute my thoughts during a discussion. My class no longer begins with, "Kids, today we're going to talk about irony."

Often students come up with ideas I never thought about. When that happens, I take notes. Days or weeks later, when I refer to a student's idea, I say, "As so-and-so said to us." I always have a clipboard in hand for taking notes from students. I know how flattering it is when teachers take notes from me when I give workshops. It's flattering for our students, too. It makes them want to contribute.

Self-selected Reading

Students select any book they want to read. No attention — within reason, of course — is paid to grade level, genre, or any of the other conventions teachers may use in curtailing which books a student may read. (Some of the favorites among my eighth graders may be found in a list at the end of this chapter.)

Initially, when I instituted self-selection in my class, I worried about maintaining the sense of community felt with whole-class reading. First, the class was very quiet and there was no discussion. I decided we'd each read our books for twenty minutes, and then have a discussion about what we read. Twenty-seven people were reading 27 different books. It didn't work in the beginning because I could not get a discussion going. I realized a big part of the problem was not giving the students enough time to think and rehearse what they might want to say. A reading log became one answer for me. It serves as a rehearsal for discussion (Probst, 1988; Romano, 1987).

The reading log, a black-and-white marble notebook, is a place for the reader to respond, whether to a book being read by the whole class or to a self-selected book. As with everything else in a process classroom, modeling is imperative for introducing logs. The teacher must keep a log and share it with the class. Students need to share in pairs or in groups. As I circulate and notice a student who is making an interesting entry, I have that student share the entry with the other students. I encourage the students to talk about what they noticed about a classmate's entry to help them realize that they can do the same things in their logs.

As I model, and as students share and discuss, they get ideas to write in their logs. As the year advances, the students collaboratively generate a list of ways to respond in their logs. Some ways in which my students have responded in their logs are:

- Writing about things that surprised them
- Predicting
- Comparing authors and books
- Giving reasons why they liked or disliked something
- Commenting about a scene they thought was well written
- Relating their lives to the lives of the characters
- Questioning the author
- Commenting on the leads to each chapter
- Quoting the descriptions they like and writing about why
- Commenting on things they've learned for their writing
- Analyzing characters

Logs Elicit Personal Response from Students

I have found that it takes me at least 3 to 4 months to get some students to write logs that resemble a personal response rather than a book report. One thing I do tell my students is they can write anything in their logs except responses that resemble book reports.

When kids make personal responses in logs, they slow down their reading because they react as they are reading. They don't wait until they're finished. I encourage students to write in their logs when they have something to say. They therefore might not write every day; however, I discourage them from waiting until the end of the chapter to write.

At first, students find this very difficult and even a little frustrating. They don't want to stop. After a while, though, they get used to the response log and find that they don't mind taking the time to write in their logs. In fact, they find that the more they write their ideas, the better their thinking.

My eighth grader Cindy read *To Kill a Mockingbird* (Lee, 1960) and wrote in her log:

> There is a lot of tension around the subject of Boo Radley. I think that the author is trying to build suspense for something that will happen later. Even though I'm finding this book a bit difficult to understand, I did enjoy the courtroom scene. It is very realistic, and everything concerning the Tom Robinson case shows the great prejudice that the southerners had towards blacks even after the Civil War.

Two years ago, one of my eighth graders was hooked on books about Vietnam. That's all he read for months. He read one book he absolutely loved. As he read, he arrived at a passage he felt was not well written. He rewrote those three or four paragraphs the way he thought they should be written. The possibilities for logs are limitless.

Dorothy wrote about *Down a Dark Hall* by Lois Duncan (1974):

> I love when Kit's family is looking for the school and they drive down this road. They describe it so well. "They inched their way along for several yards and then the road curved and suddenly the trees had closed in around them. The highway behind them might never have existed for they were in a world of cool darkness where the only odor was the wild sweet smell of earth and woods." I can't believe how someone can lead their imagination to write something like that.

When I conferred with Dorothy about this entry, I asked her what made her respond the way she did. She explained that since she's been writing, she reads differently. "I look for the way authors describe things now, so I can get ideas for my writing."

Logs Require Personal Response from Teachers

Kids need responses to their logs from their peers and from their teachers. Recently, Art Buchwald (1988) said, "I think the magic of getting people to write is knowing there's an audience for the writing." We have to provide an audience for kids, whether they are drafting one piece for weeks or making a log entry for 10 minutes.

I collect logs from five students every day, read them, make comments such as "Great," "Fantastic," "What made you come to that conclusion?" "What great character analysis." I write notes at the end of the log entries. My comments may question, agree, or disagree with something the students have written. Often I will recommend other books the students may think about reading in the future.

Kim read *Rumble Fish* by S. E. Hinton (1975). At the end of her log I wrote:

> I can hear you talking as I read your log. It moves so rapidly. You personalize a great deal, you compare, you question, you quote, you analyse characters. You do a fantastic job.

To Dom who read *The Pigman* by Paul Zindel (1968) I wrote:

> Your log is fantastic. Very well done. You give your opinions and interpretations of what is going on. And you back them up with examples from your reading. Reading your log I get the impression you're really into the book. You seem so moved by the sadness and problems of Mr. Pignati, Lorraine, and John. I was intrigued too by the way Zindel alternates the points of view of each chapter between Lorraine and John. Great job. One of the best you've done.

TEACHING SKILLS AND GIVING GRADES

Reading logs are but one component that works for me and my students. Ten-minute minilessons are an additional component. During these lessons, I deal with problems in comprehension, vocabulary, literary terms, and strategies of reading. Usually, however, I direct my teaching to concerns that surface in class discussion or from the reading logs.

I find grading very difficult in a process classroom. Effort becomes an important component of a grade. About three or four times during a marking period I announce to the class that they will be required to make a log entry in a test situation and that their entry will be graded according to the depth of their thinking. If students simply recount the story, they will not get a good grade.

Often I ask the students to grade their own papers on a scale of 1 to 10 and write a paragraph that includes reasons for their grade. When I agree with their evaluation, fine. When I don't, I meet with them and we discuss the grade. Sometimes we compromise. Sometimes they convince me that they deserve the higher grade, and sometimes they don't. The reading log is only one component of my language arts grade. Vocabulary development and grammar usage are also included. My most important assessment tool is the clipboard full of notes collected while observing my students reading.

I enjoy teaching much more now than I ever did. I feel more like a coach than an oracle of knowledge. My students respond more to themselves, each other, and me, than they ever did before in my 24 years of teaching. Students are reading more than ever. And I know they're reading because they could never respond the way they do if they didn't read. Students in my school are required to read 10 books a year — a book a month. My students read 4 books as a class, and, on the average, 16 self-selected books.

When students say to me, "Mr. G., I don't know what's happening, but I read more than ever," "Mr. G., I haven't read a book cover to cover since the third grade until this year," "Mr. G., those book reports I've always done, I never read the books, but I'm reading now," I know a process approach to reading for my eighth graders works.

MY EIGHTH GRADERS' FAVORITE BOOK LIST

After the First Death, Robert Cormier
Angel Dust Blues, Todd Strasser
Animal Farm, George Orwell
Anne of Green Gables, L. M. Montgomery
Breakaway, Ruth Hallman
Bridge to Terabithia, Katherine Paterson
Can You Sue Your Parents for Malpractice?, Paula Danziger
The Cat Ate My Gymsuit, Paula Danziger
Don't Care High, Gordon Korman
Down a Dark Hall, Lois Duncan
A Gift of Magic, Lois Duncan
The Hessian, Howard Fast
I Never Loved Your Mind, Paul Zindel
I Want to Go Home, Gordon Korman
Johnny Tremain, Esther Forbes
A Lantern in Her Hand, Bess Aldrich
The Light in the Forest, Conrad Richter
My Brother Sam is Dead, Collier Brothers
The Outsiders, S. E. Hinton
The Pearl, John Steinbeck

The Pigman, Paul Zindel
Roll of Thunder, Hear My Cry, Mildred Taylor
Sounder, William Armstrong
Summer of Fear, Lois Duncan
Summer of My German Soldier, Bette Greene

REFERENCES

Atwell, N. (1987). *In the middle: Writing, reading, and learning with adolescents.* Portsmouth, NH: Heinemann.

Buchwald, A. (1988, July). *Art Buchwald speaks about his writing.* Paper presented at Martha's Vineyard Writing Institute, Northeastern University, Boston, MA.

Calkins, L. (1986). *The art of teaching writing.* Portsmouth, NH: Heinemann.

Duncan, L. (1974). *Down a dark hall.* New York: Dell.

Frank, A. (1952). *Anne Frank: The diary of a young girl.* New York: Doubleday.

Gies, M. (1956). *Anne Frank remembered.* New York: Simon and Schuster.

Hinton, S. E. (1975). *Rumble fish.* New York: Delacorte.

Lee, H. (1960). *To kill a mockingbird.* New York: Warner.

Probst, R. (1988). *Response and analysis: Teaching literature in junior and senior high school.* Montclair, NJ: Boynton/Cook.

Romano, T. (1987). *Clearing the way.* Portsmouth, NH: Heinemann.

Zindel, P. (1968). *The pigman.* New York: Bantam.

CHAPTER 12

Reading, Writing, and Storytelling: An Administrative Bridge from the Middle School to the Preschool

JOSEPH SANACORE
Hofstra University and Hauppauge (NY) School District
with
AL ALIO
Hauppauge (NY) Middle School

In the early 1980s, the Hauppauge School District (Long Island, NY) moved toward process writing. Major staff development efforts were initiated, and they focused on a wide variety of areas, including early writing experiences, the developmental appropriateness of invented spellings, writing as a recursive process, writing and reading links, and communication across the curriculum. Not surprisingly, several of the full-day staff development sessions concerned children's literature and storytelling, and this exposure seemed to ignite a special response from us and from some of our colleagues. We brainstormed the many conventional and novel uses of storytelling, and eventually considered ways of motivating secondary school students to write authentic children's stories and then to engage in storytelling sessions with preschool and kindergarten children.

Four teachers, including Al Alio, a seventh- and eighth-grade English teacher, discussed ways to involve middle school students in writing and telling children's stories. As the district administrator responsible for language arts, Joseph Sanacore joined this group of volunteers and supported their efforts as a facilitator. Initially, we focused on the need for children's literature and storytelling as an important foundation for young children's subsequent success as readers and writers. We also considered different ways in which adolescents could serve as a resource for nurturing preschool and kindergarten children. In addition, we pursued ways to promote bet-

151

ter communication among the elementary, middle, and high schools. Finally, we talked about the components of reading, writing, and storytelling in an enjoyable context. In this chapter, we describe how we implemented this project.

UNIQUE LINKS BETWEEN READING AND WRITING

The students in Grades 6, 7, and 8 experience a variety of writing activities that one would expect in the typical language arts classroom. They write narrative, descriptive, and expository passages, and they complete journal entries on a regular basis. They also write for a variety of purposes, including to inform, to persuade, and to entertain.

A unique aspect of the language arts program is a voluntary unit on writing and illustrating children's stories, to be used for future storytelling with the district's preschool and kindergarten children. A prototype for this project took place at the Hauppauge High School, and it is described elsewhere (Sanacore, 1983). In the prototype, seniors wrote stories for preschool children and shared them through storytelling activities.

The middle school teachers involved in this project provide their students with prewriting experiences, including visiting and observing their intended audience in the preschool and discussing the interests and behaviors of younger siblings at home. The teachers also guide the students to become more sensitive to young children's behavior, especially behavior concerning interests and attending ability.

When this awareness of the preschool audience is developed, the students immerse themselves in published works of children's literature for about 2 weeks. This daily exposure helps them to self-select a wide variety of books and to identify and appreciate special characteristics used by professional writers; some of these characteristics also have value for effective storytelling, an important part of this middle school project. For example, Huck, Helper, and Hickman (1987) believe that stories worth telling should "include a quick beginning, action, a definite climax, natural dialogue, and a satisfying conclusion" (p. 648). They further suggest selecting stories with no more than four speaking characters. Examples include such folktales as *The Three Billy Goats Gruff* and *Chicken Little*. In addition, the students' immersion in children's stories increases their awareness of special devices. For example, the alliteration in Kipling's *Just So Stories* gets students involved in oral reading, stressing repeated sounds. Similarly, longer repeated refrains in Slobodkina's *Caps for Sale* and incremental refrains in Raskin's *Ghost in a Four Room Apartment* entice children to participate in choral reading (Stewig, 1978). Thus, as middle school students immerse themselves in a wide variety of children's literature, they focus on ways of improving their own creative writing and on characteristics and devices for involving preschool and kindergarten children during future storytelling sessions.

Our middle school students have used a sampling of stories as examples of effective writing (see list at the end of this chapter). We add to and delete from the list each year. Fortunately, the library media specialists serve as major resources for helping the middle school teachers update this list of children's books.

Once this foundation is provided, each day, for about 3 weeks, students write and illustrate their stories while the classroom teacher (and, if available, an art teacher) offers praise, provides suggestions for improvement, and encourages individuals to share ideas. As students work in small groups, they discuss their developing stories in the context of various activities, such as reading the stories aloud while the listeners develop a "feel" for how the stories "tell." They also refine characteristics supporting the structure of text, including action, a definite climax, and natural dialogue. In addition, students focus on such story devices as alliteration, repeated refrains, and incremental refrains (see discussion questions in Figure 12.1). Based on interests and talents, students may engage independently in writing and illustrating their stories, or they may work cooperatively with others. Sometimes, one student does the writing while a partner complements the story with illustrations. The entire instructional emphasis is on guiding the process rather than on correcting the product. This immersion in the process is a major source of support for enhancing the writing and illustrating of authentic stories.

STORYTELLING

When the stories are completed, volunteers learn storytelling techniques. According to Farrell (1983) and Nessel (1985), storytellers should select literature they like and want to tell. Farnsworth (1981) also believes that a major prerequisite to effective storytelling is liking the story one plans to tell. "Any misgivings or reservations you have about the story will be communicated to your listeners. So feeling that it is 'your' story comes first" (p. 164). Farnsworth's concern is well-received and fits nicely in the context of the course unit, since students who volunteer to "tell" their stories are, in fact, the authors of these stories. Naturally, they like their own stories, and they are ready to communicate this feeling to younger children.

With this accomplished, the volunteers learn and practice a variety of

FIGURE 12.1. Some discussion questions used by students to improve their developing stories

---

1.   Does the story have enough appeal for young children?

     Comments:_____

2.   Does the story "feel" appropriate for storytelling?

     Comments:_____

3.   Is the intended audience able to understand the story?

     Comments:_____

4.   Does the story include

     A.   a quick beginning?

     B.   action?

     C.   a definite climax?

     D.   natural dialogue?

     E.   a satisfying conclusion?

     F.   no more than four speaking characters?

     Comments:_____

5.   Does the story contain special devices, such as

     A.   alliteration?

     B.   repeated refrains?

     C.   incremental refrains?

     Comments:_____

---

techniques for about 2 weeks. Although comprehensive sources concerning storytelling are available, Stewig (1978) offers excellent suggestions for teachers that are easily adapted for students. These adaptations at the Hauppauge Middle School are as follows:

1. The teacher or librarian models storytelling techniques with a variety of children's literature.
2. Students divide their plots into separate units of action, and they practice them in sequence. "This does not mean memorizing the story word for word, but rather learning the sequence necessary to moving the story ahead" (Stewig, 1978, p. 340).
3. Students identify sections of their stories that should be memorized. For example, a repeated refrain that contributes significantly to the mood of a story should be committed to memory and be incorporated into the storytelling.
4. Students develop fluency by practicing about twice a day for at least a week. During these practice sessions, storytellers blend the memorized sections with the sequenced units of action. Becoming accustomed to the sounds of their voices during storytelling is necessary; students therefore rehearse in a comfortable environment, for example, with friends, with parents, or in front of a mirror.
5. Students monitor their progress by tape recording the "telling" of their stories. To assure objectivity during the evaluation of their oral presentations, they wait several days before they listen to the tape recordings. Then, thoughtful analysis focuses on achieving greater fluency, modifying aspects of the stories to generate more effectiveness, choosing different words to inspire mood clarity, and changing paralinguistic elements (pause, tempo, pitch, etc.).
6. Students change aspects of their presentations, based on their thoughtful analysis. They also continue to practice their storytelling until they are finally ready to share their stories with children.

The storytelling environment at the Hauppauge School District involves kindergarten children in two elementary schools as well as preschool children who attend the Child and Family program. The preschool program is sponsored by the home economics and careers department, and it is offered in the Hauppauge High School. Home economics students work with the children and gain concrete insights concerning the physical, emotional, social, and intellectual development of the children. The preschoolers also derive benefits by being exposed to a variety of activities, including listening to and participating in storytelling. Rather than provide the children with a great deal of storytelling during a short period of time, we believe that the children gain more benefits from experiencing storytelling several times a week throughout the school year. This approach also keeps this unit "alive" by supporting the middle school students' continued sense of authorship.

As the students "tell" their stories, the home economics students observe the children's behavior. Usually, the storyteller prepares the children with an introductory approach adapted from Burns, Roe, and Ross (1988, p. 52). The student says: "This morning I'm going to tell you my story, and I think you may already know something about it. It is called _____. How many of you know something about it? This story is about [the storyteller reveals a brief summary of the plot]. I want you to help me tell the story. When the rabbit says [the storyteller mentions a key sentence or repeated refrain], I want you to say it along with me. Let's try it now, all together." The children practice saying this line with the storyteller. Then the student tells the story and signals to the children when it is the right time for them to say the line.

Some of the storytelling activities are videotaped so that the storytellers can view what they have done effectively and, if necessary, consider strategies for improvement. In addition, future storytellers are able to view the videotapes and to experience vicariously the excitement and challenge of working creatively with young children. These viewing experiences also help new students improve their own storytelling techniques. Some videotapes appear on local cable channels, enabling the Hauppauge community to observe and respond to warm, creative happenings from the middle school.

BENEFITS

The benefits to students and community are numerous, including:

1. Students enjoy writing and telling stories. Here are some of their comments: "I had a lot of fun with storytelling. Working with my friends in a small group was really helpful" (Mary, Grade 6). "I never believed I could get up in front of others and tell my own story. I feel more confident. Now I speak up more in all my classes" (John, Grade 7). "The kids actually enjoyed my story! I don't believe it! I feel great! I think I'll become a professional writer!" (Charlie, Grade 8).
2. Students increase their sensitivity to a range of audiences by communicating with a unique public, namely young children. The anticipation of a real audience, eager to hear the stories, is both a valuable motivation for the students and a useful simulation of the working conditions of professional writers.
3. Children become excited about book language and story events. These experiences build a background of knowledge and create a desire to read.

4. Storytelling also provides opportunities to involve children. For example, motivating children to help "tell" the stories and encouraging them to use gestures concerning the stories are examples of creative involvement. This active participation reflects a more satisfying experience than passive listening to stories; it also serves as an introduction to creative drama (Stewig, 1978).
5. The relationship between the middle school students and the young children reflects genuine warmth. This relationship seems to provide the children with a positive introduction to school, and it appears to provide the middle school students with realistic insights concerning the capacity of young children to use and appreciate language.
6. Copies of the children's stories are placed in the library media center. They are available for parents who plan to use them with their children, for children who can use them independently, and for middle school students who are new to storytelling. Similarly, the videotapes of storytelling are available for parents' and students' viewing.
7. The interdisciplinary and interage activities generate positive public relations.

SUMMARY

Thus far, the writing unit and the storytelling activities represent a rewarding bridge from the middle school to the preschool. Older and younger children benefit from their creative involvement, and teachers also gain useful insights about the importance of language stimulation for young children. As we support these process-oriented approaches, we continue to observe and interview the preschool and kindergarten children who are active in the program. We also survey the children's parents as well as the students and teachers who participate. Subjective responses, in the form of self-reports, support the continuation of the Hauppauge School District's efforts. Major findings include:

- Most of the preschool children read more books, select a wide variety of materials, maintain a desire to read, and tell their own stories.
- Most of the middle school students who participate increase their sensitivity for communicating with a unique audience (the preschoolers).
- Teachers who participate read extensively about children's literature (Cullinan, 1987; Huck et al., 1987), about using it with young

children (Coody, 1979; Stewig & Sebesta, 1989), and about how young children learn to read and write (Strickland & Morrow, 1989).

From preschool children to middle school students to classroom teachers, everybody benefits from this innovative project.

Acknowledgments. We are grateful for the support we received from classroom teachers Charlie Dodd, John Moore, and Alma Olafson; library media coordinator Caren Donnelly; library media specialist Joyce Sullivan; and home economics and careers teacher Catherine Hempson.

CHILDREN'S LITERATURE LIST

Bloch, M. H. (1964). *The cat and chanticleer, Ukrainian folk tales.* New York: Coward-McCann.
Brown, M. (1972). *The bun: A tale from Russia.* New York: Harcourt.
Brown, M. (1957). *The three billy goats gruff.* New York: Harcourt.
Cauley, L. B. (1983). *Jack and the beanstalk.* New York: Putnam.
Diamond, D. (1983). *Rumpelstiltskin.* New York: Holiday.
Galdone, P. (1978). *Cinderella.* New York: McGraw-Hill.
Galdone, P. (1982). *Hansel and Gretel.* New York: McGraw-Hill.
Godden, R. (1982). *The mousewife.* New York: Viking.
Jarrell, R. (1972). *Snow White and the seven dwarfs.* New York: Farrar, Straus, and Giroux.
Kellogg, S. (1985). *Chicken little.* New York: Morrow.
Kipling, R. (1972). *Just so stories.* Garden City, NY: Doubleday.
Raskin, E. (1969). *Ghost in a four room apartment.* New York: Atheneum.
Shub, E. (1973). *Clever Kate.* New York: Macmillan.
Slobodkina, E. (1947). *Caps for sale.* New York: W. R. Scott.

REFERENCES

Burns, P. C., Roe, B. D., & Ross, E. P. (1988). *Teaching reading in today's elementary schools* (4th ed.). Boston: Houghton Mifflin.
Coody, B. (1979). *Using literature with young children.* Dubuque, IA: Wm. C. Brown.
Cullinan, B. (Ed.). (1987). *Children's literature in the reading program.* Newark, DE: International Reading Association.
Farnsworth, K. (1981). Storytelling in the classroom — Not an impossible dream. *Language Arts, 58,* 162–167.
Farrell, C. (1983). *A guide to storytelling.* San Francisco: Zellerbach Family Fund.

Huck, C., Helper, S., & Hickman, J. (1987). *Children's literature in the elementary school* (4th ed.). New York: Holt, Rinehart and Winston.

Nessel, D. D. (1985). Storytelling in the reading program. *The Reading Teacher, 38*, 378–381.

Sanacore, J. (1983). Creative writing and storytelling: A bridge from high school to preschool. *Phi Delta Kappan, 64*, 509–510.

Stewig, J. W. (1978). Storyteller: Endangered species? *Language Arts, 55*, 339–345.

Stewig J. W., & Sebesta, S. L. (Eds.). (1989). *Using literature in the elementary classroom*. Urbana, IL: National Council of Teachers of English.

Strickland, D., & Morrow, L. M. (Eds.). (1989). *Emerging literacy: Young children learn to read and write*. Newark, DE: International Reading Association.

Part IV

SPECIAL POPULATIONS

IRENE W. GASKINS
Benchmark School, Media, PA

Last summer my 5-year-old granddaughter said to me, "Grandma, I'm writing a story for you. Will you tell me the sounds?" Helen told me the first word and I responded with the initial letter. "The sounds, Grandma, not the letters. I know the letters." I gave Helen the sounds for her words and soon she showed me her story. When I asked Helen if she would like to read it to me, she replied incredulously, "Grandma, you learn to write first. Reading comes later."

During the early years of Benchmark School, a school for bright underachievers ages 6 to 14 who exhibit reading and writing problems, writing was not an important part of our remedial program. We concentrated on teaching children to read before we expected them to write. In 1970 when the school was founded we believed that it was not reasonable to ask children with reading problems to write when they could not read; thus, we did not expect our beginning readers to write more than a few words each day. Today, however, 20 years later we are doing it Helen's way. Students who have not yet succeeded in learning to read, write first. Reading comes later. Let me begin at the beginning and tell you the Benchmark writing and reading story (Gaskins, 1980).

WRITING: A FELT NEED

In the mid-1970s Benchmark School's follow-up data on students whom the Benchmark staff had sent back to their neighborhood schools suggested that we were doing a good job of teaching poor readers to read. Our program included daily book conferences on books students read at home each evening; small-group, directed-reading–thinking lessons; sustained silent reading; and literature read orally by the teacher featuring different genres each month. When our graduates returned to their regular schools they tended to read at or above the median for their regular classes, with many scoring in the top quartile on achievement tests. Reports about their writing abilities, however, were not so glowing. In analyzing our program in search of an explanation for these discouraging reports, we discovered that our writing program fit Graves' description of "writing instruction that really isn't writing instruction at all. The teacher provides the appointment for writing through assignments and then responds to the mechanical errors contained in the child's writing after it is completed" (Graves, 1977, p. 823). We realized that there must be more we could do to help our students develop writing skills. As a result, the staff decided to make writing the focus of a schoolwide curriculum development project.

During the school year 1977–78 a literature search was conducted to find guidelines for improving the writing skills of our poor readers. This search resulted in a handbook, *Suggestions for the Direct Teaching of Writing* (Gaskins, 1978b), in which the literature review was synthesized and recommendations were made for teaching writing.

We sensed that those who, like Graves (1975), were beginning to talk of the process approach were on the right track. Yet, we also knew that the children who attended our school were there because they had not learned in programs that worked for most children. They were the very children who often learned something only when it was directly taught. We wondered if the process approach would meet our students' need for explicit guidance. Our solution was to attempt to combine the best of process writing and direct teaching. For example, like process-approach advocates, we believed that teaching children to write should take place in the context of writing and in a supportive affective environment. Yet, we believed it was in the best interest of underachievers to hold them accountable for applying what they had been taught, as well as accountable for working through, on a regular basis, the drafting and revising phases to produce a final draft. Past experience with Benchmark's poor readers suggested that when we did not hold them accountable, the students tended to write many brief first drafts, but rarely took a piece to a final draft.

As I reviewed the professional literature, I was most intrigued by the seemingly unconventional, but common-sense, ideas of Donald Graves (1975, 1978a, 1978b), who contended that children learn to write by writing, not by completing grammar exercises, adding capitals and punctuation marks to someone else's sentences, or completing worksheets with "story starters." Further, he maintained that students do not learn to write by having their compositions marked and edited with a red pen, nor by concentrating on neat handwriting and correct spelling. Instead of following these timeworn practices, Graves suggested that teachers encourage students to write daily on topics about which they know a lot. Graves believed that on initial drafts students should focus on capturing their great ideas, leaving the mechanics of writing for later drafts.

MAKING A BEGINNING

In the fall of 1978 the staff put their hearts into making some drastic changes in their classroom writing programs, but the idea of process writing was so foreign to us that what we considered drastic proved to be more window dressing than substance, and our applications of process writing tended to feel stiff and uncomfortable. However, despite the fact that our translation of the process approach left much to be desired, our enthusiasm was genuine. In the fall of 1978 I wrote:

> *The Little Engine That Could* has always been a favorite read-aloud book at our house. I am reminded of that story this fall as the pushing and tugging of children's pencils seems to be pulsating to a rhythm that says "I think I can, I think I can" and now picks up speed to a tempo of "I know I can, I know I can." (Gaskins, 1978a, p. 1)

We knew that we were not going to change our poor readers into great writers overnight, yet as quickly as possible we needed to change the perception that our graduates' receiving schools held about Benchmark students' writing abilities. For our students, composition was not the major problem. Their dictated compositions were often exceptional. It was the act of getting their thoughts on paper in a form someone could read that was their stumbling block. Teachers often commented that they knew the Benchmark students understood the information presented in their science or social studies classes, but if one depended solely upon what these students wrote to measure their understanding, there would be little evidence.

As a staff we agreed on 10 "survival" writing skills that would be emphasized regarding everything students wrote, whether it be a sentence answer in social studies or a composition in language arts. The survival skills, ranging from "Writes enough that makes sense and gets the job done" to "Writes a paragraph that sticks to the topic," were listed in priority order, with the recommendation that when one of the skills was consistently exhibited by a student, the next skill on the list would become the student's goal. As a guideline for responding to what students wrote during the time set aside for writing, the teachers were told to consider content, organization, effectiveness, and mechanics in that order.

The 1978–79 school year was launched with an August in-service focusing on writing. I encouraged the staff to leave the English textbooks and writing worksheets in the curriculum library and, instead, to use what the students wrote as the basis of instruction. I sensed uneasiness among the Benchmark teachers regarding this plan. It was obvious that they did not feel that several handouts and a four-page handbook were enough guidance to enable them to create a writing program. They were also worried about what would happen to our students when they returned to regular classes if they did not know how to complete grammar exercises and punctuation worksheets. The English books continued to be present in their classrooms; but as the year progressed, they were used less and less. To help us in this transition, we invited Donald Graves to present an all-day workshop in December.

Only one Benchmark teacher, Rebecca Hemphill, was new to teaching that fall as we inaugurated a process approach to writing. Becky knew a lot about teaching reading, but the only conviction that she brought with her about teaching writing was that the way she had been taught was not effective. She had never used an English textbook for teaching, so she had not come to rely on it as others had. The new writing handbook and the two lists of priorities were to shape her program until our workshop later in the year.

In December Graves arrived. Reading professional journals and books had given us a framework for teaching writing, but it was Donald Graves who breathed life into our writing program. What we learned that day is as applicable today as it was when it was shared with us.

Initially the staff proved to be a formidable and skeptical audience for Graves. The following are examples of problems we presented to him and his solutions:

- *Poor motivation.* We were reluctant to believe that a process approach would work for students with a history of failure, especially considering their lack of motivation to write. Graves suggested that we assure them of success by letting them draw pictures as a means of rehearsing their ideas and that we expect them only to "write about what they know."
- *Inadequate spelling ability.* We insisted that our poor readers could not spell, thus could not write. Graves asserted that if they knew six sound/symbol relationships and could draw a line, they could write. He suggested that we write with the students and let them write unhampered by the need to spell words correctly. "Tell them, 'Don't stop to worry about the correct spelling; just get your great ideas down. We can worry about spelling later.'"
- *Resistance to change.* We said students were resistant to making

changes once their ideas were on paper. Graves suggested that we have students write on every other line and revise as they wrote. "It doesn't have to be right the first time." We learned it was often best to give 30-second miniconferences to listen to portions of their pieces and to ask questions, then to move on. It was their choice whether or not they made changes.

• *Not enough time.* We said we did not have time to grade the compositions. Graves taught us about "share time" and three types of responses that would help the writer. He suggested that the teacher ask those listening to the author present his/her piece: (1) What does the person know? (2) What questions do you (the listener/reader) want to ask to get more information about the topic? (3) What is the one thing the writer should work on for the next draft? The goal was for students to add information and redraft independently. As Graves interacted with students we heard him make comments such as, "That's a neat story, but it's not all there" or "It's not wrong, it's just not done." Graves emphasized that we needed to "be specific about what the child knows that is not clear or not included."

• *No teacher's guide.* We said we needed more information about how to teach using this method. Shouldn't we wait for the teachers' manual to be published? Graves said there would be no manual and outlined what he saw as the teacher's primary responsibilities: (1) to provide the appointment for learning, (2) to help all children realize that they are experts on something, and (3) to establish a routine. Graves led us to realize that on any one day students would be at different places in the writing process. The teacher might begin the writing session by asking, "How many need someone to listen to their piece today?" "How many are having trouble getting started?"

The 1970s were the days of "back to basics," and many of our questions were about when and how to teach "the skills" of writing. Graves' answer never changed, no matter how many varieties of the question we asked, "You teach the students what they need at the time for the writing they are doing." "Anything done as a group lesson comes from the children's writing." "Skills are taught only as an extension of a skill a student just discovered in his/her own writing." "Skill teaching evolves whole to part — not isolated skills to the composition."

It was a responsive model. We were to teach what our students needed. That concept matched our beliefs about how to work with students who were struggling in reading and writing. Maybe this approach would work with our special population after all!

When we asked Graves what the critical skills were that our students should know, his skills list read very differently from the skills that were being emphasized in most writing programs of that day. His skills really did not sound like skills, rather they were goals: (1) to feel comfortable about writing alone; (2) to discover what they know; (3) to know how to interview; (4) to know how to use secondary resources; (5) to be able to limit a topic; (6) to know how to write a "discovery" draft; (7) to be able to plan one's use of time and how to deal with the problems one meets; and (8) to be able to find an audience to read early and final drafts.

PUTTING PROCESS TEACHING INTO PRACTICE

After the December in-service with Graves, various interpretations of a process approach were put in place in the 14 Benchmark classrooms. Teachers talked among themselves about their successes and problems, gaining a little each day from each other in their understanding of the processes of writing and reading, but it was Becky (our new teacher) who was most daring. What she learned was quickly put into place and daily she shared what was happening with Sally Ross, the teacher of our 6-, 7-, and 8-year-old nonreaders. Exciting things began to happen in both of their classes.

Becky taught a class of ten boys who were 9 and 10 years old. All were average or above in intelligence, but were virtually nonreaders. After the Graves in-service she challenged her boys to "plaster the walls" of the classroom with their writing. That was a challenge the boys could not resist. Each page that the boys wrote was to be taped to the preceding page and hung on the walls until every inch of the four walls from the cathedral ceiling to the floor was covered.

Initially, all that Becky cared about was that these boys who resisted writing wrote on every other line and produced a full page of writing. In the past, most of them had considered their compositions finished after completing one or two sentences. Now pages began to be filled, although for some writing a page required several hours of student effort and teacher cheerleading and coaching. The written compositions in the early days of this project often looked more like Morse code than alphabetic writing. Words frequently consisted of little more than an initial consonant and a line. Becky and her teaching assistant were kept busy moving from one boy to another asking them to "read what you have written so far." As the boy read, Becky or her assistant would write above the consonants and lines the words the student was reading. This procedure facilitated the students' being able to read their compositions, using a form of echo reading, during the share time. Similar activities were taking place in Sally Ross's class of beginners.

There was an enthusiasm present in both rooms that winter and spring that had not been present in the fall of that school year. Becky's students were as engaged in, and determined about, papering their room with their writing as they might have been about building a fort in the woods. They began slipping in before school began in the morning to get a head start on writing. Day after day many or all of them chose to stay inside and write rather than go to recess. How they loved to see their writing displayed from ceiling to floor. The students in both Becky's and Sally's classes enjoyed reading their pieces to one another and hearing pieces read during share time. When Miss Hemphill and Miss Ross said it was time for reading groups, their students would beg to spend more time writing. Reading groups were often replaced by students working in pairs, reading their pieces to one another or editing each other's piece. Becky would not accept a page for the wall until two students had read and reacted to it.

Weeks went by without a reading group being conducted in Becky's class, although no one in the school was aware of it at the time. Who had time for reading groups when these children had research to do for their pieces in real books, reading of classmates' pieces to give them feedback, and reading of published pieces to learn about subjects in which their peers were experts? Later Becky confided that she began to feel so guilty about not holding reading groups that on days they did not have reading groups, she had the students take the basals home and read them to their parents. The parents of Sally's students helped at home, too, by brainstorming with their children possible topics about which they could write and by jotting down two or three key words the children could use to trigger their memories when writing the next day.

Although we did not know that the reading of student-authored compositions had replaced reading group in Becky's room, we all did know that the "wallpapers" in Room 2 totally covered not only the walls, but the doors and windows, too. By spring the boys moved on to extra layers of papers, and they would bring anyone they could find into this room, now devoid of sunlight due to papers over the windows, to show off their work. Each time I visited I would ask one of them to share what he had written. Not only could these September nonreaders read their pieces to me, but they enjoyed sharing their understanding of the processes of writing and reading and the relationship between the two. Their grasp of what literacy is all about was remarkable. And best of all, they obviously had become writers and readers! And Sally's beginners were joining the "literacy club," too!

When Benchmark held its annual Recognition of Accomplishments ceremonies that June, many of Becky's students made trips to the stage to receive certificates for their accomplishments. Some of her students had made the most extraordinary progress in reading and writing that anyone to date had achieved at the school. Another historic occasion at the ceremonies was the recognition of our youngest students (Sally's class) for their writing — something that we had never done before because we previously had not expected them to write.

THE WRITING/READING CONNECTION CONTINUES

With a year of attempts at teaching process writing behind us, the staff was anxious for Graves to return to answer our continuing questions. That fall, Graves sat at a Benchmark conference table for 8 hours answering teachers' questions and talking to them about their students' writing.

Our story does not end here. I have only shared with you the beginning. With each passing year the process writing and reading programs at Benchmark become a little better and our students reap the benefit of our gains in expertise. Donald Graves continues to visit the school and share his wisdom with us, as do other writing experts such as Jane Hansen (1983) and Taffy Raphael (Raphael, Kirschner, & Englert, 1988). As a result of Hansen's influence, we present a monthly Author's Day program where exemplary books authored by students are introduced and added to our library collection. Each year since 1985, Raphael has visited the school to spend time demonstrating how to interact with children around the pieces they have written and to guide us in teaching our students to write using various text structures. This guidance has given us a big boost in developing a more sophisticated writing program for our older students.

By 1982 we were absolutely convinced that the process writing/reading program we were implementing was playing an important part in the success of our students when they left our program to enter a regular school (Gaskins, 1982). We were delighted when others (Allington & McGill-Franzen, 1987; R. Gaskins, 1988) confirmed that students with reading problems benefit from remedial programs that emphasize not only reading as a process, but writing, too.

Based on what we have learned from the experts who visited Benchmark and on our own professional reading, a second handbook to guide the teaching of writing among our older students was developed (Hemphill, 1987). It took 10 years, but we finally had developed a writing program that met the needs of students in Grades 1 to 8. Bringing about the change in the way we viewed and taught reading and writing was not quick or easy (I. Gaskins, 1988; Gaskins & Elliot, 1991). However, when we witness the skill and enthusiasm with which our students write and read, we realize it was well worth the effort. Nevertheless, we are still learning, and will continue to for a long time to come.

CONCLUSIONS

Does a process approach work for special populations? Yes, it certainly does! We have discovered that our poor readers experience the same developmental stages in writing and reading as their agemates in other schools, though often at a more irregular pace, and that meeting students where they are in the process of writing and reading is what good teaching is all about. Like my granddaughter Helen, Benchmark students write first and read later. Because they are writers, they understand that reading must make sense. Because they are readers, they have a wealth of information about which to write.

In the chapters that follow you will find that other teachers of children with unique learning needs have discovered that a process approach works for them, too. Justina Henry explains the Reading Recovery program that uses immersion reading and writing activities to teach at-risk first graders to read. Special education teacher Jane Beaty describes how her students read, write, and learn through real-world texts such as newspapers, trade books, and the video screen.

Leslie Funkhouser, who brought her beliefs about process-oriented teaching to her work with gifted children, shares many wonderful examples of her students' writing. Rita Bean and Rebecca Hamilton, who work with remedial students in the Pittsburgh schools, describe how their approach has been changing from a skills-oriented one to a model "built within a context of strategy and process," with reading teachers and classroom teachers working collaboratively.

In the last chapter of this section, three teachers of bilingual children in Austin, Texas, tell how they teach reading, writing, and language (both Spanish and English) through literature. While Julie Guzman plans themed literature units for her kindergarteners, second-grade teacher Modesta Trevino engages her students with Latino folktales, and Stella Mata capitalizes on the humorous Amelia Bedelia books to help her fourth graders understand idiom.

The special-needs students described in this section, like all children who engage in many realistic and enjoyable reading, writing, and speaking activities in a responsive social environment, are well on their way to gaining control over oral and written language.

REFERENCES

Allington, R., & McGill-Franzen, A. (1987). *A study of the whole-school day experience of Chapter 1 and mainstreamed LD students* (Final Report of Grant #G008630480, Office of Special Education Programs). Washington, DC: U.S. Department of Education.

Gaskins, I. W. (1978a, Fall). Director's point of view. *Benchmark News*. Media, PA: Benchmark Press.

Gaskins, I. W. (1978b). *Suggestions for the direct teaching of writing at Benchmark School*. Unpublished manuscript, Benchmark School, Media, PA.

Gaskins, I. W. (1980). *The Benchmark story: The first ten years 1970/1980*. Media, PA: Benchmark Press.

Gaskins, I. W. (1982). A writing program for poor readers and writers and the rest of the class, too. *Language Arts, 59*, 854–861.

Gaskins, I. W. (1988). Helping teachers adapt to the needs of students with learning problems. In S. J. Samuels & P. D. Pearson (Eds.), *Changing school reading programs: Principles and case studies* (pp. 142–159). Newark, DE: International Reading Association.

Gaskins, I. W., & Elliot, T. T. (1991). *Implementing cognitive strategy training in a school setting: A how-to manual for teachers*. Cambridge, MA: Brookline Books.

Gaskins, R. W. (1988). The missing ingredients: Time on task, direct instruction, and writing. *The Reading Teacher, 41*, 750–755.

Graves, D. H. (1975). An examination of the writing processes of seven year old children. *Research in the Teaching of English, 9*, 227–241.

Graves, D. H. (1977). Research update—Language arts textbooks: A writing process evaluation. *Language Arts, 54*, 817–823.

Graves, D. H. (1978a). Research update—We won't let them write. *Language Arts, 55*, 635–640.

Graves, D. H. (1978b). We can end the energy crisis. *Language Arts, 55*, 795–796.

Hansen, J. (1983). Authors respond to authors. *Language Arts, 60*, 970–976.

Hemphill, R. M. (1987). *Writing instruction for middle school students*. Unpublished manuscript, Benchmark School, Media, PA.

Raphael, T. E., Kirschner, B. W., & Englert, C. S. (1988). Expository writing program: Making connections between reading and writing. *The Reading Teacher, 41*, 790–795.

CHAPTER 13

Reading Recovery Through Reading and Writing

JUSTINA M. HENRY
Warren (OH) City Schools

A first grader has been reading *All By Myself* by Mercer Mayer (1983) during a Reading Recovery lesson. He comes to the word "fur" and says "hair." He rereads the sentence, glances at the picture, checks his prediction with the features of the print and self-corrects.

His Reading Recovery teacher responds, "I liked the way you read that. You stopped at the tricky part and worked it out. You reread the sentence, thought about the story, and looked at the picture. Then you looked closely at the word. These are all good ways to help yourself."

The purpose of the interaction between the Reading Recovery teacher and the student is to help the child monitor and use available information, including meaning, language structure, and visual cues. A distinguishing feature of the program is the "teaching for strategies." Strategies are the "in the head" processes that readers use to construct meaning from written text.

This viewpoint is very different from the one I had before becoming a Reading Recovery teacher leader. I no longer define reading instruction as the sequential mastery of isolated skills. My beliefs about the reading process have changed as I have learned to carefully observe and reflect on children's reading and writing behaviors. The special training I received through Reading Recovery has helped me learn to support children so they can make accelerated progress in reading.

READING RECOVERY: A PROGRAM FOR CHILDREN

Reading Recovery, an individualized intervention program for at-risk first graders, was developed in New Zealand by child psychologist and educator Marie Clay (1979a, 1979b). Concerned that many children found learning to read difficult, Clay looked at competent readers to observe what they were doing that low-progress readers were not. She concluded that high-progress readers search for meaning. They predict what the text will say next and check this with whether it sounds right, looks right, and makes sense. If they encounter a difficulty in their reading, they search for more cues and self-correct. In this way they learn something new and improve their own reading each time.

Low-progress readers fail to establish this self-improving system. They stumble along, using a narrow range of strategies. They may seem to operate on the idea that reading is inventing text and disregard the visual details of the print. Or they may focus on looking for words they know and forget the meaning of the text. Their attention may be at the letter level, and they become intent on "sounding out." Meeting with little success, they become more inefficient in the ways they operate on print and fail to become independent readers.

From the results of her research, Clay (1979a) devised the Diagnostic Survey, a set of six measures used to detect children who are at risk of failing. She then formulated efficient intervention procedures to help them get on the right track in reading so that they can perform at satisfactory levels without continued supplementary instruction. The results of this program indicate that at-risk children can make accelerated progress in reading and catch up with the average of their classroom.

Reading Recovery has been a nationwide program in New Zealand since 1979. Since 1984, Reading Recovery has been established in more than 228 school districts in Ohio (DeFord, Pinnell, & Lyons, 1988; Pinnell, DeFord, & Lyons, 1988). Also, separate school districts in several other states and Ontario, Canada, and Victoria, Australia, have implemented this project.

READING RECOVERY: A PROGRAM FOR TEACHERS

Reading Recovery is a year-long in-service for teachers as well as an intervention program for first-grade readers. Teachers attend weekly in-service sessions at a training site in their area while simultaneously conducting daily, 30-minute, one-on-one lessons with four students at their own schools. By observing demonstration lessons behind a one-way glass and participating in discussions with their colleagues, they learn to be better observers of children's writing and reading behaviors. They learn more about the reading process and how to use this knowledge to make better instructional decisions.

This on-going interaction with their peers helps each teacher develop new ways of thinking abut how children learn to read. They consider their own observations of the student and teacher during the demonstration lessons and may challenge each other's ideas. These experiences have an impact on the teachers' theoretical orientation of the teaching of reading. Over a period of time, teachers shift their focus from a skill-oriented activities approach to a view that reading and writing involve the child acquiring strategies for problem solving.

OBSERVING BEGINNING READERS

Teachers learn to observe children by using Clay's (1979a) Diagnostic Survey. This set of six measures is administered individually at the beginning and end of a child's program and often a year or more later in follow-up studies. The Diagnostic Survey is used to assess children's understanding of written language and includes:

1. *Letter Identification.* The children are asked to identify 54 letters (upper and lower case and two forms of a and g). A point is scored by naming the letter, saying its sound, or telling a word that begins with that letter. This is not to say that learning the alphabet is a prerequisite to learning to read. Rather, beginning readers simultaneously learn more about the visual features of letters and words as they become competent. This measure may provide some information. Do the children notice differences in letters? What are the children's correct responses and substitutions?

2. *Word Test.* The children are asked to read a column of twenty words. This shows to what extent they are accumulating a reading vocabulary of the most frequently used words in first-grade books.

3. *Concepts About Print.* The children respond to questions as the teacher reads a special little book. This test reveals each individual's confusions about directionality, one-to-one matching of words, and specific concepts such as "word," "letter," "first," and "last."

4. *Writing Vocabulary.* A writing vocabulary inventory is established by encouraging the children to write as many words as they are able in 10 minutes. The children are asked to read what they have written, and a point is scored for each word said and spelled correctly. This test reveals the core of words they can control as well as their directionality, letter formation, and visual discrimination of print.

5. *Dictation Test.* This test uncovers the children's awareness of letter-sound relationships and their ability to record them in sequence. The children are asked to write two or three dictated sentences, and a point is given for each sound written accurately.

6. *Text Reading.* Using a type of shorthand, the teacher records the

substitutions, omissions, and insertions the children make as they read orally. The teacher wants to know: Can they match words one-to-one? Do they have directionality under control? Do they monitor their own reading? What is the highest level they can read with at least 90% accuracy?

"ROAMING AROUND THE KNOWN"

Using the information from the Diagnostic Survey, the Reading Recovery teacher plans the starting point for each child's individualized program. A child's Reading Recovery program begins with ten, 30-minute daily sessions called "Roaming Around the Known." The purpose of these first lessons is to help the child go over what is known in different ways until the child is responding fluently around the personal stock of known letters, words, and messages. The teacher does not present anything new, but observes more of what the child knows as they read and write together. The teacher and the child get to know each other, and the children can discover things they didn't think they knew.

It is a time for the reading of many books. Natural language texts are chosen because they support beginning readers with predictable stories and patterns and refrains.

Another aspect of "Roaming Around the Known" is the writing of little books. There are opportunities for the child to generate sentences, and the teacher writes what is dictated, encouraging the child to contribute as much as possible. There is much rereading, and soon the child is able to read most of these simple books with little help.

By the time the child is ready for more intensive instruction, new behaviors may have emerged. The child may seem to control one-to-one matching on simple texts and may notice errors in reading and attempt to self-correct.

A TYPICAL READING RECOVERY LESSON

The purpose of Reading Recovery is to help children use effective strategies for reading texts, not to accumulate items of knowledge. Each day the teacher prepares a lesson plan and chooses the books to be read. The Reading Recovery book list includes over 500 books from different publishers and is arranged in levels 1 to 20, comparable to classroom reading levels from readiness to the end of Grade 1. Books at the lower levels include predictable stories and language structures; higher-level books present more difficult and varied texts.

During and after the lesson, the teacher documents the child's reading and writing behaviors by making notations on the lesson plan. From these observations instructional decisions are made for this particular individual.

Each daily lesson follows a specified sequence:

1. *Familiar reading.* First, the child selects two or three familiar books to read. Since these books have already been read, the child has an opportunity to practice fluent reading.

2. *Taking a running record.* Next, the teacher takes a running record of the text introduced to the child in the previous lesson. Using checks and other symbols, the teacher can record exactly what the child reads, analyzing the errors and determining what strategies the child controls as she or he attempts to get meaning from the text. The Reading Recovery teachers observe whether children monitor their own reading, are aware of unknown words, and notice information such as meaning, structure, and visual cues and use these to crosscheck and self-correct. After the child has read the book, the teacher will use what has been observed to support the child in the use of strategies. The teacher may go back to the part of the book where the child had difficulty and was able to solve the problem, making a teaching point by getting the child to do some more reading work on the part that was difficult. The teacher may ask the child to find the "tricky part," reread it, and think of something that would make sense. Children are encouraged to take risks, try to work things out, and think about their responses.

3. *Writing a story.* In the writing part of the lesson, the child composes one or two sentences and writes the sentence(s) on unlined paper using a marking pen. The child is helped by the teacher to hear sounds in words and is encouraged to write as much of the story as possible. The link between reading and writing is evident as the child writes and rereads until the message is complete.

4. *Cut-up story.* The teacher quickly rewrites this message on a strip of heavy paper. The words of the story are cut apart, and the child then reconstructs the message, attending to the print, scanning the errors, and self-correcting, if necessary. The cut-up story is put into an envelope and taken home to be reassembled for practice.

5. *Introduction and attempt of new book.* At the end of each lesson, a new book is introduced to the child. The teacher selects a book that is within the control of the child and yet still provides some opportunities for the child to apply new responses or procedures. The child attempts to read the new book, and the teacher strives to help the child become independent.

Instruction continues and, typically after about 12 to 16 weeks, the children are released from the program. The goal of Reading Recovery is to help children develop effective reading strategies so they can catch up with their peers. This accelerated progress is possible because the children have become more independent in their learning and have developed a self-improving system.

The following case study describes an individual child's Reading Recovery program.

JOSHUA: A CHILD'S PROGRAM

When school started in the fall, Joshua was identified as being among the lowest-level readers in his first-grade classroom. The Diagnostic Survey indicated Joshua's strengths and confusions about written language. He seemed to have some book handling skills and appeared to be aware that it is the print, not the pictures, that contains the message. He was able to identify almost all the letters of the alphabet, but was only able to write one word and had little concept of letter-sound relationships. An analysis of Joshua's reading showed he was able to use the meaning of the story and language structure, but ended up inventing text and did not always match words one-to-one.

The goal for Joshua's early lessons was to help him learn how to look at print. At first he did not notice discrepancies in his reading of *Plop!* (Melser, 1981b). A running record of Joshua's reading during Lesson 3 showed that he used meaning and structure cues. He seemed to match words one-to-one, but did not monitor his own reading (Figure 13.1). In the writing part of the lesson, Week 1, Joshua generated this sentence (Figure 13.2). The underlined letters indicate the letter-sounds Joshua was able to hear in the words he wanted to write. But as the lessons progressed he began to notice the visual features of letters and words and to use this knowledge to learn new things. He learned to fluently read and write a core of words, locate them in a simple text, and integrate this with what he knew about the meaning of the story and language structure. From the beginning of his program, Joshua read little books such as *Toot, Toot* (Wildsmith, 1984) and *Little Pig* (Melser, 1981a). The language patterns and predictability of these stories supported his early efforts.

By reading and writing whole texts each day, he learned to monitor his own reading. Because I encouraged him to orchestrate these strategies for problem solving, his self-correction behavior increased.

Questions such as, "I liked the way you did that. But can you find the

FIGURE 13.1. Record of Joshua's reading during Lesson 3

									CUES USED	
Accuracy : 83% Self-correction rate: 1:nil TOTALS							**5**	**0**		
PAGE	TITLE AND LEVEL: Plop! (3)						E	SC	E	SC
2	Plop|R|A ✓ ✓ ✓ ✓ ✓ Little Frog can see the flowers.						1		Ⓜ̶S V	
3	We|A ✓ ✓ ✓ ✓ He |T can see the dragonfly.						1		{ M S̶ V M S̶ V̶	
4/5	✓ ✓ ✓ ✓ ✓ He can see the ducklings.									
6	✓ ✓ ✓ ✓ He can see the fish.									
7	He can ✓ ✓ ✓ ✓ Can he see the big bird?						2		M S̶ V M S̶ V	
8	✓ We ✓ Yes, he can.						1		M S̶ V̶	

Symbols

✓ = correct response
R = repeat
A = appeal
M = using meaning cues

S = using information from the structure of language
V = using visual cues, including letter-sound relationships

FIGURE 13.2. Joshua's writing during Week 1

'tricky part'?" and, "Why did you stop? What did you notice?" encouraged Joshua to self-monitor and try to solve the difficulty.

After 35 lessons, Joshua had progressed as a reader and a writer. He was able to fluently read in texts such as *It Looked Like Spilt Milk* (Shaw, 1947) and *The Chick and the Duckling* (Ginsburg, 1972). These were comparable to those levels being read by the average group in his classroom. There was evidence of successful problem solving in his reading of *Pat's New Puppy* (Leaming, 1971). Joshua was using strategies independently. He monitored his own reading, searched for cues, and often self-corrected (Figure 13.3). By Week 11, Joshua wrote almost all of his message independently (Figure 13.4). His writing vocabulary had increased to at least 36 words. Using this and his ability to analyze the sounds in words, he was now able to generate simple sentences and write them easily. Most

FIGURE 13.3. Record of Joshua's reading by Lesson 34

PAGE	TITLE AND LEVEL: Pat's New Puppy (7)	E	SC	CUES USED E	SC
2	Pat got a new puppy.				
3	The puppy was brown and white.				
4	The puppy had big feet and a long tail.				
5	Pat named the puppy Happy.				
6	Pat put Happy in the|she|she|c|R her wagon.		I	MSV / MSV	MSV
7	she took him R for a walk ride.		I	MSV	
8	Happy jumped out of the wagon. He ran into the park.				

Symbols

✓	= correct response	S	= using information from the structure of language
R	= repeat		
A	= appeal	V	= using visual cues, including letter-sound relationships
M	= using meaning cues		

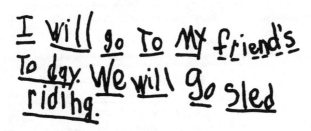

FIGURE 13.4. Joshua's writing during Week 11

importantly, he viewed reading and writing as tasks he could tackle, working patiently and independently to make meaning.

THE TEACHERS' RESPONSES

Reading Recovery teachers feel that their views of the reading process and beginning reading instruction have changed as a result of the Reading Recovery training. One teacher said, "I used to think of beginning reading as the acquisition of isolated skills and mastery of a controlled vocabulary. My idea of a good reader was one who knew all the words and could answer my comprehension questions. My concept of teaching has changed dramatically. I used to think of 'activities' and 'correctness.' Now I think of the child's responses and his efforts to solve new problems in his reading."

Teachers gain an understanding of the importance of teaching strategies. They help children by giving them time to orchestrate their responses. In this way, children learn to take responsibility for their own learning.

Reading Recovery teachers learn to observe children's reading behavior and look for evidence of progress in new ways. The child who knows how to monitor his own reading and searches for more information becomes an independent processor of print.

As for myself, I have realized that the questions we ask and the comments we make to children during the lessons are based on our belief systems of how children learn. Paradoxically, a part of learning to be better observers of children is for us to take the time to close our eyes once in a while and reflect on our own responses to the children and the quality of our interaction with them. I have learned to become more reflective and analytic of my own teaching and encourage other teachers to do this so we can share our insights. In this way, we continue to refine our knowledge of our own theories and develop our own self-improving system of putting theory into practice.

REFERENCES

Clay, M. M. (1979a). *The early detection of reading difficulties*. Auckland, New Zealand: Heinemann Educational Books.

Clay, M. M. (1979b). *Reading: The patterning of complex behavior*. Auckland, New Zealand: Heinemann Educational Books.

DeFord, D. E., Pinnell, G. S., & Lyons, C. A. (1988a). *The Ohio reading recovery project: Vol. XII. State of Ohio Year 3*. Columbus: The Ohio State University.

Ginsburg, M. (1972). *The chick and the duckling*. New York: Macmillan.

Leaming, H. (1971). *Pat's new puppy*. Glenview, Illinois: Scott Foresman.

Mayer, M. (1983). *All by myself*. New York: Western Publishing.

Melser, J. (1981a). *Little pig*. Auckland, New Zealand: Shortland Publications (Distributed by The Wright Group).

Melser, J. (1981b). *Plop!* Auckland, New Zealand: Shortland Publications (Distributed by the Wright Group).

Pinnell, G. S., DeFord, D. E., & Lyons, C. A. (1988b). *Reading recovery: Early intervention for at-risk first graders*. Arlington, VA: Educational Research Service.

Shaw, C. (1947). *It looked like spilt milk*. New York: Scholastic.

Wildsmith, B. (1984). *Toot, toot*. Oxford, England: Oxford University Press.

CHAPTER 14

Reading Workshop with Technology in a Special Education Class

JANE BEATY
Metropolitan Nashville (TN) Public Schools

At the beginning of the school year, I locate the third-, fourth-, and fifth-grade special education students with whom I will be working. They have already been certified by the state as either learning disabled, seriously emotionally disturbed, or educable mentally retarded. Ten to twelve fourth-grade students with the greatest need for service will be with me for 4 hours a day before returning to their homerooms for mainstreaming in science and social studies. Other special education students will receive service for varying amounts of time during the rest of the day.

My fourth-grade class and two adjacent regular fourth-grade classes, known as Apple Classrooms of Tomorrow (ACOT), are part of a nationwide research project funded by Apple Computer, Incorporated. My classroom is in an open space surrounded by one of the regular fourth-grade classes and a technology centrum. All of my students have their own Apple IIgs computers and share a printer with three other students. A Macintosh II computer and videodisk player are on loan from Vanderbilt University. My IIgs and printer are on a table behind my desk.

A CHANGE IN PERSPECTIVE

Sometime around 1985 I noticed that my students were not making the reading progress that I had anticipated. This was in spite of my best efforts to make individual daily plans for each student, assemble enough first- or second-grade materials each day to keep the students busy, check stacks of completed worksheets and workbooks, and try to follow our system's mandated sequence of communication skills. The 1986 International Reading Association national convention in Philadelphia was the precipitating event that changed my teaching philosophy. There I encountered many "whole language" educators who were incorporating good literature into their language arts programs in a variety of ways. At first I dutifully took notes, not fully understanding what I was hearing, but by the time I came home, I was sold on trying out some of the strategies. It made so much sense to me.

I remember the first day back in class with my students trying out a story-mapping lesson on a story I had read to them. They listened to the story, filled in individual story maps with story details, and then wrote their own versions of the story. It worked! It was so easy to do, and the students were so proud of their writing. We made a wall display entitled "From Story Maps to Stories" and displayed their story maps along with their stories. From that point on, I started to add the bits and pieces of strategies and materials to my classroom instruction. Many good ideas led to others; any strategy that didn't work for my students was replaced with another one that did. This process continues to this day.

One of the most difficult parts of my transition to process-oriented instruction was gradually discarding the huge assortment of out-of-date basals, worksheets, workbooks, and task cards that I had been accumulating over the years. They were the security blanket that got me through each day. If I got rid of them, what would I do with the students? Would they ever learn to read? Yet, my experience with these students has shown me that they are learning to read because they are reading and writing meaningful text daily.

MATERIALS

Unlike many of their peers, my students are unable to read or write well enough to function successfully in a regular classroom. Their cumulative records indicate increasing difficulty and/or failure to succeed with language-based activities. Much time is spent during the first few weeks of school convincing the students that they are all readers and building enough confidence in them so that they believe that they can read material that at first glance might be perceived as too difficult. This means exposing students to a wide variety of reading material drawn from newspaper current events and weather stories, the best of children's literature, and stories written by individual students and entire classes, present and past. Basal readers are still used upon occasion when the story meshes with a topic under study.

Using the Newspaper

One of the most exciting uses of the newspaper for my students is the ongoing study of the weather combined with learning the locations of the various states. Before the school year begins, I post the names of the months all around the room at the juncture of the wall and ceiling, leaving room under each month name for four weekly weather maps for that month. Every morning I post the current weather map from *USA Today* on the chalkboard. Each map shows the temperatures and weather conditions expected for that day all across the United States. We look for the hottest and coolest areas and talk about weather systems as they move across mountain ranges, rivers, the regions of the United States, and other map features. If there is a newsworthy weather story, I cut it out and paste it on paper, number the paragraphs to help the students keep their places, underline particular vocabulary words, add some higher level questions to enhance comprehension at the side of the article, and make a copy for each student. We might use this one story as part of our reading, writing, and class discussion for several days. In the past we have also used the newspaper to read about national and local elections and issues, major sports events such as the Olympics, and natural disasters such as hurricanes and earthquakes in this country and worldwide. At first I am the one who picks out the newspaper stories, but as the students get used to following current events, they often suggest the topics for our reading.

Choosing Good Literature

I try to provide a variety of genres to meet the interest levels of all students at one time or another. Finding good quality stories with predictable language that will appeal to 9-, 10-, and 11-year-old disabled readers is not always easy. At the beginning of the year when the students are feeling somewhat insecure about their reading abilities, I start off reading poetry from a good anthology such as *The World Treasury of Children's Literature* (Fadiman, 1985). Copyright laws permit limited copying of certain copyrighted works under certain conditions for nonprofit educational purposes (American Library Association, 1977). Keeping those regulations in mind, I make student copies of a favorite poem or two and use them as a source of minilessons in reading and as the springboard to the enjoyment of poetry throughout the year. The poems are short enough to be easily mastered, and the students experience almost immediate success. This leads naturally into my reading and rereading of such story/poems as *The Terrible Tiger* (Prelutsky, 1972) with its predictable refrains and humor. It is always a favorite with the students and in great demand for independent reading.

Bringing the Rain to Kapiti Plain (Aardema, 1983) is the first book I use for total group reading at the beginning of the year. It fits perfectly into our study of the weather and climatic conditions. It also is written in rhyme, has predictable language, and is beautifully illustrated. There are so many ways to integrate this story into our curriculum that it is no trouble to keep the students interested for many days. All students become successful readers of this story and beg to take their copies home to share.

It is important to expose my students to stories printed on the highest quality paper with outstanding word pictures and exceptional illustrations. Three such books are *The Mare on the Hill* (Lockert, 1985), *St. George and the Dragon* (Hodges, 1984), and *Dear Mili* (Grimm, 1988). *The Mare on the Hill* is a realistic fiction book printed on slick paper that enhances the reproduction of its oil painting illustrations. It is a story of two young boys' attempts to befriend a wild mare brought to their farm by their father. The other two books are fairy tale/fantasies that excite the imagination of children and adults alike. In *St. George and the Dragon* a brave knight seeks to find and destroy a loathsome dragon who has terrorized the small kingdom ruled by the Lady Una's parents. The subject matter of *Dear Mili* is somewhat complex for some of my students, but Maurice Sendak's lush and greatly detailed illustrations enhance their comprehension. The story deals with a little girl who is sent by her mother into a forest to take refuge from a frightening war that is about to come to her village. The author's treatment of death in this book is sensitively handled and in no way maudlin nor disturbing. These three books are the basis of ongoing discussion, reading, and writing. The students' differing opinions about the books make for exciting and interesting lessons for all of us.

I model my own enjoyment of beautiful books when I touch the paper in these books and read them to my students; then I watch the students touching the pictures and reading my copies after they have been returned to our room library.

HOW THE PROGRAM WORKS

Language arts takes up around 2½ hours a day. My program immerses the students in reading, writing, and discussion of connected text of varying lengths. Each day I try to include independent reading in student-selected library books, directed teaching, and application of some word recognition or comprehension skill either in groups or individually. I use a variety of materials so that my students have opportunities to write, share, and discuss what is being read. I also read aloud the best literature that I can find. It is a most flexible time, designed to maximize the amount of time spent in actual reading and writing of connected text.

Sustained Silent Reading

We begin with 10 to 15 minutes of schoolwide sustained silent reading (SSR) at the beginning of the day. The students are allowed to choose anything they want to read, providing they can make some sense of it. I have an extensive classroom library with an adequate selection of books on levels from pre-primer to Grade 4. I keep a book to read in my hand, but am available to the students if they need help. They signal for help by raising their hands and pointing to the difficult part; after I help out, they reread the sentence before proceeding. If students have chosen books that are too difficult for them, then I help them make more suitable choices. After SSR, the students move on to a writing activity related to their reading. Sometimes they talk with a partner about some part of the book they have been reading and then write in a teacher-directed or self-directed way about the book in an ongoing response journal. Sometimes they copy a favorite part of the story or recount a short sequence of events they were reading that day. Sometimes I ask them to find examples of writing conventions such as how their authors used conversation and quotation marks. In order to induce the students to sample different kinds of literature, I also try to highlight at least two or three books from our room or school library each week.

Teaching Reading as a Process

Regardless of the source of material, I follow a fairly standard procedure in getting students ready to read and write no matter what their functioning levels might be. This process is applicable to small- or large-group reading instruction and also can be used when I read stories to the class from any genre of literature. There are five possible areas to incorporate in my lesson plans.

Pre-reading.   Pre-reading is most important in any reading class, but of paramount importance when teaching students with reading/learning problems. Extensive concept development prior to reading eases their reluctance to tackle printed material and helps them feel more comfortable, if not immediately successful. Visual aids — such as maps, diagrams, pictures, concrete objects, semantic mapping (Heimlich & Pittelman, 1986) on the chalkboard, a wall chart, or paper—help to elicit what students know and to determine their readiness to read and understand a passage. Vocabulary can be introduced either at this point or as the story progresses. Sometimes I model a skill—such as using the context of a sentence to figure out a new word, predicting what will happen next, outlining, or making a timeline—that will come into play during the reading of the story under study or as a follow-up activity.

Story Introduction.   This is the time to generate interest in the story to be read. I give the background of the story, describe the setting, or introduce a character. Telling the class the reasons for my choice of the story, introducing the author and/or illustrator, recalling other works by either or both, and noting any special awards the book may have won are all ways to attract the students' attention and enhance their enjoyment of the story. At this time I focus the students on something to anticipate as the story proceeds.

Story Reading.   I practice reading aloud some of the story to myself ahead of time so that I can be thoroughly familiar with it. If this is a group reading lesson, I read aloud while the students read along silently with me in their own copies, thus making it easier for them to become involved in the story without concern over decoding problems. We stop to clarify troublesome ideas and vocabulary, identify and discuss points that were highlighted before listening, and discuss inferential and critical comprehension questions.

Either that same day or the next we begin a series of assisted reading episodes in which the students and I read in unison. Those who know the words carry the poorer readers along so that no one struggles with unfamiliar words. Again we stop to discuss the story in much the same way as was done the first time through. In the beginning stages of assisted reading we usually read a paragraph at a time. I usually introduce each paragraph by connecting it to the one we just read and then either tell the students what the new paragraph will be about or ask them what they think will happen next. This oral modeling enhances their enjoyment and understanding of the story and models some strategies that good readers use when they read. As the students become familiar with the story, the prompts are gradually withdrawn until they are no longer needed.

Story-related Activities.   These activities are based on the objectives to be accomplished, the amount of time available, and the interest and ability levels of the students. In a literature unit, after much class discussion, we often rewrite the story as a group project, print student copies, and then use the story as the basis for reading instruction. While I am giving special attention to an individual or small groups, other students work at their own pace on a variety of projects related to the story, eliminating the need for drill-and-practice worksheets. Students form groups to talk about and/or illustrate their favorite parts and then share with other class members. Students make story maps to help recall narrative texts and then use them to write about the story. Some students might rewrite the lead to the story after researching the various ways different authors begin their stories. Students of different ability levels might respond to the same questions or projects in ways that challenge them individually and reflect their own ideas. Others plan and execute the best way to display important story elements (Cohen, 1972). Some students practice reading the story in pairs to improve their fluency and comprehension. As a culminating activity, the story or article can be rewritten and illustrated as a class project, published, and shared at home.

Cross-curriculum Integration. Integration of reading and writing across the curriculum can begin at almost any point. For social studies, students compare and contrast the life of early settlers in *The Ox-Cart Man* (Hall, 1984) to the lives of settlers in our own state of Tennessee. For science and health, students who are researching insects might bring in newspaper articles about the effects of tick-borne Lyme disease on people and research the life cycle of ticks.

Our fourth-grade social studies curriculum has a unit on American Indians. I have found two books, both based on Native American legends, that can be successfully integrated into a unit of this type. One is *The Gift of the Sacred Dog* (Goble, 1980), a story about a young Sioux brave who saved his tribe from starvation by seeking help from the Great Spirit. *The Legend of the Bluebonnet* (DePaola, 1983) is about a young Indian girl who sacrificed her most precious possession to break the drought that had brought her tribe great misery. These two stories form the basis of ongoing writing and reading activities. Whole-class discussions help the students to see similarities and differences between the two books. Students might work together to fill in a wall chart comparing the contrasting common story elements and then use the chart to help them write about either or both of the stories.

Bartoli and Botel (1988) have many good suggestions on integrated thematic units for both regular and special education students.

INTEGRATING THE COMPUTER INTO THE TEACHING OF READING

In 1988, when I was ready to graduate to the next higher step from just booting up games for my students to play on my one computer, I read a book that started me using the computer in the teaching of reading (Strickland, Feeley, & Wepner, 1987). There is still controversy among certain educators over the effectiveness of the computer as an instructional tool in the classroom, but I am completely sold on its use. In 1989 Fisher studied classrooms equipped with computers and found that students become more independent and assertive learners when they have ready access to computers. They develop more confidence in their abilities as learners when they have some control over their assignments. Observation over 3 years in my classroom would substantiate these research findings.

Careful selection of software coupled with appropriate teaching strategies are the key to an exciting classroom environment in both the regular and special education ACOT classrooms. One of the most significant applications of the computer in my classroom lies in the use of selected utility software to enhance the teaching of reading and writing in any curriculum area. Utility programs allow the teacher or students to enter their own words, phrases, or stories at any reading level from any source of material. The students' writings then form the basis of a language-experience reading program. These programs are natural tie-ins to whole language teaching and to content-area subjects at different levels. The possibilities for use are limited only by the imagination of teachers and students.

AppleWorks (Apple Computer, 1983–1986; see list of software cited at the end of this chapter) is an integrated program that has wide application in business and education settings. Its word-processing program is used daily by all of my students in basic language arts assignments. It does not take long for even second- or third-grade students to learn how to use *AppleWorks*. It is as simple or complex as one needs to make it. Some students enjoy using the database to organize their own categories for books read or to store information about states or countries in social studies, or plant and animal life in science. There are simple commands which greatly assist students in such activities as writing stories with predictable text or moving text around.

Teacher Support Software has produced some outstanding utility programs that are the backbone of my reading/literature program. *The Language Experience Recorder+ (LER+)* (Mason, 1987) is a multidimensional word-processing program that prints text in 20-, 40-, and 80-column print. Students take great pride in printing their best work in large type for bulletin board display or making it into a big book with their own illustrations. There are many other useful features to this program, including banner print for wall charts and captions for displays, word and sentence counts, alphabetical word lists, and readability estimates. Students practice reading fluency on the *LER+* with the installation of a speech card.

Other Teacher Support programs promote whole language teaching and provide numerous and varied opportunities for students to become totally familiar with any reading material. *Word Works* (Domenech, 1987) is a series of computer games that reinforce vocabulary words. *The Semantic Mapper* (Kuchinskas & Radencich, 1987) is a multipurpose program that I use as a concept developer, a pre-writing activity, and comprehension checker. *The Sequencer* (Kuchinskas, 1989) helps students review important steps in content-area material as well as learn to summarize. The utility disks for each of these programs allow us to use any material that we choose. They work equally well in classrooms with one computer or many.

Another favorite program is *Reading Realities* (Wepner & Mason, 1989). These highly motivating stories are designed for at-risk teenage students, but many of them are entirely appropriate for my fourth-grade students. Among other issues they deal with drugs, alcohol, and peer pressure. There is no problem building or maintaining interest in the many activities this program provides.

Using the Macintosh II computer with videodisk technology is showing great promise for enhancing students' reading and writing opportunities. (A videodisk player is linked to a monitor and a Macintosh II computer.) For example, I showed my class the videodisk of a film entitled *Visions of the Deep* (Vestron, 1984), which features underwater photography of all sorts of sea life coupled with the photographer's explanations of the pictures. The students chose a short segment of the film about a mother whale and her calf to write about. We recorded the videodisk frame numbers for that segment and programmed the computer to play only that segment when a screen button was "clicked on" with the Macintosh mouse. Then we listened very intently as the photographer described what was happening in that segment. As the students listened to the photographer's voice and watched the film, they focused on certain video details and wrote a class story on the Macintosh computer. We compared the film with our class story for accuracy as many times as necessary by clicking the button to replay the film portion.

Along with this technology, the students use books and encyclopedias to research whales. Then they write their own individual stories on their computers and share information with classmates.

DOES MY PROGRAM WORK?

My goal, like that of teachers everywhere, is to expose my students to the best materials available, increase the amount of time they spend in meaningful reading and writing experiences, add to their store of knowledge about the world, and promote a sense of self-worth about themselves.

After many false starts on books that he found "boring," one fourth-grade student, who came into the program reading on the pre-primer level, finally found a fairly simple book, *The Magic Fish* (Littledale, 1985), that he simply could not put down. He read it many times to himself and then to others, each time with great relish. One day as he sat at his computer writing about the book, I asked him how he was getting along. His answer reflected his new self-image: "I'm doing just great. It's easy once you learn how."

REFERENCES

Aardema, V. (1983). *Bringing the rain to Kapiti plain*. New York: Dial.

American Library Association, National Council of Teachers of English, National Education Association. (1977). *The new copyright law: Questions teachers and librarians ask*. Washington, DC: National Education Association.

Bartoli, J., & Botel, M. (1988). *Reading/learning disability: An ecological approach*. New York: Teachers College Press.

Cohen, E. G. (1972). *Designing groupwork: Strategies for the heterogeneous classroom*. New York: Teachers College Press.

DePaola, T. (1983). *The legend of the bluebonnet*. New York: G. P. Putnam's Sons.

Fadiman, C. (1985). *The world treasury of children's literature*. Boston: Little, Brown.

Fisher, C. W. (1989). *The influence of high computer access on student empowerment*. Cupertino, CA: Apple Computer.

Goble, P. (1980). *The gift of the sacred dog*. New York: Macmillan.

Grimm, W. (1988). *Dear Mili*. New York: Michael di Capua Books.

Hall, D. (1984) *The ox-cart man*. New York: Penguin Books.

Heimlich, J. E., & Pittelman, S. D. (1986). *Semantic mapping: Classroom applications*. Newark, DE: International Reading Association.

Hodges, M. (1984). *St. George and the dragon*. Boston: Little, Brown.

Littledale, F. (1985). *The magic fish*. Jefferson City, MO: Scholastic.

Lockert, T. (1985). *The mare on the hill*. New York: Dial.

Prelutsky, J. (1972). *The terrible tiger*. New York: Macmillan.

Strickland, D. S., Feeley, J. T., & Wepner, S. B. (1987). *Using computers in the teaching of reading*. New York: Teachers College Press.

SOFTWARE CITED

Apple Computer. (1983–1986). *AppleWorks*. Cupertino, CA: Apple Computer.

Domenech, L. H. (1987). *Word works*. Gainesville, FL: Teacher Support Software.

Kuchinskas, G. A. (1989). *The sequencer*. Gainesville, FL: Teacher Support Software.

Kuchinskas, G. A., & Radencich, M. C. (1987). *The semantic mapper*. Gainesville, FL: Teacher Support Software.

Mason, G. E. (1987). *Language Experience Recorder+*. Gainesville, FL: Teacher Support Software.

Vestron. (1984). *Visions of the deep* [videodisk]. Romaine, CA: Image Entertainment (Distributor).

Wepner, S. B., & Mason, G. E. (1989). *Reading realities: Real life issues*. Gainesville, FL: Teacher Support Software.

CHAPTER 15

Gifted Students Respond to Their Reading

LESLIE LYNN FUNKHOUSER
A. Scott Crossfield Elementary School, Herndon, VA

One of my goals as an elementary teacher has been to give students an early foundation for lifelong literacy. I feel that it is critical in the primary grades to nurture a love for reading and writing. In this chapter I will focus on showing ways these students use reading, writing, and talking as tools for understanding the world around them.

A FOUNDATION FOR LITERACY

The students described are second and third graders. Some are in the Gifted Program in Fairfax County, Virginia. They achieved an I.Q. score of 140 or above on the Otis Lennon School Ability Test administered in second grade. Others are from regular classrooms but have qualified for differentiated services due to talents noticed in reading, writing, and speaking.

Although these students are bright and articulate, the strategies used are appropriate for any students, no matter what their capabilities. My classroom is structured so that students share responsibility for everything that happens in it. They take turns organizing and being in charge of small- and large-group discussions. They control the questioning and the conduct of the groups. When problems arise, they decide as a class how to solve them.

Students need to be prepared to read for a variety of purposes throughout their lives. Two purposes I focus on are reading and writing for pleasure, and reading and writing as tools for gathering and sharing information for use with family, community, work, or school.

To help children learn about reading for enjoyment, for getting a job done, or for finding out more about a topic, I focus on children as literate citizens of the future. Such a focus requires that the children have plenty of time to read, write, and respond each day. In my class, children choose what they will read during our reading workshop time. Their selections come from a variety of sources: literature or trade books; magazines such as *World, Cricket, Ranger Rick*, and *Sports Illustrated for Kids*; the children's own published books; literature and poetry anthologies; book tapes; and selected author's works to read as a special focus. As with the children's daily writing, I have learned that choice of materials is a topic I frequently ask the children to discuss and evaluate. They are asked to think about whether the level of their book is appropriate for them and if they have reading material in mind to work on next.

As an example of an activity related to the second purpose, a group of students sit down and compose a letter home about what we are doing in school. The students design the letterhead and decide what format to use for their letter. Below is a typical letter in which the children use reading and writing as tools, for communication to their parents. Jamie, Jenny, and Travis review the authors we have studied and announce we are now reading Bill Peet. Note that on a subsequent day, Brian, Mark, and Adam mention that one of them wrote a letter to Bill Peet. The authors for Friday point out how we study phonics. Just about every day the children mention our read-aloud books. Parents can get a good sense of what we are doing, and the children know their letters are conveying important information.

RUNNING THROUGH THE WEEK WITH MS. FUNKHOUSER

Thursday, January 4 — Today in school Ms. Funkhouser read us *Helga's Dowry*. It is a troll love story. Jamie, Kia, Charney, and Davey read with their first grade buddies. We have had four author studies. We have studied Chris Van Allsburg, Carol and Donald Carrick, Steven Kellogg and Tomie dePaola. We are now on Bill Peet. In gym we played Bronco Tag. We are having our pictures taken with our fifth grade buddies.
    Authors: Jamie, Jenny, and Travis.

Friday, January 5 — Ms. Funkhouser read *Cappy Boppy* during Read Aloud. In art, we made push-pull animals out of clay. Kids brought in words with silent e and long vowel letters. Some of the words were: *alive, Folkstone, space, plate*, and *disgrace*. On Monday, we are starting a new unit called *Attributes and Shapes* for science. In music we are learning about a new instrument. It is called the Vibraslap.
    Authors: Nate, Damian, Lang, and Johanna.

Monday, January 8 — Brian and Greg are publishing a book called *Snow*. We are learning about attributes. Attributes means things can have different characteristics. In Read Aloud, Miss F. read *Merle The High Flying Squirrel*. Mark is writing a letter to Bill Peet. We worked on a poem called *Ice* for penmanship. Then we drew icy pictures. We are going to the library with our fifth grade buddies. We are learning about the parts of a book such as *The Table of Contents*. We have music at the end of the day.

    Authors: Brian, Mark, and Adam.

Wednesday, January 10 — Today two teachers visited our class to learn about reading and writing workshop. The teachers learned about our journals, small group reading conferences, writing conferences, and sharing. The Mammal Group is graphing their weekly data about the gerbils. One of our anoles died and Erik and Mark buried him.

    Authors: Erik, Mark and Cindy.

STUDENTS DIALOGUE WITH TEACHER AND PEERS

Students write about books they are reading each week. We call these reading journals. In the beginning of the year I am the partner who responds to each child's journal. Later the children have a buddy within our class and respond to each other. The following are examples from student journals. They reflect the many interests students have as they choose books.

The Playful Dolphins
By NATIONAL GEOGRAPHIC

A dolphin named Betty shakes hands with her trainer. A dolphin named Mo jumps to the reward pole. Dolphins are playful animals. They do tricks for people. They can catch balls on their noses.

                                Patrick

Dear Patrick,
    Dolphins sound like fun animals. How do they learn to do so many things? Who trains them? What will you read next?

                                Love,
                                Ms. Funkhouser

Dear Miss Funkhouser,
    The trainers are the people who want a job with the dolphins. I

will probably read about horses because they are one of my weakneses!

Love,
Patrick

Marissa receives an interesting response from Jamie, who provides places for her to answer her questions about her journal entry.

Polar Express
By Chris Van Allsburg

One day a boy woke up. He was waiting for slagh bells. But instead he heard hissing steam and clashing wheels. It was a train. He got on his robe and got on the train. He got a slagh bell from santa clas. He had a hole in his robe so it fell out. He got it back on Christmas day. It was on the slagh.

Marissa

Dear Marissa,
　　Did santa clus give the boy preses?
　　Answer: Onley a slagh bell.
　　Did you read all of this book?
　　Answer: yes
　　Do you read lots of books that have santa clus?
　　Answer: no.

Love,
Jamie

Damian retells in great detail his reading of the H. G. Wells classic. He warns his reader that the entry is long with his unique check-off boxes at the end. Through our dialogue in the journal, I learned this adult novel was easy for Damian.

War of the Worlds
(Part 1)
By H. G. Wells

In 1894 mysterious bursts of flaming gas come from Mars and head earthward! Wells meets his old friend Ogilvy. Ogilvy is an astronomer and studies the flames. Then it turns out to be Martians! They made heat-rays that shot a white flame that killed Ogilvy and lots of other people! Wells ran away and told everybody he could tell in London. Then Wells saw the fighting machines that the martian's made. They were destructive and killed more people. Soldiers were trying to destroy the fighting machines but got killed. Then fighting machines attacked people in the Thames River! Their heat-rays made lots of steam in the river. Then some soldiers hit one of the fighting machines and killed the Martian inside. The other Martians killed the soldiers and started to go to London.

If you want to see the second part check the boxes below. This is a very long journal.

yes☒   no☐

Damian

Dear Damian,

Thank you for so much information. I like your little boxes for answers and your little illustrations too. What made this book challenging for you?

Ms. F.

Ms. F.,

This book was not challenging for me.

Damian

STUDENTS' DIALOGUE WITH PARENTS

Parent volunteers often help during reading and writing workshop and learn how to respond to the children. I have shown them that first we need to tell the child what we like about the story or journal and secondly we need to ask questions about the story or journal. As parents listen to many reading and writing conferences in the classroom they begin to use the same strategies with the children's homework.

The children work on a piece of writing one night a week. They also read and write in their journals one night a week. They are encouraged to spend about 30 minutes reading or writing. Their parents then spend about 10 minutes writing down a comment about the child's content. The following examples show parents responding to their children's reading journals.

Jason's mother praises his effort and prompts him to think about his own brother.

Here Comes Tagalong
BY ANNE MALLETT

In this book a boy named Steve is 5 years old and just moved into a new house. His mother allowed him to visit three houses away on one side and three on the other. Steve always followed his brother and his friends around. They decided to build a treehouse. Steve's brother and his friends didn't let Steve in the treehouse.

Jason

Jason,

  I found your journal fun to read and full of information. Do you have a tagalong for a brother too?

Hugs & Smiles,
Mom

Jamie's mom compliments her on her illustration and highlights her control of a stylistic point, her use of the nonsexist "he/she."

The Interupters

This is another chapter in *Mrs. Piggle-Wiggle's Magic.* "Everybody is interupting shouts Mr. Franklin. They have to find a cure. Mrs. Piggle-Wiggle! Of course! Mrs. Franklin calls her. She has a cure! It is . . . little blowers that you fill up with white powder. You blow some powder on the interupter. He/She can not see or feel the powder. The person will start interupting but won't finish.

Jamie

Dear Jamie,

  Your illustration is a great one! How did you know to write He/She? Have you found any traits you'd change in the character Mrs. Piggle-Wiggle?

Love,
Mom

Patrick and Marissa worked on pieces of writing at home after they had finished first drafts in class. They had shared these pieces in small group conference but wanted more input. Here are excerpts from Patrick and Marissa's writing and their mothers' responses. Patrick's mom responds appropriately to the wealth of details in the book coauthored by Patrick and Chris, displaying her obvious pride in being "a mother of one of the authors." Her questions will no doubt send the authors back to their source materials.

Hi our names are Patrick and Chris If you want to learn more about the Galaxy read our book!

By Patrick McGarry and Chris Montague
The Galaxy

There are nine planets in our galaxy. Our galaxy is called the Milky Way galaxy.

My favorite planets are Jupiter and Saturn. Jupiter has sixteen moons, and Saturn has a ring of gas and acid around it. It is not true when on cartoons they show people walking on the ring around Saturn. You would fall right through.

My least favorite planet is Pluto. Because nothing could live there. . . .

Uranios looks like a big bulls eye in space. If you droped a half dollar on Venus it would melt.

Mercury is the closest plant to Earth, not counting the moon. If you where in space flying over Mercury you would see green, purple, and yellow lights. That is if you were on the night side of the planet. . . .

Dear Patrick,

This story has a lot of details that are informative. As a mother of one of the authors, one of the things I like best about this story is that it is nice and long! The length of this story tells me how hard the authors worked on it. I like the illustrations too.

Which planet has the most moons? Do all the planets have moons?

Love,
Mom

Marissa's mother compliments her on mechanics and content. Her provocative question prompts Marissa to think about the details she presented so she can come up with some connecting statement about the various birthplaces of family members.

All About My Family

In my family we have five people. Their names are Annelyse, Rosamond, Marcia, and Glyn. Our house has four rooms. We have new carpet in our house. The carpet is white. My family is going to refinish our basement. My dad works at a machine tool Association. Annelyse was born in Georgia. Rosamond was born in Kanas City. Mom was born in Fayeteville, Ark. And my dad was born in Edinburgh, Ark. I was born in Kanas City.

Marissa

Dear Marissa,
    I like how slim Dad and I look in your picture. What is interesting about our family?

Love,
Mom

AUTHOR STUDIES

I spend about three hours a day working in the language arts area. I read aloud to my students at least twice a day and often a third time if I have something to read relating to a math concept or science unit. During these read-alouds I will also focus on the work of a particular author, such as Tomie dePaola, Bill Peet, or Steven Kellogg. If we are studying an author I read as many as 20 to 30 books by that author for a period of 2 to 3 weeks. As the year goes on, children begin to compare and contrast author's style as well as illustrator's style. This is also a springboard for the children's own writing. Frequently, children will begin to write letters to some of these authors. In her correspondence with Tomie dePaola, Stacey reveals the deep emotions she feels when reading two of Tomie dePaola's books.

Dear Tomie daPaola,
    You are one of my favorite authors. Your pictures are wonderful and so are your books. I'm in second grade and I'm almost 8. My favorid book you wrote is *The Legend of the Blue Bonnett*. I did not know if I wanted to cry or smile. I also felt like that when I read *Now One Foot, Now The Other*. We are studying you and your books. Do you like being an author and an illustrator? I wrote 2 books in school. They are *My Dog* and *My Best Friend*.

Your Friend,
Stacey

SHARING BOOKS THROUGH DISCUSSION

Each day during a small-group reading share, four or five students of varying abilities meet to read from a book they have been working with. It can be a big book, a chapter book, or even a book they may have read before. Each child may give us a brief summary, depending on how far they have read, and then read orally from a part they have really liked. The children are in charge of small-group sharing and decide the questions they will ask and the kinds of things they want to discuss during the sharing session. My role is the same as the children's role. I ask questions about the book and tell what I've liked about the child's reading. Often the small groups operate with a child in charge while I hold individual conferences.

A few weeks ago Patrick shared one of the National Geographic Society books called *The Blue Whale*. This was the beginning of a discussion:

ERIK: Patrick, What's your favorite whale? How do the whales kill the fish? How long is the blue whale?
PATRICK: Whales don't kill the fish; they swallow them whole. It's about 200 ft. long.
LAUREN: This book was a good choice. I learned a lot from your sharing today Patrick.
REBECCA: I've read this book too, and I liked the way you read today. This book gives a lot of information.
MARK: Did you know about the blue whale before you read this book?
CHRISTIAN: Where did you find this book?
PATRICK: I knew a little about the blue whale before I read this book. I found this book on the shelf where the National Geographic Books are kept. The blue whale is my favorite whale.

In my classroom a whole-class sharing session takes place daily; we share both books and writing and then talk about them as a class. Children have the opportunity to ask questions, make comments about the selection shared, or connect it to something from their own personal experience by using a "remember" or "reminder" type comment. When I read to the class Charlotte Zolotow's *Mr. Rabbitt and the Lovely Present*, some of the children made the following comments:

LAUREN: That story reminds me of choosing a gift for my mom at Christmas.
MARISSA: This reminds me of reading this book every Easter. We have this book at home.
KEVIN: What's your favorite color that the little girl picks?
Ms. FUNKHOUSER: My favorite color would be the blue but it wasn't my favorite fruit.
JASON: Why did they say blue grapes when they aren't blue but purple?
Ms. FUNKHOUSER: They are meaning the purple ones. They are a bluish-purple.
NICK: If you had written this book would you change anything? I like the illustrations.

Ms. FUNKHOUSER: I don't know exactly what I'd change, but this isn't one of my favorite books. I got tired of reading it to you and felt it was too repetitious.

One of the most important aspects of both small-group and whole-class sharing sessions is the event itself. It's a chance for the children to validate themselves as readers and writers and to have opportunities to talk and further refine their thinking.

A second purpose behind having sharing sessions built into the daily schedule is to build a supportive community of readers and writers and learners. The children are always encouraging each other. They look forward to sharing their reading and writing and become very upset if the schedule changes.

As I've listened to tapes of children's sharing, I've found that lively discussions result from sharing sessions. Many of their questions are about the way the author might have felt as he or she wrote the book, as well as how the children felt about their own pieces of writing. Students have frequently said that the feedback they receive when they share is a good way to measure how successful they are as writers. Many students list titles from the class library written by their classmates as favorite books to recommend to fellow readers.

Providing opportunities to share reading and writing lets the children see that I value responses and new ideas. Children are always encouraged to produce their own ideas and to ask each other questions about their reading and writing processes. These questions do not come from workbooks or teacher's manuals. The children are stretching themselves to grow as they gain greater confidence in their own ideas. As the teacher, I find that I have gained confidence in accepting the children's ideas and their individual differences without needing to rely on manuals and specified questions made up by others. By building our classroom community as one where all learning and teaching are shared responsibilities, we all become experts. As I reflect upon my own growth in sharing learning with children, I'm reminded of my own risk-taking with colleagues at the Mast Way School in Lee, New Hampshire. During a 2-year research study connecting reading and writing instruction, University of New Hampshire professors Donald Graves and Jane Hansen taught our staff about accepting children's ideas and divergence. They were our teachers in showing us the importance of sticking our necks out and stretching ourselves. For 2 years the researchers and teachers shared writing every Monday for one hour after school. As our writing group met for the last time, I remember how confident I felt about sharing my own piece, a poem about teaching and learning.

CHAPTER 16

Collaboration: Key to Implementing Process Teaching in a Remedial Reading Program

RITA M. BEAN
University of Pittsburgh

REBECCA HAMILTON
Pittsburgh Public Schools

Current concerns about remedial reading programs include issues about the content, the setting, and the reading specialist's role. Criticism often focuses on the lack of long-term effectiveness, particularly beyond the primary grades (Kennedy, Birman, & Demaline, 1986; Slavin, 1987). Recent studies of remedial reading programs indicate an emphasis on isolated skill instruction, with little congruence between what the student receives in the remedial class and in the classroom or developmental program (Allington & McGill-Franzen, 1988; Bean et al., 1989; Johnston, Allington, & Afferbach, 1985).

In this chapter we describe our plan for how reading specialists, in collaboration with classroom developmental reading teachers, can implement process teaching in remedial instruction, whether that instruction is provided within the classroom or in a pull-out setting. The plan that we present is based on two important notions: (1) Collaboration is important when students receive reading instruction from more than one teacher (Bean & Eichelberger, 1985; Allington & Brockou, 1988); and (2) instructional congruence between the developmental and remedial program is essential (Walp & Walmsley, 1989). Background for our plan is provided by describing one child's perception of reading and writing; then, research findings that have influenced our thinking are discussed. We describe five process strategies that teachers in the Pittsburgh school district have found to be both useful and effective, and conclude by presenting our plan for implementing process teaching in the remedial setting.

A CHILD'S PERCEPTION OF READING AND WRITING

One of the authors of this paper, a reading diagnostician, often assumes the responsibility for assessing reading capabilities of students. Described below is an interaction that she had with one of them.

One afternoon last September, I remember working at a small desk in a room to the left of the main office in one of my district's 50 elementary schools. Sitting across from me was a round-faced, smiling third-grade boy named Jasper. We had been together for almost an hour, and Jasper was patiently wading through each of a series of activities and tests I had selected for him in order to help me make some decisions about his reading strengths and needs. As a reading diagnostician, I had administered these kinds of assessments dozens of times before and so resisted the temptation to slip into a kind of mechanical and impersonal repetition of directions and interactions with Jasper. The tests may have been familiar and unthreatening to me — but they certainly weren't for Jasper, who was meeting me for the first time too. He demonstrated an admirable perseverance and was not showing any signs of fatigue as we worked — but I was, and so I suggested that we take a break. I asked him if he liked to read and write — a standard question I posed to most students — usually eliciting typical responses of either yes or no. Jasper's answer, however, was unique. "Yes — *and* no," he replied in a matter-of-fact tone that suggested he had somehow anticipated my question. I asked him to explain what he meant. "Yes, I like to read," he answered, "and no, I do *not* like to write. Reading is easier," he continued, pushing his glasses back up on his nose. "All you have to do is look at the words, figure out what they are — and well . . . just read them. But not writing. Writing is too hard." Jasper was winning me over with analytical third-grade confidence, and suddenly I didn't care if we finished all the testing that afternoon or not. "Tell me why writing is too hard," I persisted. "You have to think too much to write," he responded. "You have to find all the words yourself. When you read — somebody's already done that for you so you don't have to think when you read." He asked to be excused, and it occurred to me as he skipped toward the boys' room that Jasper managed to summarize at 8 years of age what teachers and researchers of reading and writing have been debating and analyzing for years. The remainder of my afternoon with Jasper was spent reading to him and inviting him to read to me. I asked him to make predictions about what we were about to read, to tell me what he already knew about the topic of the stories we chose together. As we discussed each of the passages and argued a few ideas, we discovered together the exciting and inevitable connection and interdependence of reading and thinking. Once I was able to assist him in discovering that, he looked up at me about an hour later and said, "OK — you *do* have to think a lot to read. But I *still* say writing is too hard." I tend to agree somewhat with Jasper — writing is indeed hard — but not, as he insisted, *too* hard.

CHANGES IN READING INSTRUCTION

There has been a gradual and significant departure in today's definition and understanding of reading and writing — and consequently, its instruction — from that of even 10 years ago. In her article "Some New Approaches Toward Teaching," Shaughnessy (1970) states that writing "is the act of creative reading." Such a conclusion certainly challenges teachers of reading and writing to reflect on and prepare for instructional changes. Perhaps the nature of these changes are best summarized in *Becoming a Nation of Readers: The Report of the Commission on Reading* (1985): "Research has shown that children's learning is facilitated when critical concepts are directly taught by the teacher . . . so comprehending information in textbooks is easier if students are instructed in strategies that cause them to focus their attention on the relevant information, synthesize the information and integrate it with what they already know" (p. 71). Though the notion of the integration of subject matter and its instruction is not new, the instructional strategies available to today's teachers are. The shift is characterized by a philosophical and practical commitment to the construction of meaning as opposed strictly to its instruction. If we give students opportunities, they will discover that authorship impacts and improves readership, and conversely, more practiced readers evolve into more proficient writers.

Those of us teaching reading for longer than ten years can well remember the emphasis placed on skills: teaching students to read by systematic introduction of isolated skills in the various areas of phonics, vocabulary, and comprehension; teaching students to eventually write through instruction about grammar, parts of speech, and sentence structure. The reciprocal nature of the processes of reading and writing was not yet completely recognized — let alone emphasized. The notion was that the whole reliably and inevitably equalled the sum of its parts. It seemed educationally sound to assume that successful reading would eventually result from internalized skill-acquisition, practice, and orchestration. Successful writing would likewise result from topic elaboration, errorless grammatical usage, and "correct" reproduction of character or author purpose and motivation. Yet the startling and ever-rising drop-out rate and illiteracy statistics suggest that such skill-based instruction is inadequate, or at the very least, short-sighted. That is not to imply that we do not acknowledge the importance of skills, but that we view them as a means to an end, not an end in and of themselves. Therefore, the repeated and contrived practice of an isolated reading skill for its own sake may not provide students with what they need to become effective readers.

We propose that a marriage of process and skill is essential for all students, including those who find themselves placed in remedial reading programs. Texts inspire writing by evoking students' thoughts and feelings; writing improves the knowledge, understanding, and interpretation of texts. One inevitably enhances and improves the other as process and skill are interdependent and interactive in nature. Consequently, those of us responsible for diagnosis and remediation in reading face a challenging and unique undertaking. If we no longer believe that reading and writing proficiency is best achieved through repeated practice of isolated skills in the developmental reading or English classroom, then as reading specialists we must strive for expanded remedial techniques.

TRADITIONAL APPROACH TO REMEDIATION

What might a weekly set of lessons in remedial reading have looked like for at-risk students 10 years ago? Supplementary reading laboratories, which provided practice in reading short passages, might have been used to improve literal comprehension. After teacher-directed lessons about what sequencing is, grade-leveled workbooks for practice in that skill might have been provided. Practice in differentiation between cause and effect in a series of sentences or identification of superficial main ideas in short paragraphs would have been likely as well. Sight word drills, phonetic review, and vocabulary flashcards might have been included. Little or no attention may have been given to the students's writing, since it would have been perceived as pertinent to English class. The problem remains that the set of lessons described above can still be found in remedial reading programs today!

PROCESS APPROACH TO REMEDIATION

We propose that reading specialists develop integrated language arts remedial programs that build on what we have learned about teaching reading and its relationship with teaching writing. Further, the value of listening and speaking activities must be acknowledged. Practice with these oral language activities helps to stimulate thought, improve fluency, and provide important information about students' prior knowledge. Therefore, we offer an approach to remediation based on process teaching with comprehension in reading and communication in writing as the ultimate goals.

Instructional Strategies

The model we propose, built within a context of strategy and process, strives to improve not just the child's cognitive skills, but metacognitive skills as well. Though skill deficiencies are addressed, there is not as much emphasis placed upon their isolated practice. Described below are the six specific strategies our remedial teachers in Pittsburgh have found to be most successful.

Concept Map.   The first strategy, also known as semantic mapping (Johnson & Pearson, 1984), emphasizes the stimulation and assessment of a student's prior knowledge. It serves as an excellent technique to improve receptive vocabulary, which is a critical need for at-risk students and which prepares them for reading stories in class. The group brainstorms a critical concept from the story they are about to read. The teacher records student responses in categories that might include definitions or synonyms, people, places, or consequences related to the concept (Figure 16.1). Responses are saved, displayed, and referred to frequently, adding more categories and thoughts as needed. Students can then be encouraged to write a story draft about a personal experience relating to a concept or a character in a story they have recently read. Conferences with teachers and peers follow to revise and edit the drafts in preparation for the final product. Final drafts can be "published" in student-made books and displayed in the classroom.

Story Mapping.   Story mapping is a strategy that emphasizes comprehension development by the graphic representation of important concepts and supporting details in narrative texts. In this strategy the teacher leads the class in an analysis of a story by using a map, representing each student's interpretation and memories of specific events in the text. To the extent that each map is personal and interpretive in nature, there are no absolute "right or wrong" responses. The map serves as an excellent structure for retelling and enhancing the student's sense of sequence. It also helps the student to understand cause and effect relationships within authentic contexts, while also familiarizing the student with narrative story

FIGURE 16.1. Concept map

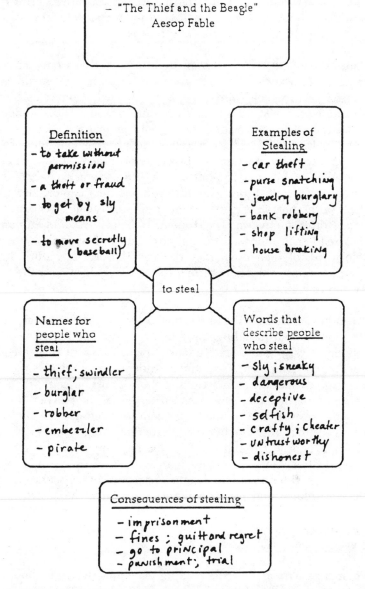

- "The Thief and the Beagle"
  Aesop Fable

to steal

Definition
- to take without
  permission
- a theft or fraud
- to get by sly
  means
- to move secretly
  (baseball)

Examples of
Stealing
- car theft
- purse snatching
- jewelry burglary
- bank robbery
- shop lifting
- house breaking

Names for
people who
steal
- thief; swindler
- burglar
- robber
- embezzler
- pirate

Words that
describe people
who steal
- sly ; sneaky
- dangerous
- deceptive
- selfish
- crafty ; cheater
- untrustworthy
- dishonest

Consequences of stealing
- imprisonment
- fines ; guilt and regret
- go to principal
- punishment; trial

Technique: Teacher leads class in brainstrorming. Teacher records
responses into these categories adding more as needed.

elements such as settings, characters, conflicts, events, and resolutions. The story map lends itself to an outline for writing as well — extending comprehension into an analysis of story themes, characters, events, ironies in problems, and resolutions. The entire process encourages critical thinking, stimulates imagination, and helps a student connect reading and writing as responses to his or her own comprehension.

Cloze Procedure.   The cloze procedure is another strategy frequently recommended for vocabulary and comprehension improvement. Students read selections in which words have been omitted at intervals, supplying the missing words. Natural reliance on context occurs as the students read or reread the selections in an effort to find logical replacements for the deleted words. Class discussions follow to analyze and review student choices, and to reveal the thought-processes of students. Cloze can be used not just as a reading activity, but as a writing one as well. Students can write their own cloze stories, deleting words of their choice, and exchanging them with another student. "Nonsense" words can be chosen to complete the stories, motivating the students to be creative and humorous. As students read each other's cloze compositions and respond to them with possible words of their own, they discover the crucial nature of logical context in writing, the strength of precise vocabulary, and the need for clarity and revision.

Dialogue Journals.   Writing is one of the best ways we have found to involve students with reading, thinking, and responding. Dialogue journals (Bode, 1989) encourage students to begin where they are already proficient and competent: speaking. Students are told to simply write down personal experiences, reactions to class discussion, and problems that are personal or academic in nature. In response, the teacher "dialogues" with them, answering any questions, commenting and sharing personal ideas and feelings of his or her own. The dialogue journal might also be kept with a "buddy" (Bromley, 1989). Teachers are often very receptive to this modification when they find it difficult to keep up with the class journals. Over time and with enough practice students improve in mechanics and usage, and perhaps more importantly, they learn to express themselves on subjects of personal interest. They learn to think and to summarize, to construct their own meaning, and to convey ideas and opinions to a specific audience.

Response Writing.   While reading selections, students should be encouraged to respond to what they have read without the threat of "right and wrong" dangling over their composing heads. Over time, students begin to compare selections, characters, and ideas, while taking more and more risks with their responses. With enough practice, they develop a style and sense of audience. When responses are exchanged and shared, students soon discover the diversity in thought and feeling that exists among their peers. For example, one second grade student responded to a story he had recently read with his classroom group, "The Three Wishes" (Swedish folktale). Later, when working with his remedial reading group, he responded by writing a short paragraph expressing his own personal wishes (Figure 16.2). His writing helped to bridge the story's content to his own life and experience, extending his comprehension by connecting the wishes of the story characters to those of his own. By writing in response to stories they have read, students begin to internalize the text's important concepts — and the fragile line of separation between text and reader diminishes more and more.

The literacy response form (Figure 16.3), developed by a local reading specialist, has proven to be effective with upper elementary, middle school, and high school remedial students. This structured form was built on the notions of Bleich (1978) who writes that students need to react to what they read in three ways: (1) describe what they as readers see in the text; (2) react to the text, discussing what they think or feel; and (3) make associations between the text and their own thoughts, feelings, or experiences.

Read-Around Groups.   Teachers who use Read-Around Groups emphasize how helpful this strategy can be in improving fluency and in helping students to see connections between reading and writing. Students share compositions, exchanging them with each other for the purpose of evaluation. Each composition is numbered, so that they remain anonymous. After writing, the class is divided into groups with a designated

Wishes

I Wish I had a Corvet and a Limo.
I Wish I had a pot of gold.
I Wish I Was Spiderman.
I Wish My eyes were gray.

FIGURE 16.2 Writing sample

FIGURE 16.3. Reading specialist M. Gardner's "Literary Response Form"

LITERARY RESPONSE FORM

NAME:_____   DATE:_____

1. I read the story entitled "_____."

    I remember (or the part I liked best was)_____

    _____

    _____

2. This part reminded me of a time when_____

    _____

3. I feel/I think_____

    _____

    _____

4. I think the whole story was_____

    _____

    _____

    because_____

    _____

    _____

This form may be reproduced. For a more "open-ended" response, the following questions can be used:

1. What part of the story do you remember? (OR What part of the story did you like best?)

2. Describe an incident you are reminded of by the part of the story you remember. (OR Describe an incident you are reminded of by the part of the story you described in the first question.) Tell the whole story!

3. What do you think about your answer to the second question? (OR How do you feel about your answer to the second question?)

4. What is your opinion of the whole story?

---

leader. The leader of each group passes its set of papers to the next group. Eventually, each group in the class reads all sets of papers except its own, until each group comes to a consensus as to which paper or papers serve as models for each set. The teacher then reads the model papers aloud and engages the class in a discussion, listing characteristics common to each one. Varied opinions are encouraged and students derive a list of criteria that they agree enhance communication and improve writing. The following day, the list of characteristics is used in revising individual papers. Students practice reading and writing, discovering as *readers* what constitutes good *writing*.

Plan for Implementation

Given the above instructional strategies, the problem remains as to how to implement them into a cohesive remedial program. The plan that we present is based on the notions of *collaboration* and the *congruence* that can be developed through that collaboration. In our plan, reading specialists must not only extend and reinforce the instruction begun by developmental teachers, but they must also initiate additional activities crucial to children's reading progress. We begin by discussing the plan as it works in Pittsburgh, in an inclass configuration, and then go on to discuss variations or modifications for use in a pullout setting.

Inclass Setting. For the purpose of illustrating a coherent program for a specific set of circumstances, we describe three third-grade children whose test results, writing samples, and performance scores typify what reading specialists might see when working with students of that age. Sight vocabulary of these students is limited, and they demonstrate little or no memory of vocabulary words repeatedly taught to them from basals. Although they may pass most phonics tests given to them, they have virtually no strategy for recognition of words in context. Their oral reading is frequently slow and labored. They have difficulty comprehending much of what they read silently or orally. Yet their listening comprehension of common and everyday topics is adequate and equally strong in both literal and inferential areas. Samples of writing produced in the classroom reveal short sentences, limited vocabulary, and little or no originality.

With this third-grade group as an example, we share an intervention strategy plan for a week's instruction by the reading specialist in conjunction with the classroom teacher (Figure 16.4). The plan, which was developed cooperatively by both the reading specialist and reading teacher, illustrates the sequential and complementary nature of classroom instruction and remediation for this group. For example, on Monday the class-

Students: Joe, Mike, Sue   Classroom Teacher: Mrs. J. Instruction   Reading Specialist: Mrs. M. Model

	Monday	Wednesday	Friday
Classroom Teacher	– Concept Map : based text story "The Storm" (review "using word "will") – Category diagram	– Read story silently – Re-read : paired-oral reading – Discussion, questions to aid comprehension, sequencing	– Guided and independent practice of skills (especially synonyms/ antonyms / sequencing of story events)
Reading Specialist	– Discuss, review concept map; focus on specific vocabulary: synonyms/antonyms – CLOZE exercises – using vocabulary of Map & Split – Dialogue journal writing (to make predictions)	– Story Map (emphasize sequencing of story events) – Activities: oral reading, writing – write summary of story using Map as guide; author. – Dialogue journal writing (personal response to story)	– Read-around – Group activity using summaries of previous class – Identify and review skills – Read – aloud – novel – Dialogue journal writing

FIGURE 16.4. Week's implementation plan

room teacher, with a larger group that includes our three students, uses a concept map during direct instruction, preparing the students to read a basal text story. In so doing, the teacher is able to access students' prior knowledge of the story's critical concepts. During the brainstorming session, the teacher complies and categorizes vocabulary words that are crucial to the understanding and enjoyment of the text. The reading specialist then begins working with the group of three by reviewing and discussing students' map responses and by focusing on specific vocabulary skills such as synonyms and antonyms of the given words. Using prepared cloze exercises in which the most critical words of the map and the text have been deleted from the sentences, the specialist guides the three students through the passages by encouraging them to predict and justify their responses. Finally, the specialist provides time for the three students to write in their dialogue journals, perhaps to make predictions about what they are about to read, using their concept map and newly acquired vocabulary as clues for logical predictions.

By Wednesday of the same week, this group of three students has read the story silently in their classroom. The classroom teacher provides opportunities for rereading, and conducts class discussions to check for comprehension of the story's main points and issues. Later, the reading specialist guides the three students in the completion of a story map, reviewing and reinforcing essential skills such as text-based sequence of events, or cause and effect relationships inherent in the story's plot. As an extension activity, the specialist encourages the students to write a summarization of the story's plot with the map as their guide. Finally, the specialist shares responses to the dialogue journal entries of Monday, verifying predictions made about the text at that time.

On Friday, the classroom teacher prepares activities for the guided and independent practice of skills taught within the context of the story. The reading specialist conducts a Read-Around Group activity using the story summaries written during the previous class for shared reading. In addition, the specialist reviews and reinforces the story's essential skills such as synonyms, antonyms, and sequencing, referring students to both the original concept and the story maps of the week. As a culminating activity for the week, the specialist reads aloud to the students, perhaps from a novel that contains similar subject matter, or that has the same author, modeling fluent and expressive oral reading.

Pull-Out Setting. How can this plan be modified for use when the remedial program exists in a pull-out setting? We assert that in many cases a similar plan (see Figure 16.4) could be used by the remedial teacher if there is close collaboration with the classroom teacher and an agreement that the total reading program for these students would be presented by the two teachers together. Teachers would need to communicate frequently, indicating possible changes or modifications in the instruction (e.g., dental checkups scheduled during the developmental reading period), and discussing student progress and needs.

However, given the realities and different contexts in which we live, this plan may need to be modified. In schools where the group coming to remediation pulls from three different classrooms or where an individual classroom teacher hasn't gotten the "word" about process teaching, reading specialists may need to implement such a program with much less involvement from the classroom teacher. In these situations, we suggest that the specialists begin by implementing the plan discussed in Figure 16.4 on their own. The need for congruence could still be met. A reading specialist could focus on the specific needs/skills identified by classroom teachers by selecting a novel or text that would be appropriate. For example, if students need help with multiple meaning words and figures of speech, any of the Amelia Bedelia (Peggy Parish) books could be used. If comprehension has been identified as a weakness, many texts can be used to generate discussion and activities related to this need. (We have had lots of success with the Ramona books written by Beverly Cleary, and with Sobel's Encyclopedia Brown novels.) Our younger readers have enjoyed predictable books such as Bill Martin's *Monday, Monday, I Like Monday* (1970), and Joanne Nelson's *There's a Dragon in my wagon* (1989). And if students have difficulty with various phonic skills, reading specialists can develop minilessons that reinforce or reteach those skills, using words from the text being discussed.

Moreover, reading specialists should continue to strive for collaboration by *sharing* their instructional strategies with classroom teachers, requesting ideas regarding the reading needs and strengths of the students, and planning related extension activities whenever possible. For example, one of our reading specialists makes a point of researching the author of the basal selections being read in the classroom and immediately gets the complete version of the story or another story by that same author for use in the remedial classroom.

SUMMARY

The described strategies and the suggested implementation plans are by no means the only ones available to teachers of process-based reading and writing. For the purpose of this chapter, however, we have tried to summarize five of the most successful strategies as reported back to us by the remedial and developmental teachers with whom we have worked over the years. Admittedly, teachers are occasionally reluctant to rely on these techniques, particularly as remedial strategies. Surely, they argue, the student needs isolated practice and drill. Yet it is the at-risk student who is most in need of the consistency of structure that the strategies of process-based teaching affords. If our remedial students would practice underlining main ideas in a workbook for an entire year, it would not guarantee their understanding of *why* the idea is indeed main, and more importantly, it would not help them to perceive subtleties of meaning, or the debatability of crucial literary concepts. Authentic texts frequently convey more than one main idea. The process-based teaching and strategies described in this chapter are an important means of improving reading and writing and of helping students to see the interrelatedness of the two processes. These strategies encourage students to use their own experiences to analyze and respond to text; they provide the practice, exposure, and imitation of teacher modeling that develops student expertise and competence with literacy tasks.

In summary, our process plan for remediation provides students with: (1) understanding of and experience with the purposes and functions of literacy, (2) experiences with authentic reading and writing activities, and (3) the combined support of both the developmental and specialist teachers that enable students to become more effective readers and writers.

REFERENCES

Allington, R. L., & Brockou, K. A. (1988). Development of shared knowledge: A new role for classroom and specialist teachers. *The Reading Teacher, 41*, 806–811.

Allington, R. L., & McGill-Franzen, A. (1988). *Coherence or chaos? Qualitative dimensions of the literacy instruction provided to low achievement children.* Final Report to U.S. Department of Education, Office of Special Education Programs (Project #G008630480). Albany: State University of New York at Albany.

Bean, R. M., Cooley, R., Eichelberger, R. T., Lazar, M. K., Morris, G. A., & Zigmond, N. (1989). *Critical features of remedial reading programs: Effects of setting on instructional practices, student activities, congruence, and achievement.* Final Report. Office of Educational Research and Improvement, U.S. Department of Education (Grant #008720233). Pittsburgh, PA: University of Pittsburgh.

Bean, R. M., & Eichelberger, R. T. (1985). Changing the role of the reading specialist: From pullout to inclass programs. *The Reading Teacher, 38*, 648–653.

Becoming a Nation of Readers: The Report of the Commission on Reading. (1985). Washington, DC: National Institute of Education.

Bleich, D. (1978). *Subjective criticism.* Library of Congress Catalog # 77–12968, ISBN 0–8018–2032–4. Baltimore, MD: Johns Hopkins University Press.

Bode, B. (1989). Dialogue journal writing. *The Reading Teacher, 42,* 568–571.

Bromley, K. D. (1989). Buddy journals make the reading-writing connection. *The Reading Teacher, 43*(3), 122–129.

Johnson, D. D., & Pearson, P. D. (1984). *Teaching reading vocabulary* (2nd ed.). New York: Holt, Rinehart and Winston.

Johnston, P., Allington, R. L., & Afferbach, P. (1985). The congruence of classroom and remedial instruction. *The Elementary School Journal, 84,* 465–477.

Kennedy, M. M., Birman, B. F., & Demaline, R. (1986). *The effectiveness of chapter services.* Washington, DC: Office of Educational Research & Improvement, U.S. Department of Education.

Martin, B. (1970). *Monday, Monday, I like Monday.* New York: Holt, Rinehart and Winston.

Nelson, J. (1989). *There's a dragon in my wagon.* Englewood Cliffs, NJ: Modern Curriculum Press.

Shaughnessy, M. (1970). Some new approaches toward teaching. In S. W. Youdovin (Ed.), *Foundations for learning: Language* (pp. 1–10). Boulder, CO: Foundations for Learning Press.

Slavin, R. E. (1987, October) Making Chapter 1 make a difference. *Phi Delta Kappan,* 110–119.

Walp, T. P., & Walmsley, S. A. (1989). Instructional and philosophical congruence: Neglected aspects of classroom coordination. *The Reading Teacher, 42,* 364–368.

CHAPTER 17

Learning Language from Story (in Three Voices): Talking, Reading, and Writing in Bilingual/ESL Classrooms

STELLA J. MATA
MODESTA BARBINA TREVINO
JULIE GUZMAN
Austin Independent School District

with
NANCY L. ROSER
JAMES V. HOFFMAN
CINDY FAREST
The University of Texas at Austin

For many children in America today, entry into a public school marks their first significant contact with the English language. In many ways these children are like most others: They are excited to learn and expect to be successful, they form new friendships easily, they regard their teachers as positive role models, and they draw from their homes the physical, psychological, and emotional support needed to sustain their efforts to learn.

But children who enter school with a first language other than English face some enormous challenges: They must negotiate the "world of school" with limited flexibility in their communication skills; they must take the same kinds of risks associated with learning a first language, but without the time and personal context that served their first-language learning; and they must consciously ignore the judgments and actions of individuals who treat them as "behind" from the very beginning lest they begin to think of themselves as likely to fail. If the school receiving the learner is inflexible, then success is unlikely. Repeated failure, embarrassment, and even ridicule may force language learners to seek shelter within themselves. And when the risk-taking stops, the learning stops. If, on the other hand, the system is flexible, if it not only accepts but builds connections between the learners' first language and the learning of English, then a successful school experience is likely if not assured.

The teachers of these children face an enormous challenge as well, for it is the teachers, through the classroom learning environment they create, who directly represent the system to the learners. What does it mean to establish a classroom learning context that is flexible and responsive to the needs of second-language learners? Over the years there have been debates (sometimes heated) as to the best ways to meet the needs of these children in schools. There are advocates for bilingual approaches (transition and/or maintenance varieties), immersion approaches, intensive ESL approaches, and so on. Although these represent very different philosophies, all share the view that some kind of special attention must be given to these children if they are to succeed. All agree that the old "sink or swim" approach is indefensible. To ignore language differences is to perpetuate a society in which those who possess a first language other than English are relegated to low social status and given limited access to the opportunities afforded by our democratic society.

We will not enter the debate in this chapter on the "best" approach for meeting the needs of second language learners. Rather, we will describe some of the rich opportunities for helping children learn language and literacy through literature. In this chapter, we look briefly into three elementary-grade classrooms in Austin, Texas, serving children for whom English is a second language. Despite the brevity of the look, you will notice that the three teachers and their students engage in language learning in joyful ways. The first, a kindergarten teacher (Ms. Guzman), uses themed literature units during storytime as a stimulus for talk, drawing, and writing. The second teacher (Ms. Trevino) uses folktales of the Latino culture as a base for storytelling, drama, retellings, writing, and discussion in her second-grade classroom. The third, a fourth-grade teacher (Ms. Mata), helps her children relish their new language as they command it. In this example, her children explore English idiom using a favorite character—Amelia Bedelia—as their language guide. In these three case accounts, each individual teacher's personal voice is prominent. We conclude the chapter by highlighting the common themes that characterize these classrooms, as well as the challenges these teachers' stories offer to all who work to meet the needs of bilingual/bicultural learners.

JULIE GUZMAN: STORYTIME AND STORY TALK

Ms. Guzman, a kindergarten teacher at Ortega Elementary School, has been helping her students grow toward literacy through the sharing of quality literature using a thematic approach, and by encouraging their divergent responses to literature through talk, writing, and the arts. These are features of a literature project titled "Language to Literacy," a program in which Ms. Guzman and the other two teachers featured in this chapter) are participants. (For a description of the program's features, see Roser, Hoffman, & Farest, 1990.)

Sharing literature is an important part of my classroom. We start each day by reading and talking about a storybook. I don't think my children are read to at home. Their parents are too busy working and trying to take care of the family. So, from the beginning, I offer them chances to listen to good books and to talk about them. Storytime this year is organized into units — related groups of books — pulled together because they encourage children to explore a theme or a subject or an author's works.

When it's time for a new unit, I put out the new books and put up what we call the "language chart" on Friday afternoon. The language chart is the huge piece of butcher paper that we use to write and dictate responses to the stories in a unit. It holds children's drawings as well. When the children arrive on Monday morning, the first thing they do is look through the new books for the storytime unit. They're curious to see what we are going to be reading!

At the beginning of the year, when I read books aloud, I translated back and forth as I saw need. Later, I just read the books in English. They understand so much now. I can tell because they ask questions or say things about the story. And, when they don't understand, they make a little face. Sometimes they ask me questions in Spanish, like "Que estaba haciendo?" ("What was she doing?") — and I know they need help, so I translate.

After we read the story, I record their ideas about it on the language chart. I put the chart on the floor and the children sit around it. We talk about the book and I write what they say on the chart. Sometimes they lie on their stomachs as I write. They like to see their language in written form. They see letters and they recognize them: "Oh, that's the letter in my name and that's the letter in my friend's name and that's the letter that starts Strega Nona's name." Sometimes they contribute in Spanish and sometimes they talk about the story in English. I record what they say in the language they use. No one would ever get the idea that it is "wrong" to answer in Spanish. They understand that you can talk about the story in either language. They like it when I write their names beside what they've said about the story. They'll say, "I said this," and they compare what they said with what others said about the book.

I think recording their ideas on the language chart helps them better understand the stories, too.

For a unit of cumulative tales, I organized a column of the chart to receive the names of the characters from the stories. At first, I didn't think they really understood what the characters were, but later, they started talking more about the characters. For example, when we read several versions of Henny Penny, they noticed when the characters were the same and when they were different and discussed it long and hard. They know a lot of authors, too. They can tell who wrote what. They talk about favorite authors, like James Marshall or Tomie dePaola, and they notice their illustrations.

Stories have become a part of their daily language. They use the words of stories in their conversations with their friends and in their writing. Sometimes at lunch I overhear story words. Recently, someone said that her neighbor was "gobbling up" his hamburger just like the Big Bad Wolf. When they go to the writing center, they write about the stories and the characters. For example, after we had read several different illustrated versions of Little Red Riding Hood, Erica wrote her own version of the story and called it "Little Pink Riding Hood." Sometimes they change the story by using their own characters and ideas. They wrote lots of stories about Henny Penny; some of them added new characters like Horsey Lorsey and Dopey Lopey.

I think they live the books. Blocks in the block center get made into beds for the three bears; they bring three chairs over, they take bowls from housekeeping, and they're off. I hear the language: "This is the small bed, the medium-sized bed, and the large bed." They play Strega Nona in housekeeping, pretending to stir a pot and saying, "Boil, boil, magic pot." And when they play school, they dress up in dresses and high heels and someone is always Miss Viola Swamp, saying things like "You do your work!"

And sometimes I notice the values from stories taking hold. After we read the George and Martha books, we were outside one day and the children were pretending to be George and Martha. I could hear them saying, "You're still my friend, no matter what happens" and things like that.

I know literature brings out the children's language because it gives us so much to talk about. There is so much in their minds and they want to express their thoughts. I know that they had heard some of the books I've read in their prekindergarten classes. They'll say, "Oh I know that book, my teachers last year read that story." But I think they saw it one way in prekindergarten, and now that they're older, they experience it another way. As we read these stories again, their language continues to grow. I think my children feel successful about themselves and their language. I think that literature brings language out.

MODESTA TREVINO: STORYTELLING AND STORY READING

Modesta Barbina Trevino is a second-grade teacher at Sanchez Elementary School. She teaches bilingual children in her morning language arts class, all of whom are labeled Limited English Proficiency (LEP) and Spanish-dominant speakers.

I grew up as a project child. I didn't have access to any books except for the basal readers in my classroom at school. Even so, my mother was a great storyteller and I became a lover of language. I'm determined that literature will dominate in my own family and in my classroom. I'm convinced of the need to provide all children, regardless of reading level, age, or language dominance, opportunities to be exposed to quality literature — to take pleasure in its content, its message, and its relevance. I see too many students who are frustrated simply because they do not meet the teacher's expectations for fluency or answer their basic comprehension questions in complete sentences. It is little wonder that children become uninterested when their growth in literacy is being accounted for solely by the number of words they read per minute.

I have always relied on literature, but this year I'm trying something different. I am using the literature that the children may be most familiar with — Mexican folktales from an oral tradition — and I'm learning to tell the stories in Spanish rather than read them. So the children's first school experience with the tales is sitting close on the story rug with the lights dimmed a bit as I take the role of storyteller. I tell them this is how I imagine the stories were originally told in the evening when people gathered after their work was done. I think my children feel comfortable in the story circle, secure, but at the same time excited by my excitement.

I'll give an example. I began a unit on Leyendas (legends) by telling a very popular legend of the Southwest, "La Llorona," or "The Weeping Woman." The legend probably originated in Mexico, but there are many different versions, all designed to explain to children the soft "weeping" sounds they will hear at night if they disobey their parents! One version tells of an Aztec mother who killed her children because she did not want them to become victims of the Spanish Conquistadors and suffer the same agony she had experienced during the Conquest. Another version explains the weeping sounds as those of a mother who drowned her children because of her frustration with their life of hardship.

After the first telling, volunteers get a chance to retell the legends in their own words. This is how Rodrigo told La Llorona (in Spanish):

Un día, había una señora que tenía dos niños que les pegaba.	One day there was this lady who had two children whom she used

Los niños tenían una mamá que no los quería, y los dejaba andar sucios. Ni los dejaba bañarse, ni les compraba ropa nueva. Se fastidió con ellos y su esposo la dejó. Se enojó, y así que los llevó a la presa a la orilla del pueblo, y los aventó a la corriente. Todas las noches se levantaba a los doce de la noche, y buscaba a sus dos niños. La gente del pueblo le tenían miedo. Siempre seguía llorando por sus hijos.

to spank. The children had a mom who did not love them and let them sometimes run around dirty. She wouldn't even make them bathe themselves, nor would she buy them new clothes. She became frustrated with them and her husband left her. This made her mad, so she took the children to a dam at the edge of town and she threw them into the water current. Every night she would wake up at twelve at night and go looking for her two children. The people from the town were scared of her. She was crying for her two children thereafter.

Retellings were followed by written and illustrated versions. The children could choose to work together or alone on those; ultimately, we assembled a class book. Both the books of legends I relied on for the storytime and others for the children to read on their own were made available to those who wanted to prepare a storytelling session. But we didn't just tell legends, we read them, too.

Another that I chose was Nuestra Senora de Guadalupe, retold by Tomie dePaola. It's the legend of the Virgin who appeared to Juan Diego in the valley of Tepeyac in 1531, and is very popular among Mexican people. The Virgin requested that Juan Diego relay a message to the bishop of Mexico, saying that a church should be constructed to honor her and her people on the same site where she had appeared. The bishop found it difficult to accept Juan Diego's request without some sign of proof. On his third visit to the bishop, Juan Diego presented a bouquet of roses, out of season at the time, and on his tilma, miraculously, was painted a picture of the Virgin.

In Yolanda's retelling, details were not unnoticed:

Cuando Diego llegó a las montañas de Tepeyac, le dijo a la virgencita lo que deseaba el obispo. Ella le dijo a Diego que fuera al lugar adonde primero

When Diego reached the mountains of Tepeyac, he told the Virgin what the bishop wanted. She told Diego to go to where they first met and there he would

se encontraron, y allí se encontraría unas rosas para llevarle al obispo. Cuando vieron las rosas en el piso y el retrato de la virgencita pintada en la tilma, dijeron que era un milagro. El obispo ordenó que construyeran una iglesia y que pusieran la tilma con el retrato de la virgen en la iglesia. Mucha gente visita a la Virgen de Guadalupe.

find roses to take to the bishop. When they saw the roses on the floor and a picture of the Virgin on the tilma, they said it was a miracle. The bishop ordered the church to be built and to have the tilma with the Virgin's picture placed in the church. Many people came to visit La Virgen de Guadalupe.

Writing, as for all of our units of literature, had different forms and purposes during the legends unit. For example, on the unit language chart, we noted the title, characters, and plot, but led by a few, we also began to discover some features of legends that surfaced in all the stories we were reading, telling, and sharing. So, literary understandings grew from reading and writing related stories. The publishing company we organized for our writing and illustrations was titled Aztecas Ediciones. It flourished during this unit study, and got renamed during the next! Yolanda Martinez, Editor-in-chief, made room for each literary and artistic contribution.

As the children read independently from the legends that surrounded them — and as they talked and wrote — I felt from them a real sense of identity with the legends and a sort of self-validation because they were sharing what they brought from their own heritage. I think they were learning, too, that their experiences are not isolated, but instead a part of a larger fabric and pattern.

STELLA MATA: TEACH US ENGLISH, AMELIA BEDELIA

Stella Mata teaches fourth grade in the same elementary school as does Modesta Trevino. She, like the other two teachers, has worked with the Language to Literacy project with the goal of making her classroom more literature-centered as children learn their second language.

About half of my students are newcomers to the United States. The other half have been enrolled in this school since first grade. Much of their instruction is in English now, but we move rather easily back and forth between languages when clarification is necessary. Recently I learned how much fun it can be to laugh about the complexity of language with the help of Amelia Bedelia (and some additional assistance from Fred

Gwynne). We have just completed a whole unit of Amelia Bedelia books, and I'd like to tell you about the fun we had. You may remember that Amelia Bedelia is the house servant who interprets all of her orders quite literally; for example, when she is told to check the towels, she actually puts check marks on them. When she is told to dress the chicken for dinner, she puts tiny clothes on the refrigerated bird. In monolingual classrooms, I suspect that children discover English idiom much sooner than do my fourth graders. But no class could have laughed harder or enjoyed Peggy Parish's works more thoroughly.

We began this unit by my reading aloud from *Amelia Bedelia* (Parish, 1963). Then we talked about the "interesting" errors that Amelia Bedelia made, and I wrote them on sentence strips. On a second reading, children gave the thumb's up sign when they realized the mistake that Amelia Bedelia was about to make. One conversation went like this:

STUDENT: She told Amelia Bedelia to ice the fish.
Ms. MATA: What's that mean? Is icing like frosting?
STUDENT: Con hielo.
Ms. MATA: Yes, why do you think Amelia Bedelia should ice the fish?
STUDENT: Fresco.
Ms. MATA: What is she doing to the fish now?
STUDENT: Scale them.
Ms. MATA: What are the scales?
STUDENT: La balansa?
Ms. MATA: No, let's draw the fish scales. [Draws on board] Now,
    what do you think "scale the fish" means?
STUDENT: Cut off the scales!

My students spent the next few minutes drawing and then explaining an idiom of their choice from *Amelia Bedelia*. When they finished, we turned Amelia Bedelia's misadventures into theater, with one group dramatizing what she was told to do and another acting out what she actually did do. "Amelia Bedelia checked the towels like this," I told them as I put a check on the board. "But Mrs. Rogers meant that she should check them by looking very carefully to see if the towels were all there and all right. I see another kind of check on Juanita's scarf. Who can tell about Juanita's check?"

As the unit went on, there was a lot of independent reading of Amelia Bedelia books (see the list of references at the end of chapter). I got books on tape for them as well. We made a class book of ridiculous idiomatic expressions, and small groups turned out their own Amelia Bedelia adventures. Fred Gwynne's *The King Who Rained*, *A Chocolate Moose for*

Dinner, and *A Sixteen Hand Horse* also helped. In the children's original books, Amelia faced difficulties like a frog in her throat and a mole on her nose.

Best of all, in this unit I watched children laugh at language play. It takes a great deal of sophistication to be able to laugh in your second language. "Do you see . . . ?" they would ask me, struggling to understand that "to prune" means to cut, not to tie prunes to the bushes. And then — chuckles, grins, and groans.

I know how difficult some will think the investigation of idiom is. I confess that sometimes translating what a particular word and phrase means in Spanish was difficult for me. But the object was always the same — to find the humor and to laugh wisely at Amelia Bedelia.

CONCLUSIONS

Several themes stand out in the comments of these three teachers that relate to successful work with literature and writing for second-language learners. The first theme is one of personal commitment and understanding on the part of the teacher. Each of these teachers has come to understand through study, firsthand experience, experimentation, and reflection what it means to move toward a literature-based program in her classroom. Not one is buying into someone else's philosophy; instead, each has developed a personal philosophy of teaching that draws on the concepts of teacher as guide, child as learner, language as constructive, and culture as emerging. These teachers are as insightful as they are articulate about what they do and why they do it.

The second theme that stands out relates to the role of literature and response to literature in the classroom. In all of these classrooms, quality literature has been placed in a prominent position in the curriculum. The quality literature includes (but is not limited to) works relevant to the cultural background of the children. The engaging qualities of literature that transcend cultures, such as humor, conflict, and triumph, provide the occasions for students to respond both individually and collectively. The students are encouraged to find themselves in these works as they construct their personal interpretations. Culture plays an important role in all literary experiences because the total literary experience includes not only the receiving of ideas (what we most typically associate with reading) but also the personal, thought-driven, emotional, psychological, and even physical responses of the reader.

The third theme is one of integration of language processes. In these classrooms, speaking, listening, reading, and writing traverse together.

The teachers as well as the students are facile in moving between Spanish and English in their interactions with one another. Connections are made as students learn language through the study of literature. They talk. They listen. They write. They read. They learn.

The fourth theme is one of pervasiveness. Although the teachers focus on literature during "language arts time" in the classroom, its influence shows up everywhere — from the dramatic play in the "housekeeping" center, to the lunch conversations, to the units of study in social studies and science. In these classrooms the lines in the lesson plan book that so neatly divide the day into subject areas are blurred as language and literature spread across the curriculum.

The fifth theme is one of joy and excitement. It is clearly evident from the descriptions of these classrooms that the students are not only engaged in important learning activities, but enjoying themselves enormously in the process. The risks that are a necessary part of all language learning are in evidence, but there is no fear of failure on the part of students. The patterned language drills that are part of many ESL programs are not in evidence in these classrooms. There is no sense of rote memorization here on the part of students. Rather, there is a sharing of ideas through language.

We suspect that these same themes can be found in *any* classroom committed to teaching literacy through literature. Perhaps the most important message to be found in the classrooms of these three teachers is that the same kind of instruction that works well for native English-speaking children works just as well for second-language-speaking children. The extra ingredient is the need for added flexibility and understanding on the part of the teacher/guide so that important linguistic and cultural connections are made in timely and developmentally appropriate ways. In this context, the diversity that these children bring with them to the classroom becomes an opportunity rather than a deficit.

REFERENCES

dePaola, T. (1980). *Nuestra Senora de Guadalupe*. New York: Holiday House.

Gwynne, F. (1976). *A chocolate moose for dinner*. New York: Simon and Schuster.

Gwynne, F. (1980). *The sixteen hand horse*. New York: Simon and Schuster.

Gwynne, F. (1988). *The king who rained*. New York: Simon and Schuster.

Parish, P. (1963). *Amelia Bedelia*. New York: Harper & Row.

Parish, P. (1964). *Thank you, Amelia Bedelia*. New York: Harper and Row.

Parish, P. (1966). *Amelia Bedelia and the surprise shower*. New York: Harper and Row.

Parish, P. (1977). *Teach us, Amelia Bedelia*. New York: Greenwillow.

Parish, P. (1978). *Come back, Amelia Bedelia*. New York: Harper Junior Books.
Parish, P. (1978). *Play ball, Amelia Bedelia*. New York: Harper Junior Books.
Parish, P. (1979). *Amelia Bedelia helps out*. New York: Greenwillow.
Roser, N. L., Hoffman, J. V., & Farest, C. (1990). "Language, literature and at risk children." *The Reading Teacher, 43*, 554–559.
Santos, R. (1975). *Tesoros de mi raza* (la llorona). Dissemination and Assessment Center for Bilingual Education. Austin, TX: Region XIII Educational Service Center.

Part V

PERSPECTIVES FROM BEYOND THE CLASSROOM

JOAN T. FEELEY, DOROTHY S. STRICKLAND, SHELLEY B. WEPNER

The greatest satisfaction for a teacher is the feeling of being rewarded by one's students. In fact, most of the time the students are the *only* source of rewards for most teachers. Isolated in their own classrooms, teachers receive feedback for their efforts from the words, expressions, behaviors, and suggestions of the students. . . . Unlike other professionals who look to colleagues and supervisors for such feedback, teachers can only turn to children. (Lieberman & Miller 1984, p. 2)

The loneliness of teaching has concerned educators for a very long time. Unlike most professions, teaching does not provide for a continuous sharing of knowledge and experience with one's peers. Having graduated from a preservice program, most teachers find themselves in a classroom armed only with a set of preselected teaching materials, a curriculum guide of some sort, and a healthy dose of optimism about what lies ahead. Interaction with supervisors, administrators, or peers frequently takes place at the most basic or superficial levels, with attention given only to the most pressing concerns of the day.

Coupled with the loneliness of teaching is its many uncertainties. Lortie (1965) has stated that teaching is fraught with "endemic uncertainties." Teachers can never be sure about the relationship between teaching and learning. Most operate with the assumption that good planning, teaching strategies, and materials will improve student learning. But, rarely do they have the time or the expertise to reflect on what "really" makes a difference. They are aware that often the best learning seems to take place when they least expect it, something they cannot always account for. It is not uncommon for teachers to operate from a knowledge base that is controversial or in the process of change. At the same time, they may find themselves in teaching situations where the goals of the school are vague and conflicting. Thus, finding a sense of direction and purpose in order to do their best is a challenge to all teachers. For teachers like those contributing to this book, however, the challenge is even greater. These teachers are attempting to forge new territory. They want to extend their knowledge base, make sense of the research, and apply what they learn to their work. These are the teachers who are most apt to reach out to their peers and the broader community of educators for support and colleagueship. They realize that, as professionals, they must look beyond their immediate classrooms to help shape policy and practice.

Today, we hear more and more about the need to restructure the schools so that all members of the school community share in making the decisions that impact upon them. Certainly, the classrooms described in this book are excellent examples of learning communities in which decision making is shared. Terms such as "shared decision making," "empowerment," "decentralization of power," and "school-based management" are frequently used to describe districtwide efforts that promote the professionalization of teachers and a spirit of collaboration and cooperation among school staffs. Such efforts may take many forms.

For example, in many school districts throughout the country, teachers are involved to a greater degree than ever before in the decisions regarding the selection and ordering of materials. This has numerous implications for teachers who are attempting to move toward literature-based instruction. While it suggests that teachers have more to say about the materials they use, it also implies greater responsibility and the need to cooperate with other teachers, librarians, and resource people to coordinate efforts and make the best use of the funds available. Increased roles in decision making mean more work and greater responsibility for everyone. Staff must be given time and opportunity to work together. They need to discuss policy and, in some cases, even to shape it. Then they must monitor their own actions to determine whether or not what they do really reflects the policy on which they agreed.

In Omaha, Nebraska, groups of up to 33 educators, holding a variety of job descriptions within the district, meet monthly in someone's home to discuss issues of common interest. The informality of a private home and casual attire was purposely selected in order to reduce the constraints sometimes incurred when people meet in a school setting. Sometimes the large group divides into smaller groups to focus more intensely on topics of mutual concern. Often, the topic under discussion involves curricular innovations such as those described in this book. "This gathering of educators, teachers, principals and supervisors, coming together on neutral turf, with limited rules or constraints, with a shared purpose of learning more about a program and supporting each other's efforts to implement that program is what collegiality is all about" (Marcuzzo, 1990, n.p.).

Throughout the country, many peer support groups have been formed by teachers who are trying new approaches and who find the support of other interested and concerned professionals invaluable. Networks among school districts are also being formed so that teachers and administrators may work together to share ideas and expertise. One such network, the Rutgers (University) Literacy Curriculum Network, is comprised of 32 school districts in New Jersey that wish to work together and with the university in order to improve literacy instruction.

It is not by accident that many of these collaborative efforts seem to have emerged simultaneously with the trend toward a process approach to literacy. Teachers who use a process approach to reading and writing are aware of the need to restructure their classrooms so that cooperation and collaboration are in evidence. They are also very much aware of their own need for collaboration and support from fellow teachers, administrators, supervisors, and the school library media specialist as they implement change. The articles in Part V, describe such efforts from a districtwide perspective. Carol Santa describes how, as language arts coordinator, she helped facilitate the transition to a more wholistic language arts program in her school district. In an interview with a school superintendent, Joan Feeley helps define the role of the supportive administrator as teachers seek to implement a process approach.

REFERENCES

Lieberman, A., & Miller, L. (1984). *Teachers, their world, and their work*. Alexandria, VA: Association for Supervision and Curriculum Development.

Lortie, D. (1965). Teacher socialization: The Robinson Crusoe model. In *The real world of the classroom teacher*. Washington, DC: National Education Association.

Marcuzzo, T. (1990). The new wave. *Collage*. Omaha, NB: Omaha Public Schools.

CHAPTER 18

Cutting Loose: A District's Story of Change

CAROL M. SANTA
Kalispell (MT) Public Schools

This is the story of change in a school community tucked among the mountains of northwestern Montana. My community, well representative of rural America, has five elementary schools, a junior high, and a high school. On the surface, everything seems peaceful and somehow timeless. Yet appearances deceive. Beneath this tranquility is a school system in the midst of a literacy evolution. Five years from now when I look back on this time of transition, I will say that these years were mostly exhilarating, the very best of times. Yet, I will also remember the tension. Changing an entire system requires patience, sensitivity, and perseverance.

Our emergence to a more holistic view of literacy followed a progression of overlapping events. The first stage involved a new awareness about literacy. While this new awareness led to instructional changes, it also created philosophical and emotional tensions. The next stage focused on resolving this tension through a districtwide research project. We began this project by building a philosophical consensus about our literacy beliefs. From here we progressed to the stage of rebuilding. This involved developing a new curriculum that would be monitored through portfolio assessments, as well as devising a plan for developing and purchasing reading materials.

A NEW AWARENESS ABOUT LITERACY

I recall well a conversation with Bill Cooper, my superintendent 6 years ago. He asked me to dream about an ideal language arts program. Where should we all be headed? For the next hour, I talked.

Children need to read more. Let's spend the money we now spend on photocopying and worksheets on purchasing books. Let's not spend money on a new basal, but channel our resources to help teachers know what readers and writers do. Our teachers need time for learning and reflection. They need more confidence in their own knowledge about literacy. Reading is not defined as skill sheets and taught for 10 to 20 minutes a day in reading groups. Literacy emerges through teacher-student collaboration. Our reading program must mirror real life.

He leaned across the table, gently grabbed my arm and said, "You can change this, Santa. Just let me know how it is going."

For the next 3 years, life in our district went relatively smoothly. We had summer reading and writing institutes and college classes after school. I began teachers-as-writers support groups and facilitated teacher-as-researcher seminars. The language arts committee decided to spend reading adoption money on purchasing classroom libraries and sets of novels. Most skill sheets and workbooks remained in shrink-wrapped packages.

Everything seemed to be working. Talk about learning and teaching filled hallways and teacher lounges. The literacy programs in a majority of our classrooms took on a different look. They were messier, always in the process of construction. In fact, I think they will always be under construction. Literacy programs emerging and evolving from ongoing teacher student collaboration can never be confined to tidy packages.

Sometimes we worried about the messiness. The old days of marching students through prescribed programs provided a sense of neat completion. We no longer had the security of specific benchmarks such as everyone completing the 2-1 reader and passing the end-of-the-year basal tests. Yet, one only had to walk into a classroom and watch children reading, writing, and talking. Children invested themselves as readers and writers.

Then, in the fall of 1988, trouble began. Polarization of philosophies festering underground now burned on the surface. It began, as do most important events, in a teachers' lounge of an elementary school. A heated discussion occurred between a first- and a second-grade teacher. The second-grade teacher had chosen to remain static in a traditional basal program. The first-grade teacher believed that reading and writing emerged as a developmental progression. She believed that children needed to write freely without the constraint of correctness on the first try, and that they should choose their own books to read.

The second-grade teacher complained about the first-grade teacher's students who were now in his class. "Your students cannot spell. They don't know important sight vocabulary in their basal reader. They do poorly on skill sheets. Why aren't you using the basal program?"

The first-grade teacher defended her position. She talked with me and her principal. We decided to set up a meeting with the two teachers involved.

We talked openly. Both views were presented. Maybe some of our children were having difficulty making the transfer from one classroom to another when programs were so different. Even more important, we did not want philosophical differences to create such tension. We wanted harmony in our schools and teachers working together. We concluded with a plan to talk about this problem at the next meeting of the districtwide language arts committee.

The language arts committee, comprising two elementary principals and teachers from all grade levels, K–12, has the responsibility for the language arts curriculum. Each school has at least one representative on the committee. Members reflect different philosophical views. Some believe in whole language, while others are wary of that approach and follow more traditional programs. We talked about the conflict between the first- and second-grade teachers and soon realized that this was only one example of a much larger problem. Many teachers worried about the inconsistencies in programs, and the effects of different instructional philosophies on our children and on teachers.

A RESEARCH PLAN

We came up with a year-long research plan to resolve issues and provide direction. This K–6 plan focuses on three overlapping areas: collection of student data, development of a consistent instructional philosophy, and decisions regarding student assessment.

Collection of Student Data

The committee decided that the logical place to begin was with our students. Our first question was whether or not there were any differences in reading achievement between literature-based classrooms, where teachers used trade books as the foundation of their reading program, and traditional basal classrooms. We decided to use standardized test data. Given that our school board stressed standardized achievement scores, we knew we would eventually have to answer this question.

Teachers advocating literature-based instruction worried about the outcome. They predicted that students in the basal programs would probably perform better on the standardized assessments. After all, the test items measured skills more similar in content and form to those found in traditional basals.

Quite surprisingly, their predictions did not hold. In fact, at every grade level, the average percentile performance of our literature-based classes was 2 to 7 points higher than the basal classes. Thus, the old argument that basal instruction was needed to foster higher test scores was not valid in our district. Our literature-based students performed exceptionally well on standardized measurements.

Next, we decided to ask students what kind of reading program they wanted. I went around to every elementary classroom and conducted a simple survey. I walked into each classroom with a new basal reader in one hand and a trade book in the other and asked them for advice about how to spend language arts funds. "Should we buy a new reading series or should we buy more books?" Children knew exactly what they wanted — books. The response in each class varied from 96% to 100% in favor of books, not basals.

The language arts committee then prepared a brief report summarizing data collected from the standardized tests and from the student survey. We included the report in a faculty newsletter sent to all teachers and administrators. The committee was now ready to proceed to the next step, the development of a language arts philosophy.

Development of Philosophy

In order to begin our discussions, we needed to know what our K–6 teachers and administrators believed about literacy. We collected this information through a survey (see Figure 18.1) that contained two sections. The first part asked teachers to indicate their current practices: the kind of reading program they were using, how they evaluated their reading program, and whether or not they felt satisfied with their evaluation system. The second part asked teachers to dream. What would they like an ideal reading program to look like? To facilitate this "dreaming," the reading committee drafted three possibilities capturing different philosophies within our own district. In effect they represent a continuum from a literature-based curriculum utilizing trade books and writing workshop (Option 1) to a traditional basal approach to teaching (Option 2). Option 3 reflects a philosophy somewhere between options 1 and 2. We left space for teachers to expand or modify each option.

The survey provided the committee with valuable information. Even though there was considerable variability among teachers and grade levels, clear trends did emerge. For example, we learned that primary-grade

FIGURE 18.1. Survey Items with Summary of Responses

This survey is designed to gather information on the various language arts philosophies and programs in our district.

Name (optional) _____

Teaching or administrative assignment _____

Part I: Current Practices

1. Check the program that you primarily use.
   _____ a. fiction and non-fiction books incorporated within cross curriculum themes.
   _____ b. basal program
   _____ c. combination of a and b
   Results: 95% of the primary teachers (K–3) responded to c; by Grade 5 a majority of teachers (60%) were using trade books as their primary program.

2. How do you primarily evaluate your reading program?
   _____ a. basal assessment tests
   _____ b. teacher and student generated assessments
   Results: From 90% to 100% of the teachers used basal assessments.

3. Are you satisfied with your assessment program?
   Results: 100% expressed dissatisfaction.

Part II: What kind of reading program do you want for the 1990s?

Below are three options. Which option best fits your own view?

Option 1: Reading and writing workshops should form the major part of a reading program. Children should spend a majority of time reading self-selected books and writing on self-selected topics. In kindergarten and Grade 1 there should be an abundance of big books for shared reading. Language experience should be a major component of the kindergarten and first-grade program. Instruction in reading comprehension and studying takes place in science, social studies, and other content areas. Science and social studies topics are incorporated within the language arts program through nonfiction trade books and literary themes.

Option 2: A reading program of the 1990s should follow traditional basal models. Children spend most of their time reading in "readers" containing short stories or excerpts of novels. Children are grouped according

(continued)

Figure 18.1
(continued)

---

to ability and progress through the basals at varying rates. English skills and content subjects such as science and social studies are separate from the language arts program.

Option 3: A reading program for the 1990s should be midway between options 1 and 2. The look of the program is similar to a traditional basal, but the focus is more on cross-integrative themes. Skills are assessed through end-of-level tests focusing on tasks demanding writing and reading, rather than fill-in-the blank activities. The anthology selections are designed to be the link to the library and novels. Students spend at least half their language arts time reading self-selected books. Class novels, smaller sets of novels, and classroom libraries should supplement the program. Content-area instruction for the most part remains separate from language arts.

Results: The majority of the primary teachers chose Option 3 (responses ranged from 100% to 60%). The Grade 4–6 teachers responded quite differently; from 60% to 75% chose Option 1.

---

teachers (K–3) responded quite differently to Question 1 than did upper-grade teachers. Most primary teachers used a combination of materials. They used some basal materials as well as novels in their program. Their responses were quite different from those of middle- and upper-grade teachers. The fourth-grade teachers were evenly divided between options "a" and "c." However, by fifth and sixth grade, few teachers were using the basal program. Most simply taught reading through trade books.

Probably the most intriguing responses were the reactions to the questions on assessment. Even teachers not using the basal materials relied on some end-of-unit tests for assessment. While few teachers used all of the assessments in the program, most used those that reflected what they felt were essential reading skills. However, none felt satisfied with their assessment program. The committee realized that changes in assessment practices must become a priority.

In Part 2 of the survey, where teachers had an opportunity to "dream," the responses followed a similar pattern, representing differences between primary and secondary teachers. Most primary teachers wanted access to a basal program. They did not want a traditional basal, but they did want some common reading materials (Option 3). The responses were quite different for the upper-grade teachers. A majority of fifth- and sixth-grade teachers felt comfortable with a total "trade-book" approach to reading (Option 1). Few teachers at any level favored Option 2, a traditional basal approach.

The committee used the information from the survey to draft a language arts philosophy statement that elementary principals then presented to their teachers at faculty meetings. During these sessions, the principal and teachers revised the statement. The language arts committee incorporated these changes into the final statement of philosophy.

Coming to a philosophical consensus turned out to be an essential first step. We now had a place to begin for making decisions about assessment and materials.

Student Assessments

Before beginning the task of developing an assessment plan, members of the language arts committee interviewed all teachers in their schools. They conducted these interviews over a 2-week period. They asked teachers for feedback on three issues: why they were so dissatisfied with current practices, why they felt a need to continue using the basal assessments, and what they thought should be done to change the testing situation. A majority of teachers wanted some form of districtwide consistency in student expectations. The basal assessments at least provided them with some sort of scope and sequence and a system of evaluation. In reality, the tests provided a needed sense of security.

The next step for the committee became clear. We needed to develop a new scope and sequence of reading and writing behaviors based on our philosophy for students at each grade level. We could then use these behaviors as a basis for developing our assessments.

We began this process by drafting an array of reading and writing behaviors for each grade level. I met with several teachers from each grade level to draft these behaviors. We came up with four overlapping categories: phonics, main ideas, literary, and reference. Under each of these areas we listed reading and writing behaviors that seemed appropriate for each grade level. The teachers and I then presented our draft to the language arts committee for their suggestions. After incorporating their ideas, we distributed the document to all elementary staff for their review. Then the committee revised again. Finally, all teachers met after school in grade-level meetings where they came to final consensus about expected literacy behaviors for their grade level. From this point, we finalized the document and began translating these behaviors into literacy processes and products that became the basis of our portfolio assessments.

The entire process of coming to consensus about student outcomes took many hours of discussion over a 5-month period. While this task was not easy, these discussions and the resulting curriculum document became the most critical part of our change efforts. Even if individual teachers disagreed philosophically, we now had a common strand for evaluating according to district expectations. Documenting expected literacy behaviors provided needed security to whole-language teachers and served to help others cut loose from basal programs. It became key to our continuing evolution. Because accountability was reduced to just a few things at each grade level, teachers felt free to move ahead with their own literacy programs.

Literacy Behaviors

The document is concise. It contains a philosophy statement, followed by a brief description of reading behaviors categorized according to grade levels (K–6). The reading behaviors fall into four areas: phonics, main idea, literary, and reference.

The kindergarten, first-, and second-grade teachers keep a record of each child's growth in phonics awareness. This information is recorded on a district-developed phonics card kept in the child's reading folder. The card simply lists phonics elements. If children use a phonics element correctly in writing workshop, they understand the element. There is no prescribed phonics sequence. Instead, teachers introduce phonics skills when appropriate to a particular reading or writing task. For the assessment, the teacher notes whether children are using a certain phonics element in their own writing and makes a note on a class chart that at some point is transferred to the child's reading card. Teachers often choose to make periodic whole-class checks. For example, if there are many words containing the letter *m* in a shared book experience, a teacher may want to focus on this letter and then evaluate whether or not the children can use *m* in their own writing. She might ask the children to take out a slip of paper or their chalkboard slates and write several words containing an *m*. The children hold up their slates and the teacher notes those who can correctly spell the *m* element in the words.

Teachers find this assessment far simpler and more direct than those found in any published materials. It also integrates phonics into practical applications.

We assess main ideas through writing and note-taking products children create. For example, in Grade 1, an understanding of main idea is evaluated by asking children to create titles for stories they write or dictate to the teacher. Similarly, one of the evaluations for main idea in Grade 3 is noting whether or not a child can write a paragraph with clearly stated main ideas and supportive details. In the upper grades, most of the main-idea assessments occur in the content areas because main-idea strategies are essential for learning key concepts in content-area learning. Coordinating reading assessments with content subjects not only insures meaningful assessments but encourages instructional integration. Some of the assessment activities include selective underlining, note-taking, conceptual mapping, and written summaries focusing on subject matter they are learning in social studies, science, or mathematics.

A third assessment area is reference, in which children indicate through library research projects that they can use dictionaries and library sources to locate and organize information for written and oral presentations.

The fourth assessment area is literary. The assessments involve retelling stories, developing story plans, and participating in literature discussions. These discussions focus on common literature or individual novel choices.

Teachers use simple checklists to monitor student progress in these behaviors. In most cases, students staple the checklists to their reading folders and keep track of their own progress. Students keep examples of their work in folders that teachers share with parents during conferences.

Creating a united K–6 philosophy, specifying a sequence of reading behaviors, and developing assessments turned out to be an effective research plan. Teachers felt more cohesive, and tension subsided. Having a common thread made all of us feel more comfortable. We were now ready to make some decisions about reading materials.

READING MATERIALS

The language arts committee decided that we would continue to have a basal program available in each building as one of many teaching resources. Teachers choose how to use the program, but no district money would be spent on workbooks or skill sheets. The committee also increased the number of trade books available through the libraries. We acquired nine more classroom sets of trade books for each grade (see novel list at the end of this chapter), and schools increased their purchases of single titles for classroom libraries.

THE FINAL CHAPTER

We continue to evolve a literacy program based on trade books, writing workshop, and our sequence of reading behaviors. In fact, my teachers and I have just received a grant from a publishing company (Kendall-Hunt Publishing Co.) to write about our program for national dissemination.

Currently, there are about 20 of us trying to capture what we do in our classrooms on paper. As we write, we learn more about how to teach and become more committed to an integrated, cross-curricular approach to literacy where children read "real books" and write on "real" topics.

When I think back on the changes that have occurred in my own district, my primary conclusion is that we can all celebrate our own growth. Yet, the evolution has not been easy. There will always be some heat lightning on the horizon as we argue, compromise, and struggle. Our faculty lounges continue to host lively debates about literacy as we learn from one another. Who knows what the next 5 years will bring? I predict that our story of change will never have a final chapter.

BOOK LIST

Grade 1

Ahlberg, A., & Ahlberg, J. (1986). *Each peach pear plum*. New York: Viking Press.
dePaola, T. (1975). *The Cloud Book*. New York: Holiday House.
dePaola, T. (1983). *The legend of the bluebonnet*. New York: G. B. Putman & Sons.
Freeman, D. (1968). *Corduroy*. New York: Viking Press.
Giff, P. (1982). *Today was a terrible day*. New York: Viking Press.
Keats, E. J. (1962). *The snowy day*. New York: Viking Press.
Lobel, A. (1970). *Frog and toad are friends*. New York: Harper.
Lobel, A. (1972). *Frog and toad together*. New York: Harper.
Mayer, M. (1943/1968). *There's a nightmare in my closet*. New York: Dial Press.
Miles, M. (1971). *Annie and the old one*. Denver: Little.
Sendak, M. (1963). *Where the wild things are*. New York: Harper.
Steig, W. (1969). *Sylvester and the magic pebble*. New York: Simon & Schuster.
Syrat, M. (1983). *Angel child, dragon child*. New York: Scholastic Inc.
Viorst, J. (1972). *Alexander and the terrible, horrible, no good, very bad day*. New York: Atheneum.

Grade 2

Bulla, R. (1987). *The chalkbox kid*. New York: Random House.
Cauley, L. (1979). *Ugly duckling*. Orlando: Harcourt Brace Jovanovich.
Howe, D. (1979). *Bunnicula*. New York: Atheneum.
Howe, J. (1983). *Celery stalks at midnight*. New York: Atheneum.
Lobel, A. (1970). *Frog and toad are friends*. New York: Harper.
Milne, A. A. (1927). *Now we are six*. New York: Dutton.
Minarik, E. (1957). *Little Bear*. New York: Harper.
Ness, E. (1966). *Sam, Bangs and moonshine*. Boston: Holt.
Parish, P. (1963). *Amelia Bedelia*. New York: Harper.

Peet, W. (1970). *Whingdingdilly*. Boston: Houghton Mifflin.

Sandine, J. (1981). *The long way to a new land*. New York: Harper.

Schertle, A. (1989). *William and Grandpa*. New York: Lothrop, Lee & Shepard Books.

Schlein, M. (1989). *Jane Goodall's animal world: Pandas*. New York: Aladdin Books.

Sharmat, M. (1982). *Nate the Great and the snowy trail*. New York: Coward McCann.

Small, S. (1985). *Imogene's antlers*. New York: Crown.

Sobol, D. (1975). *Encyclopedia Brown*. New York: Dutton.

Wilder, L. I. (1932). *Little house in the big woods*. New York: Harper.

Grade 3

Aardema, V. (1975). *Why mosquitoes buzz in people's ears*. New York: Dial Books.

Burch, R. (1980/1925). *Ida Early comes over the mountain*. New York: Viking Press.

Cleary, B. (1984). *Ramona forever*. New York: Morrow.

Cleary, B. (1981). *Ramona Quimby, age 8*. New York: Morrow.

Clymer, E. (1973). *Santiago's silver mine*. New York: Dell Publishing.

Dahl, R. (1961). *James and the giant peach*. New York: Knopf.

Dallinger, J. (1981). *Spiders*. Minneapolis: Learner Publications Co.

Fritz, J. (1974). *Why don't you get a horse, Sam Adams?* New York: Schart Hyman.

MacDonald, B. (1947). *Mrs. Piggle-Wiggle*. Philadelphia: Lippincott Co.

MacLachlan, P. (1984). *Sarah, plain and tall*. New York: Harper.

McCloskey, R. (1914/1943). *Homer Price*. New York: Viking Press.

Peterson, J. (1967). *The Littles*. New York: Scholastic.

Rockwell, T. (1973/1976). *How to eat fried worms*. New York: Dell Pub.

Shreve, S. (1984). *The flunking of Joshua T. Bates*. New York: Scholastic Inc.

Wilder, L. I. (1933). *Farmer boy*. New York: Harper.

Wilder, L. I. (1935). *Little house on the prairie*. New York: Harper.

Wilkie, K. E. (1904/1969). *Helen Keller*. New York: Bobbs-Merrill.

Wilcox, C. (1988). *Trash*. Minneapolis: Carolrhoda Books, Inc.

Grade 4

Blume, J. (1972). *Tales of a fourth grade nothing*. New York: Dutton.

Butterworth, O. (1956). *Enormous egg*. Boston: Little.

Cleary, B. (1950). *Henry Huggins*. New York: Morrow.

George, J. C. (1972). *Julie of the wolves*. New York: Harper.

Jones, C. (1984). *Cricket in Times Square*. Nashville: Ideals Pub. Corp.

Lauber, P. (1988). *Lost star*. New York: Scholastic.

Lewis, C. S. (1963). *The lion, the witch and the wardrobe*. New York: Macmillan.

McSwigan, M. (1942). *Snow treasure*. New York: Dutton.

Mowat, F. (1961). *Owls in the family*. Denver: Little.

O'Dell, S. (1960). Island of the blue dolphin. Boston: Houghton.

Park, B. (1987). *The kid in the red jacket*. New York: Alfred A. Knopf.

Grade 5

Babbitt, N. (1969). *The search for delicious*. New York: Farrar, Straus.
Babbitt, N. (1975). *Tuck everlasting*. New York: Farrar, Straus, Giroux.
Brink, C. (1935). *Caddie Woodlawn*. New York: Macmillan.
Burnford, S. (1960). *Incredible journey*. Boston: Little.
Byars, B. (1970). *Summer of the swans*. New York: Viking.
Cleary, B. (1983). *Dear Mr. Henshaw*. New York: Morrow.
Fleischman, S. (1986). *The whipping boy*. New York: Greenwillow Books.
Forbes, E. (1943). *Johnny Tremain*. Boston: Houghton Mifflin Co.
Hamilton, V. (1968). *The house of Dies Drear*. New York: Macmillan.
Lawson, R. (1939). *Ben and me*. Boston: Little.
L'Engle, M. (1962). *Wrinkle in time*. New York: Farrar, Straus & Cudahy.
MacLachlan, P. (1988). *The facts & fictions of Minnie Pratt*. New York: Harper.
O'Dell, S. (1960). *Island of the blue dolphins*. New York: Dell Publishing.
Paterson, K. (1977). *Bridge to Terabithia*. New York: Crowell.
Raskin, E. (1978). *The westing game*. New York: Dutton.
Rawls, W. (1976). *Summer of the monkeys*. New York: Doubleday.
Speare, E. G. (1983). *The sign of the beaver*. Boston, Houghton Mifflin.
Sperry, A. (1940). *Call it courage*. New York: Macmillan Co.
Taylor, S. (1972). *All of a kind family*. Chicago: Follett.

Grade 6

Banks, L. R. (1930). *The Indian in the cupboard*. New York: Doubleday.
Burnett, F. (1915). *The secret garden*. New York: Grosset & Dunlap.
Fitzgerald, J. D. (1972). *The Great Brain at the academy*. New York: Dial.
Fritz, J. (1982). *Homesick: My own story*. New York: Putnam's.
George, J. C. (1959). *My side of the mountain*. New York: Dutton.
Gipson, F. (1957). *Old Yeller*. New York: Harper.
Juster, N. (1929/1961). *The phantom tollbooth*. New York: Random House.
Latham, J. (1955). *Carry on Mr. Bowditch*. Boston: Houghton Mifflin.
L'Engle, M. (1962). *A wrinkle in time*. New York: Dell Pub. Co.
London, J. (1904). *Call of the wild*. New York: Grosset & Dunlap.
Paterson, K. (1978). *The great Gilly Hopkins*. New York: Thomas Y. Crowell.
Paulsen, G. (1984). *Tracker*. New York: Bradbury Press.
Steinbeck, J. (1937). *The red pony*. New York: Viking Press.
Taylor, T. (1969). *Cay*. New York: Doubleday.
Wyss, J. D. (1963). *Swiss family Robinson*. New York: Airmont.
Yep, L. (1975). *Dragonwings*. New York: Harper.

Any Grade

Cole, J. (1987). *The magic school bus inside the earth*. New York: Scholastic Inc.
White, E. B. (1952). *Charlotte's web*. New York: Harper.

CHAPTER 19

Transition in a Suburban District: An Interview with Its Superintendent

JOAN T. FEELEY
William Patterson College

John LaVigne is Superintendent of Schools in River Edge, New Jersey, a middle-class suburban district of 700 students in two K–6 schools. During his 19 years as superintendent, he has seen several curriculum innovations come (mainly from the top) and go, such as Wisconsin Design, Individualized Prescriptive Instruction (IPI), and Programmed Learning. He believes they failed because they were ideas that came from outside the system (usually state promoted) rather than from within the ranks of the professional staff, and also because they were based on a simplistic, reductionist philosophy. On the other hand, because process writing and reading, based on a whole-language philosophy, came to his district through the interest and efforts of his own teachers, it seems to be catching on. In the following interview, this superintendent tells about change in his district.

How did you first become aware of the process approach to teaching writing and reading?

Well, let me backtrack a bit. In 1982–1983, we became involved in the Thinking Skills Project developed by John Barell at Monclair State College. I didn't want to foist anything on the teachers. I wanted them to take control of their own destiny. Since they were interested in staff development in this area, I gave them my fullest support but told them that they would have to take the ball and run with it.

A Thinking Skills Committee was set up and charged with preparing its own budget and selling it to the board. They found it a real education: The committee had to work harder than ever before writing rationales, making presentations, and generally taking the initiative. Also, they knew they would have to take the credit or the blame for the outcome. But they knew I would be with them either way.

Well, they won, and our Thinking Skills Committee is still active and recognized nationally. They have presented at ASCD conferences and local workshops and have taught college-sponsored graduate courses for area educators. However, we all became somewhat disenchanted with the thinking skills movement when workbooks to teach thinking began to appear. I was saying, "Let's get rid of the workbooks in reading and language arts," and now there was a suggestion for yet another set of workbooks. And to teach *thinking*, no less! I was ready to hit the roof.

Then along came Erika Steinbauer, a basic skills teacher. (She was really a reading teacher, but we eliminated the reading positions and called them basic skills teachers to meet state mandates.) Erika had been to conferences at Columbia University and other colleges like your William Paterson and was all excited about teaching writing as a process. She had interested a few teachers and, taking the lead from the successful Thinking Skills Committee, set up the Writing Process Committee in 1985. Interestingly, teachers, too, were tired of all the workbooks and wanted a new approach.

Teaching writing through a workshop approach was a natural way to teach writing, with kids drafting, reading their writing to others, revising, editing, and publishing their work. They mainly needed paper, pencils, folders, and time to write. It made so much sense. Starting in the primary grades, process writing moved slowly upward, with teachers who were excited about the results jumping on the bandwagon.

By 1987, some were ready to look at our reading program with new eyes, having learned so much about the connections between reading and writing through conducting their own writing workshops.

What did you do first to encourage a process approach?

Well, we gave the Writing Process Committee our support. It didn't need as much support as the Thinking Skills groups because we had learned so much from their work. Our teachers now *knew* they had power, that they had some control over what they do in their classrooms.

The Writing Process Committee set up workshops and got us to focus on writing for in-service days, hiring consultants and speakers to spread the word. In the summer of 1985, Sue Smith, a teacher from Glen Rock who was also a trainer from the Teachers College (TC) Writing Project at Columbia, introduced our primary teachers to process writing, following up throughout the next school year. Jim Evers, a Grades 6 through 8 teacher from Ho-Ho-Kus, taught our middle- and upper-grade teachers. This was all done with board approval. The committee sold the board and parents from the start. Again, we didn't say that everyone *had* to teach writing as process, but we encouraged those willing to try.

In 1986, the Writing Process Committee wrote a new curriculum guide, which has become a model for other districts in our area. This guide spelled out how to teach writing as a process and helped to set the tone. As superintendent, I made it clear that this was the way we would like to go, but I still did not mandate total change. (Some teachers continued to hang on to their language arts workbooks.)

Where are you now and where do you see your district headed?

A big break came in 1987 when Erika Steinbauer became our full-time Staff Development Coordinator. I recommended this new position, which was encouraged by the state, to our board, and they agreed to fund it. River Edge was among the first 100 districts to have a staff developer and probably the first for its relatively small size. A common philosophy, centered around a whole-language, process approach, permeated our staff development from then on.

Erika held this position through mid-1989, when she became principal of one of our schools. She still remains active in the transition process as a member of the expanded Reading-Writing Committee and as a teacher of our in-service courses. The staff development position has been filled by another staff member aligned with the process philosophy. My plan is to have her serve for about 2 years and then go back to the classroom or serve elsewhere as an administrator. (She is presently in a graduate program in curriculum design and administration at TC.) I will then look for someone new from the ranks to fill this position, which has become, in effect, an administrator-in-training slot in which teachers with potential can have a chance to try out working at a different level and then move on.

Besides continuing staff development in areas such as using literature to teach reading, we have invited authors like Trinka Hakes Noble and Janet Craig (*Chuckles* magazine) and storyteller Kathryn Farnsworth to visit our schools so that our children could interact with professional writers and readers. We have continued to make writing and reading through whole-language activities major curriculum goals. Also, we produce *Quill Questions*, a publication written by and for the school staff, so that our teachers can improve their own skills as writers.

As for where we're going, I see more and more teachers getting on board as children come to them from whole-language classrooms and expect to continue writing in a workshop atmosphere and reading lots of children's books. Even reluctant teachers are beginning to see that they can no longer comfortably be the center of the circle but must become a part of the circle as kids become more independent learners who don't want the teacher to just tell them everything.

To get back to curriculum development, in 1987, the Writing Process Committee became the Reading-Writing Committee, and the focus moved to examining the way we have been teaching reading. We had been using a basal approach, more or less, for years. The process writing teachers introduced the idea of a literature-based approach (which some said was not all that new since we had always used children's books along with our basals). But now they were talking about using children's books in a more direct way. Over the past two summers, teachers have been writing informal teaching guides to go with favorite books, and literature units have been developed for each grade level. Multiple copies and class sets of these titles have been purchased and put into classrooms where they are welcomed.

What are your goals for the next few years?

We expect to have a new reading-writing curriculum in place in the early nineties. The goal will be to have the reading-writing process as the center, with a basal system as backup and support. For 3 years now we have had a reading-writing network of teachers (over 20 a year) who meet once a month for 2 hours after school to share strategies for using literature and discuss process teaching research projects. This network has given us a common basis for a whole-language philosophy.

We can't throw off the basal completely because some teachers really need it. The Reading-Writing Committee is presently looking for a new basal for the primary grades. Two series are being piloted this year, D.C. Health and Silver-Burdett/Ginn. These two series both appear to use "real" literature, and writing activities are woven into each unit. At the lower grades, shared reading experiences are provided.

Basals will be ordered only for those who really want them. In fact, we are encouraging teachers to look very closely at all components and order only those pieces they really need. For example, some may order only the pupil editions (PEs), while others may still want the PEs and workbooks. We do not expect to spend a lot of money on purchasing a complete basal system and would like to avoid ordering disposables like workbooks. Some teachers will continue to develop their own whole-language programs around selected literature units.

How do you go about purchasing materials?

After we know our budget, our two principals work with their staffs, allocating equal appropriations across grades. Teachers can use their shares to buy basals, trade books, big books, magazines, or whatever print materials they think they will need. They are encouraged to consult with parents and to keep track of children's interests, so that materials reflect the needs of their students.

There is wide input in materials selection. Of our 50 plus professionals, about 20 classroom teachers and support staff are involved in the work of the Reading-Writing Committee. They meet regularly in both schools to share information about children's books and professional reading. Some of our best contributors are support people such as the art, physical education, gifted and talented, resource room, and basic skills teachers, along with the librarians. These special area people see writing, reading, and thinking as essential to all learning.

How have your children responded?

Enthusiastic, that's the word to describe our children. They love to write, to read what they write to others, and to read real books. In sheer quantity, they are reading more than ever before. Besides teachers promoting the reading of literature, the PTO sponsors reading contests such as Read-a-thon, and the librarians offer an authors-in-the-schools program. All help to create the awareness and drive to read. Kids have responded readily because they know teachers, parents, librarians, and principals are involved.

Also, our children see themselves as authors, with their published works appearing in the school and class libraries. They are more independent learners who don't need teachers to tell them what to do every step along the way. Peer conferencing has made our kids more cooperative; they have learned that they can get more done when they work together.

How have test scores been affected?

For years we have been using the Stanford Achievement Test, updating when newly normed versions appeared. We have consistently scored near the top in the reading and language subtests. There has been no perceptible change since our whole-language transition; our students continue to score in the 80th and 90th percentiles.

We are looking for a survey test that might better match our new curriculum. Presently, there is a joint committee, made up of representatives from our town, a neighboring town, and the regional schools we feed, charged with recommending a new districtwide test.

How have your parents responded?

Early on, the Writing Process Committee involved the parents by making presentations at PTO meetings, inviting parents to participate in writing workshops, and welcoming parents as volunteers in classroom writing workshops. Parents became our best supporters, at first appreciating the emphasis on more writing and later the concentrated focus on children's literature in the reading program. We continually consult parents and invite them to serve on our committees as a valuable resource. All parents, even those who don't participate directly, are kept informed through our newsletter, *Chalk Talk*, published four times a year. The Reading-Writing Committee, along with others, report what they are doing and encourage response.

How do you handle the evaluation and grading?

We look at skills globally. Teachers have been trained in holistic scoring of writing samples, and we keep benchmark samples in children's cumulative records. The writing folders provide plenty of examples for teachers and parents to look at when evaluating how children are developing as writers.

As for reading, teachers keep records of books read. Group and class book records go in children's files to avoid repetition of titles. (Teachers agree on which books will be used at each grade level when they develop literature units.) The quality of children's responses to their reading is also considered. We don't do the old book reports; we look for reflective thinking and personal response.

While we still use traditional report cards with letter grades, our teachers, who are constantly involved in in-service training and networking, are better informed about how to judge student achievement.

What are your frustrations, and how are you dealing with them?

Of course, there is continuing concern over teachers who won't change, the ones who can't survive without a basal reader and all its components. But I think that it's only a matter of time. Through continuing staff development, we're picking away at the edges. There has been almost a complete turnover of staff during my tenure here, and most new people who have been hired in recent years are open and amenable to change. The others will eventually join the group or retire.

What advice would you give superintendents who want to move into process writing and reading?

First, join the circle and learn with and from your staff. Get out of the position at the top and stop dictating down. Find good, knowledgeable people and bring them along. Be secure as a leader-participator; if you're not secure, you'll have trouble giving up power.

In New Jersey, the power now resides in law and administrative codes, and interpretation is in the hands of the state department. State monitoring procedures are burying us in mounds of paperwork and eating up precious time that we could be spending with teachers and children in classrooms.

But teachers still have power. When they close the doors of their classrooms, they can create literate environments, reading and writing with their kids. They need to take control by initiating and working for change through strong committees. Superintendents should recognize the leaders, support them, and then let them go.

Many teachers are still very dependent on administrators for guidance. They need to know where you stand and what you want. You have to let them know that you want them to take the initiative and that you will support them. Also, you need to have an identifiable philosophy yourself.

Promoting a process approach never became a union issue with us because of the success of the original committee. Early on, we diffused any concerns that all would be *bound* to change because of the Writing Process Committee's recommendations. And we kept our word, so the work of the Writing Process and Reading-Writing Committees was received with open minds. Teachers still have the power, the control over how they teach reading and writing in our district, but, as we continue our staff development and committee networks, many are making informed choices to change.

Epilogue: A Model for Change

JOAN T. FEELEY, DOROTHY S. STRICKLAND,
SHELLEY B. WEPNER

The teachers and administrators who have spoken through these pages look at children first and curriculum second. They are concerned about children's developmental needs, interests, and choices, and they want them to learn to read and write through authentic experiences with the world of print, especially through exposure to fine literature. They set the stage by modeling, providing a literate environment, and acting as facilitators and mentors as their students interact with written language, ideas, and each other. Reading and writing develop in tandem and in collaborative settings with peers and teachers providing reaction and feedback.

While the process—the act of learning by doing—receives prime focus, the product is not ignored. These educators talk about all kinds of products, such as poems, nonfiction pieces, stories, response logs, book reviews, and journal entries. These are shared for reaction and then, if important to the authors, revised and edited through a *process* of refinement, so that the product speaks to its defined audience.

Showing a strong sense of how the intellect works, the authors of these chapters are concerned about the integration of learning. They speak of thematic studies, with print and the world at large forming a resource pool from which children gather and organize knowledge. They speak of author studies in which children become immersed in the work of specific writers, such as Judith Viorst and Pat Hutchins in the primary grades, Roald Dahl in the middle grades, and Lois Lowry and S. E. Hinton in the upper grades. By comparing and contrasting the work of professionals, these young readers and writers ultimately add to their own literary development. Genre studies, too, are a recurrent theme. Children read historical fiction to learn history through narrative and to study the literary genre itself. They inspect the many ways that authors write nonfiction, with an eye toward writing informational pieces in new and interesting ways. They

251

can speak knowledgeably about personal narrative, picture books, realistic fiction, science fiction, and other popular genres.

And these educators readily acknowledge their roots. Several mention being introduced to the concept of process teaching by attending workshops at Martha's Vineyard, the Writing Project at Teachers College, or professional conferences such as those given by the National Council of Teachers of English or the International Reading Association. Those who did not have firsthand experiences with leaders who spearheaded the writing-as-process movement in the elementary school acknowledge reading articles and books by these researcher-practitioners. They learn from each other, too, often forming schoolwide or districtwide networks to meet, to share, to grow as teachers. They are an active, involved community of learners who are never satisfied with the status quo. In this book we see an exciting picture of classrooms, schools, and districts in transition from lock-step basal reading and skill-oriented composition programs to reading-writing workshop approaches centered around literature.

But how does this portrayal differ from the vast majority of American schools? According to a new National Assessment of Educational Progress (NAEP) report (Langer, Applebee, Mullis, & Foertsch, 1990), the major emphasis in beginning reading at the primary level is on phonics-based, skill-driven instruction. Even by Grade 4, instruction is focused on a single basal reader, with books and magazines used only as supplements. While more than three-quarters of these students are assigned to ability-based reading groups, more than one-fourth are rarely asked to discuss what they read in small groups. Workbooks and skill sheets are still widely used in Grade 4: 57% receive assignments such as these every day, and 40% receive vocabulary drill daily. Teachers report using these skill materials (especially with low groups) more than any other instructional resource. Analyzing, discussing, or writing about what was read are not emphasized.

And what kind of readers are these basal-driven, skill-oriented programs producing? According to the NAEP report, reading proficiency, as measured by questions on overall meaning and details, increases substantially from Grades 4 to 8 but less dramatically between Grades 8 and 12. At all levels, students have difficulty with higher-level reasoning questions that require explanation or elaboration.

Although literate, in that they can perform everyday reading and writing tasks, American students are not readers, certainly not aspiring to join Purves' (1990) "scribal society" of producers and consumers of the world of print. They report doing very little reading for school (10 pages or fewer a day) and even less for enjoyment or self-enrichment. In fact, the NAEP report indicates an inverse relationship between interest in reading and grade level. While three-fourths of the fourth graders read for fun once a week, only one-half of the twelfth graders report reading for pleasure on a weekly basis. Library usage follows a similar pattern. Although two-thirds of the fourth graders use the library weekly, only 24% of the eighth graders and 12% of the twelfth graders frequent the library regularly.

The report gives some information about the teachers in these American schools. For instance, according to demographic data, the fourth-grade reading teachers are experienced and well trained, but their expertise is apparently not trusted by administrators. The teachers reported that while they had control over the sequence of classroom instruction, they had little choice about what to teach. Curricula, which are expected to be followed, are usually tied to basal reader scope and sequence charts.

In contrast, the educators in this book are in control of what their students are learning. Trade books have replaced basals as the centerpiece for instruction. Response logs and journals have supplanted skill sheets and workbooks. Every day children are challenged to think critically and creatively about what they are reading because they are engaged in reading-writing tasks that stimulate higher-level thinking. And they want to read and write because they have some choice in selecting topics and books.

Informed by a wealth of research-based information on how children learn language, both oral and written, and how they grow in knowledge, teachers started in small ways, often beginning with writing workshop and moving to reading workshop, with literature and the children's own writing as instructional materials. Library media specialists became important sources for information on children's books and authors. Administrators recognized the inadequacies in present programs and encouraged teachers to work together to change curricula and, more importantly, the philosophy behind the curricula. They talk about "moving away from the center" and "avoiding top-down decisions" in order to promote a community of teachers and learners who have the commitment that goes with involvement in decision-making. This spirit is consistent with the school-based management movement that is sweeping the country. New York City School Superintendent Fernandez, who brought site-based management to Florida schools, is currently advocating the movement in the New York schools.

What can you, our readers, do to become a part of the "quiet revolution" that is going on in American schools? Based on the experiences reported by the authors of the chapters in this book, we offer the following guidelines:

For Teachers

• Immerse yourself in the literature concerning teaching reading and writing as process. The chapters in this book that deal with your teaching level or special area are a good place to start; their reference lists provide invaluable sources for further reading.

• Visit classrooms of teachers who are using literature-based, process approaches.

• Get to know a solid collection of children's books and authors so that you will not be dependent on basal readers for materials for your reading/writing programs. To do this, consult your school library media specialist or local children's librarian. You may also consider taking a refresher course on children's literature at a nearby college.

• Start by replacing your language arts composition program with a writing workshop. Depending upon your grade level, read Graves, Calkins, or Atwell, to help you with the mechanics of organizing a workshop.

• Move away from a prescriptive use of basals when you feel comfortable with a workshop situation. Use them as anthologies, giving children choices about which stories to read. Model and encourage response to stories via reading logs and discussion groups. Once you gather books by buying and borrowing, introduce these as choices to be read individually or in groups. For beginners, look for "big books" to share and model reading (see resources mentioned in primary section).

• Keep your administrator informed and enlist other teachers to join you in attending conferences and planning for in-service courses. Network with other teachers, sharing ideas and books, both children's and professional.

• Evaluate continually what is happening in your classroom. Keep notes and logs so that you can augment what works and delete what doesn't. Look for alternative ways of reporting children's progress.

• Inform parents face-to-face and through newsletters about what you are trying to do. Invite them to "Celebrate Writing" assemblies and author visits so that they, too, will "get the spirit."

For Administrators

• Read some of the seminal works suggested in this book (e.g. Graves, Atwell, Calkins) to become familiar with a process philosophy.

• Visit classrooms in which teachers are experimenting with process reading/writing. Start with your own district and move to others that are recommended. Take notes and ask questions of the teachers and administrators in other districts. Find out how they got started, how they moved ahead, what they are doing now. Set up collaborative networks with other administrators.

• Invite all teachers who are interested in change to attend round-table discussions. Have a predictable structure with real information being shared by teachers, staff developers, or outside consultants; encourage interclass visits.

• Initiate work on the reading/language arts curricula, suggesting that they be aligned with the latest research in language learning.

• Establish an instructional leader within your school or district (usually a teacher who has been successfully using a process approach) to head up the reading/writing committee and to help teachers by demonstrating in their classrooms.

• Involve the school library media specialists as resource personnel. Encourage them to work with individual teachers or small groups of grade-level or special-area teachers to bring books into the classroom and initiate action research. Periodically, they can present information about books, authors, and school-based reading initiatives at faculty meetings.

• Encourage teachers to spend their budgets on children's books; arrange for visits by children's authors.

• Start Silent Sustained Reading in your school and encourage students to share their writing with each other in class or with others in school assemblies.

• Inform parents by informal talks at parent meetings and through newsletters.

• Encourage teachers to attend appropriate conferences given in your area; support efforts to network, and provide continued staff development.

Process-centered teaching is not magical; it simply requires a belief that present-day prescriptive approaches are not necessarily the best for children in American schools. We hope that by reading this book and saying to yourself, "I can do this," you will find a way to initiate change in your classroom, school, or district.

REFERENCES

Langer, J. A., Applebee, A. N., Mullis, I. V. S., & Foertsch, M. A. (1990). *Learning to read in nation's schools: Instruction and achievement in 1988 at Grades 4, 8, and 12*. Princeton, NJ: National Assessment of Educational Progress.

Purves, A. C. (1990). *The scribal society*. New York: Longman.

About the Contributors

AL ALIO teaches at the State University of New York at Stony Brook and also is on the English faculty of the Hauppauge Middle School, Hauppauge, New York. He has co-authored journal articles and book chapters, and his special interests include computer education, creative writing, journalism, and storytelling.

MAUREEN W. ARMOUR is a lecturer at the University of South Florida at Fort Myers and a supervisor of teacher interns in Collier County, Florida. As an elementary school teacher in New Jersey, she taught reading and writing to middle graders and conducted teacher-training workshops and seminars. She has co-authored a book for reluctant readers, written for a basal reading program, and has been published in *Language Arts*.

RITA M. BEAN is Professor of Education at the University of Pittsburgh and Director of the Institute for Practice and Research in Education. Before coming to the university, she taught in an elementary school and served as reading specialist and reading supervisor. Her publications include research and applied articles specifically focused on the role of the reading specialist, remedial reading programs, and instructional procedures for teaching children and adults with reading problems. She is co-author of a monograph, *Effecting Change in School Reading Programs: The Role of the Reading Specialist*, and is a co-author for a basal program. Currently she is studying the effects of an integrated language arts model for teaching literacy and is also involved in several research projects focused on adult literacy instruction.

JANE BEATY is an Apple Classroom of Tomorrow (ACOT) special education/resource teacher for the Metropolitan Public Schools of Nashville, Tennessee. She was a former elementary classroom teacher in Kentucky schools and a special education teacher in New York and Minnesota. Author of *Link to Literature*, she is currently co-authoring a resource guide/computer program based on children's tradebooks and real-life issues. She also is participating in an Apple Computer–sponsored study of the impact of technology on classroom writing programs.

FREDERICK R. BURTON is principal of Granby Elementary at the Worthington City Schools in Worthington, Ohio. He received his Ph.D.

from the Ohio State University, where he completed his dissertation as a classroom teacher of a literature-based, third-and-fourth-grade combination class. Having written over 20 articles and chapters of books, he teaches graduate courses at the Ohio State University on literature-based reading, the writing process, and whole language curriculum development and evaluation.

CINDY FAREST is a doctoral student and teaching assistant at the University of Texas at Austin, where she is a member of the Language to Literacy project. A former classroom teacher of bilingual/ESL children, she earned her master's degree from Houston Baptist University.

JOAN T. FEELEY is Professor of Reading/Language Arts at William Paterson College in Wayne, New Jersey, where she coordinates the master's program in reading. Having taught language arts at the elementary, secondary, and college levels, she is a frequent contributor to the professional literature. Her book publications include *Using Computers in the Teaching of Reading* and *The Administration and Supervision of Reading Programs*. She is past president of the North Jersey Council of the International Reading Association.

LESLIE L. FUNKHOUSER is an elementary teacher in Herndon, Virginia. Having received her M.Ed. in administration and supervision from the University of New Hampshire, she serves as a consultant for schools implementing an integrated language arts approach. While teaching in New Hampshire, she worked with Donald Graves and Jane Hansen on a 2-year research project that connected reading and writing instruction. During this project, she contributed several pieces to *Teachers and Learners* and had a videotape, *One Classroom: A Child's View*, highlighting her second-grade classroom, published by Heinemann.

IRENE W. GASKINS, an educational psychologist, is founder and director of Benchmark School in Media, Pennsylvania. She received her Ed.D. at the University of Pennsylvania, where she taught graduate and undergraduate courses in reading for 15 years. She has taught in both elementary and secondary schools and has served as a reading specialist and district reading coordinator. She was the guest editor of the April 1988 issue of *The Reading Teacher*. She co-developed a decoding program that features using known words to decode unknown words and is a principal investigator in the James S. McDonnell Foundation Program in Cognitive Studies for Educational Practice and co-author of *The Benchmark Model for Teaching Thinking Strategies: A Manual for Teachers*.

RALPH GIOSEFFI is an educational consultant and coordinator of English K–12 in the Leonia Public Schools in New Jersey. Before moving to Leonia, he was a seventh- and eighth-grade language arts teacher, vice-principal, department supervisor, and staff developer in reading and writing in the Tenafly, New Jersey, schools. Presently a doctoral candidate at Teachers College, Columbia University, from which he received a Writing Project teacher-researcher grant, he has published in *The Reading Instruction Journal* and *RE-AD*.

JULIE GUZMAN teaches in a bilingual kindergarten at Ortega Elementary in the Austin (Texas) Independent School District. Ms. Guzman graduated from St. Edwards University in Austin with a B.S. degree in bilingual education. She has 10 years of teaching experience and is a teacher-participant in the Language to Literacy project at the University of Texas at Austin.

REBECCA HAMILTON serves as the Reading Diagnostician for the elementary grades in the Pittsburgh Public Schools. Before her present position, she was a classroom teacher and a reading specialist in both in-class and pull-out models. Currently she is enrolled in the doctoral program in reading at the University of Pittsburgh.

DAWN HARRIS-MARTINE is an elementary school teacher in the Mahalia Jackson School located in Harlem in New York City. Currently finishing her master's in curriculum and teaching with an emphasis in whole language at Columbia University's Teachers College, she has participated in the Teachers College Summer Institute on the Teaching of Writing for 6 years. *The Reading/Writing Connection*, a videotape highlighting her second-grade classroom, was produced by the Center for the Study of Reading at the University of Illinois.

JUSTINA M. HENRY, an adjunct professor at Ohio State University, is a Reading Recovery teacher leader and a Chapter 1 teacher for Warren City Schools, Warren, Ohio. Her 23 years of experience include teaching first grade, kindergarten, Chapter 1 reading, Adult Basic Education, and Head Start. She is currently a doctoral student at Kent State University, specializing in language arts/reading development and early childhood education.

JAMES V. HOFFMAN is Professor of Curriculum and Instruction at the University of Texas at Austin, where he teaches graduate and undergraduate courses in the teaching of reading. Past president of the National Reading Conference and co-editor of the *Reading Research Quarterly*, he is co-director of a project entitled Language to Literacy, which focuses on teachers reading aloud to students and encouraging their responses.

JIM KLIKA teaches at the Tenakill School in Closter, New Jersey, working in a second-, third-, and fourth-grade team-teaching program. Having received a National Council of Teachers of English award as a Center for Excellence, the program was also chosen to receive a New Jersey Governor's Grant for its literature-based language arts curriculum called "Building a Community of Readers and Writers." In 1990, Jim was awarded a teacher-researcher grant by The Writing Project at Teachers College, Columbia University.

MARIANNE MARINO is a teacher in the Glen Rock, New Jersey, public schools and a doctoral student at New York University. Her publications include research and applied articles on using a literature-based reading program and talking to learn. She has been awarded several grants and is researching children's self-initiated talk in constructing meaning through literature.

STELLA J. MATA has taught in the Austin Independent School District since 1977. She obtained her B.S. and M.Ed. degrees from the University of Texas at Austin. Her teaching experience includes 10 years as a second-grade and 2 years as a fourth-grade bilingual teacher.

MARY MULCAHY is the Primary Unit Coordinator at Richard E. Byrd School in Glen Rock, New Jersey. She received her master's degree in curriculum and instruction from Teachers College, Columbia University. She has been using a process approach to teach reading and writing for the past 5 years.

ELIZABETH POMEROY O'BROCHTA is an elementary school teacher in the Informal Alternative Program in the Upper Arlington City Schools in Ohio. Currently working on her master's in language arts at the Ohio State University, she has presented workshops on the reading/writing process for various school districts and university conferences.

BEVERLY PILCHMAN is a teacher in South Orange/Maplewood, New Jersey. A member of the district's Language Arts Leadership Team, she serves as a language arts mentor in her school and on the Grades Five through Eight Steering Committee, which is responsible for designing and organizing a new middle school program. In 1989, she was recognized by the WCBS radio station program, "A World of Difference," for her use of literature as a way for students to understand, respect, and appreciate diversity.

NANCY L. ROSER is Professor of Curriculum and Instruction at the University of Texas. A former classroom teacher, she is co-director of a project titled Language to Literacy, which focuses on teachers reading aloud and encouraging student response to literature.

JOSEPH SANACORE is on the faculty of Reading, Language, and Cognition at Hofstra University, Hempstead, New York, and is Language Arts Coordinator for the Hauppauge, New York, School District. Having served on the editorial advisory board for *The Reading Teacher*, he co-edited the second edition of *Handbook for the Volunteer Tutor*, a publication of the International Reading Association. His more than 100 articles have appeared in a variety of journals, including *Reading Research and Instruction, Journal of Reading, The Reading Teacher, Language Arts, Phi Delta*

Kappan, Educational Leadership, NASSP Bulletin, The Clearing House, The High School Journal, and *The Education Digest.*

CAROL MINNICK SANTA is the language arts coordinator for Kalispell Public Schools in Montana. She also directs a National Diffusion Network project, Project CRISS, designed for teaching students how to learn content information. She received her Ph.D. in psychology of reading from Temple University and has been a classroom teacher, reading specialist, and college professor. Her publications include articles in *The Reading Teacher, Reading Research Quarterly,* and *The Journal of Reading.* She is a past member of the International Reading Association Board of Directors.

MARILYN STAMPA is an elementary school teacher in Closter, New Jersey, where she is part of a team that teaches in a multi-age program that has received a New Jersey Governor's Grant and a National Council of Teachers of English Center for Excellence award. For the past 2 years she has led a reading circle among colleagues. In 1990, The Writing Project at Teachers College, Columbia University, awarded her a grant as teacher-researcher; she is indebted to Lucy Calkins and Shelley Harwayne for their inspiration and support.

DOROTHY S. STRICKLAND is the State of New Jersey Professor of Reading at Rutgers University. Formerly the Arthur I. Gates Professor of Education at Teachers College, Columbia University, she has been a classroom teacher and reading specialist. Her publications include *Family Storybook Reading, Using Computers in the Teaching of Reading, The Administration and Supervision of Reading Programs,* and *Emerging Literacy.* She is past president of the International Reading Association and a member of the Reading Hall of Fame.

DAVID F. TAYLOR is an English/reading teacher at Santa Barbara Junior High, Santa Barbara, California. As a Fellow with the South Coast Writing Project, he became intrigued with the process approach through the writings of Donald Graves and Nancie Atwell and has been a full-time practitioner of reading and writing workshop for 3 years. An occasional writer on socio-educational issues for the *Santa Barbara News-Press,* he is the author of *Doublespeak: Critical Thinking in a Nuclear Age.*

MODESTA BARBINA TREVINO is a second-grade bilingual teacher at Sanchez Elementary in Austin, Texas. She graduated with honors from Saint Edward's University in Austin, Texas. A past officer of the Austin Association for Bilingual Education and an advocate for bilingual issues, she has recently been awarded a grant to implement a bilingual Language to Literacy project in her school.

CINDY PERKINS WEAVER teaches in the Informal Alternative Program in the upper Arlington City Schools in Ohio. Having received her master's degree in reading and writing education at the Ohio State University, she has presented workshops on reading and writing across the curriculum at local conferences.

SHELLEY B. WEPNER is an associate professor at William Paterson College, Wayne, New Jersey. Her book publications include *Using Computers in the Teaching of Reading* and *The Administration and Supervision of Reading Programs*. Formerly editor of *The Reading Instruction Journal*, her software publications include *Read-A-Logo*, *Reading Realities*, and *Reading Realities Elementary Series*.

EDITH R. ZIEGLER is one of three team teachers in the multi-aged unit at Tenakill School, Closter, New Jersey. Her program in language arts for children ages 7 to 10 has been recognized for its innovations by the State Department of Education, the National Council Teachers of English, and the New Jersey School Boards Association. Having studied with Lucy Calkins and Shelley Harwayne at the Teachers College Writing Project for several years, she is currently working as a staff developer for writing in the Closter schools.

Index